To Diogo Seixas Lopes
Fazes falta.

CARTHA

# On Relations in Architecture

 PARK BOOKS

PROLOGUE

6

Ø
WORTH SHARING

20

I
CONFRÈRES

64

## II
## MANNSCHAFT
138

## III
## SANTÍSIMA TRINIDAD
194

## EPILOGUE
264

# PROLOGUE

8  Rebekka Kiesewetter
Foreword

16  CARTHA
Editorial

# Foreword

The decision to make a book nowadays often involves a welter of grave questions. Especially those new to publishing might end up pondering the book's very right to exist; a significant amount of time will also be spent weighing the "digital" vs. "physical" options; one might even speak of the responsibility that making a book implies. Novice editors often put themselves under pressure, prompted both by the expectations they place on themselves and an anxiety for the outcome to correspond to different pre-conceived ideas of what a book should be. This is fuelled by a strange combination of idealism and a desire to "make it right", in which "right" usually remains a rather vague concept. This charged mental predisposition, combined with a massive amount of working hours, is enough to suppress all the joy this kind of endeavour can bring. These are also times in which we are constantly told of the imminent death of printed media, and in which – even if not acknowledging this as a valid speculation – some people fear that books may become objects of pure luxury and speculation. Publishing a book has never been so frightening a task. It seems that in this context, books have become the holy grail of the savvy, the last bastions of durability, heavy not only physically but also in their contents. In all the musing, one has lost a certain impartiality.

It is time to calm down a little, to recoup ease and pleasure, to veer away from the overheated and somewhat dogmatic discussions, to regain a certain nonchalance in dealing with books and their "capacity", their meaning and position within the broader context of publishing. This is not to say that one should not ask the "existential" questions, but they should not weigh so gravely. They should be asked from a slightly different perspective and in different terms.

I, for one, do not see much hope in the attempts small independent publishers have made to compete with the larger, commercially successful ones. This has involved internalising a profit-driven mindset and reproducing their strategies and evaluation criteria. There is however a huge potential for small, ephemeral initiatives such as CARTHA and their aims to take on the pioneering task of redefining the concept of publishing and opening new paths towards alternative market ideas and distribution networks. Initiatives born out of shared beliefs and interpersonal relationships, rather than out of imposed institutional structures or a financial necessity. Initiatives which base their undertaking on a variety of skills, interests, and means possess the mental and structural ability (and agility) to work towards a radical change in our understanding of publishing and its aims.

Rather than thinking about what a book should be, they can think about what it can be; what value it might have beyond the one determined by the market or the most widespread, thus non-directional transmission of all the knowledge that can fit into a book case; where a book's position might be in the whole process of a recalibrated publishing. Initiatives such as CARTHA are in a position to re-align their value systems, shift them away from the businesses' prevalent evaluation criteria, away from numbers and an obsessive search for exposure. They can avoid considering maximum coverage of the distribution network as a synonym for success, break away from a project-imposed time frame, stop thinking of digital versus analogue as a relevant dichotomy, and develop entirely new ways of understanding the concept of publishing, and the related motivations and practices. Because – despite all prophecies of doom – the profound changes the field of publishing is undoubtedly undergoing, may not only lead towards segregation, exclusion or a capitalization of knowledge or of the means of publishing but – with the attentive and proactive concern of the people involved – also towards its democratization.

How? By cherishing and fostering the value embedded in the manifold networks underlining the construct, and by embracing and exploring the potential of current technologies for cross-overs, sampling, remixing, appropriation, and sharing; and by challenging ostensibly fixed poles. This would allow for established genres and perceptions to become more fluid, opening up new possibilities for experimentation.

If publishing which sets aside all prejudice is understood in its very basic meaning – making information available to the public, one can imagine publishing breaking free from its formal or medial confines, conquering three-dimensional space and slipping away from the accepted notion of printed or digitalized matter as its only modes of expression. A book in this context appears to be only one of many valid publishing strategies, one expression, one of the channels under the roof of "publishing". Each channel has its own means, outcomes, languages and possibilities, each of them offers a ground for specific yet internally diverse collaborations, relationships, exchanges and degrees of participation; each channel is connected to the other, all of them complementary and conjoined. Rather than merely depicting a reality, stating a fact or capturing a specific moment in time, a book, a magazine, a physical encounter, a blog or a flyer, are complementary facets of one endeavour, each of them revealing intermediate insights, which only make sense in a very specific time, environment, and in front of a specific public. A book in this sense could be seen as a material expression of (spatial and interpersonal) processes and experiments with no final outcome, not offering one truth but many truths for the editors as well as for the recipients.

Departing from this idea, let's look at publishing as a post-representational process: A form of publishing that is not about depicting, objectivizing, illustrating, communicating or drawing conclusions, but lays the ground for an intellectual and socio-political practice. The process of publishing under these premises becomes a gathering of empathic individuals, working and thinking together, sharing ideas. Post-representational publishing is about allowing communication to happen. Publishing in this sense also asks for a specific mind-set: being aware, being informed, being critical, being incredulous, letting a multi-vocal choir evolve and persist without excluding its cacophonic voices, without following the desire to smoothen them. The publishing context can be a unifying pretext for experimentation, a heterotopia where resonance (rather than competition), reverberation, exchange, humanity, subjectivity, absurdity, ephemerality, the refusal of utilitarianism, shared hope, empathy and friendship become the base and direction of publishing work; a place to find a sense of joy and ease that should be inherent in the pursuit of our practices.

CARTHA, born out of shared beliefs, have united under their "publishing roof" diverse personalities, professions and aims, drawing from a network of guests and friends. They have implemented a variety of digital and physical means of making public. In their own words: "A geography under construction shaped by diverse forms of representations. It is a map where opinions relate, diverge, collapse. A foggy world in which borders are constantly questioned, shifted, moved by its own tectonics but never ceasing to exist. (...) An evergrowing system of references that allows us to position ourselves. It shows us what we can get to know and what surrounds us, waiting for us to reach for it, if we so wish."

For CARTHA this book seems a way to look back on their production through their interpersonal relationships, their common work and shared beliefs. It is a moment to reflect on things that happened and might happen, a pause which enables them to sum up and collect, a way to explore the different means of publishing with which they are operating (the website, the book, the event) in relation to the published content and their personal structure, to explore possibilities and specificities, creating a tool for themselves as well as for others to generate knowledge in the realms of their topic for this year: on relations in architecture. CARTHA are also well aware of the public's prevalent reception – and without giving it too much importance, they are consciously playing with it: they are aware that printed matter transmits a sense of reliability, which is – in the eye of the recipient – different to the one of digital means: the printed, according to the predominant perception, creates a different kind of response, and "enhances" the value of the published content as well as the credibility of the publishers.

Initiatives such as CARTHA take on a crucial role in the process of re-purposing publishing: They are the enablers and guardians of a heterotopic publishing sphere and custodians of its outcomes.

Rebekka Kiesewetter

PROLOGUE

# Editorial

"Relations in Architecture", the steering topic for the first cycle of CARTHA in 2015, explored the triad formed by the ways in which architects relate to architects, to collaborators from other disciplines, and to clients and users.

As stated in our inaugural issue WORTH SHARING, we aimed at attaining a committed, but surely partial, overview of architecture's reality. Indeed, looking back at CARTHA's first cycle, we cannot help but feel that the four issues produced barely scratched the surface that covers this layered web of interactions. The complexity of the relations in architecture and all of its different interpretations can make it difficult to achieve this overview, even after many years in the field.

Nevertheless, a valuable collection of testimonials and reflections collected from around the globe made this quixotic task a tangible one. We did not approach this task with the objective of finding the ultimate truth, but with that of drawing conclusions that are imbued with the momentary character of our time. As we reflect on our inaugural issue and the context and moments in which these discussions were born, we can see the rich debate that arises. The ever-pressing question of the role of the architect in the modern world amongst the infinite web of relations that weave architecture together; is a debate that is both unresolved and keeps us pressing forward with more questions.

Throughout our discussion within "Relations in Architecture", architecture was not discussed through the analysis of the architectural object, but through that of the ensemble of interactions that make architecture possible. An approach that seems increasingly important in an ever-scrolling flux of architectural imagery.

Although varied, the contrasts and similarities amongst the 42 contributions featured in the 2015 cycle questioned the systems of coordination and dependencies between the roles of the many different entities surrounding architecture. Even more interesting and hinting towards deeper complexity within the field, those differing roles are constantly being negotiated amongst themselves and the society in which they are embedded.

In Issue I, CONFRÈRES, we balanced the constant forces "I" versus "We" within the relations amongst architects, and we confirmed a greater interest in collaboration as an elementary tool to face a new era for the profession. In MANNSCHAFT, this era seemed to lead our peers to embrace the maxim of "there's no "I" in "team" when it comes to weighing the role of the architect in relation to the growing number of members from other disciplines involved in the act of building. This phenomenon of expansion is as present within the technical environment of planning as it is in the core trinity of building: the client, the architect and the user. The third issue explored an unforeseen paradox: these last three entities are always present, even when one or more than one of them is absent. The inevitability of this triangle reinforces the strength and responsibility of architecture as a social event, yet questions the role of the architect as a persona. SANTÍSIMA TRINIDAD!

By teasing out the threads, we partially untangled the complex web of what is the field of architecture, in doing so its complex and intriguing mechanisms were also revealed. We now have a more ample knowledge of the context of our field, however we have also realized that we have only just started the process of discovery that, by its sheer dimension and appeal, has to be followed-up with new queries.

"Relations in Architecture" acknowledged architecture as a discipline in constant mutation, a discipline that keeps redefining itself. This cycle of CARTHA also confronted architecture considering the complex entanglement of economical, ecological and political variables amongst others. This state of a seemingly permanent crisis will most likely be present for generations to come. And as much as this socio-economic landscape has re-shaped the profession, the architect has neither become a guide into a new future for society nor entirely bequeathed the power of decision to others. It is therefore worth taking a few steps back in order to reconsider Architecture from within, and to approach it with the autonomy of the discipline that we overlooked in this first cycle. With this in mind, CARTHA will dedicate its 2016 cycle to the subject of "The Form of Form", as an Associated Project of the 3rd Lisbon Architecture Triennale.

This editorial project was born out of the will to reclaim time to apprehend the ever-increasing pace of the world today and in which architecture is produced. To be an open platform that channels caring, critical and fresh voices regarding our society and the built environment we all inhabit. We are proud to acknowledge that CARTHA is achieving these aspirations and we want to thank our contributors and readers in this regard. This book is a celebration of CARTHA's first year and a stepping-stone for future endeavors.

# Ø WORTH SHARING

| | | | |
|---|---|---|---|
| 22 | **CARTHA**<br>Editorial | 42 | **Mark Minkjan**<br>How to Move from Architectural Cheerleading to Architecture Criticism |
| 24 | **Francisco Moura Veiga, Interview**<br>Diogo Seixas Lopes | 46 | **Antoine Prokos**<br>This Changes Everything – Architecture of the Commons |
| 30 | **Roland Remaa**<br>Curated Hermit | 50 | **AbdulFatah Adam**<br>Under Demand |
| 33 | **Rubén Valdez**<br>Sharing – A Reflection on Contemporary Dwelling | 54 | **Visual Contribution**<br>Guido Guidi |
| 36 | **Vera Sacchetti, Juan Palencia**<br>Towards the Edge of Knowledge – Lessons Learned from Sharing what (we didn't Know) we Know | 61 | **Ganko on Guido Guidi**<br>Living Traces |

Ø WORTH SHARING

The number of existing outlets of architectural production has never been as great as it is today. At a mouse-click, one can access an immense, apparently never-ending, constantly updating stream of images and factual information related to architecture. The volume of work being shared is positively overwhelming. So overwhelming, in fact, that one almost drowns in this frenetic stream without having the chance to look more closely at a subject and analyse it in depth. The great majority of these publishing media rely on novelty to attract their audiences: there is no time to go beyond the thin cosmetic veneer that images offer. The other publishing media, which actually allow themselves the luxury of time to observe, absorb, process and react to architectural production, rely on "experts" to do so.

CARTHA was born as a naive, experimental alternative to this scenario. It is a space which does not simply rely on researchers and "qualified people" to dissect architectural production, but functions instead as a platform where one can observe how architecture is digested, used, and perceived, as a medium which goes beyond "slick imagery" and provides us with time to observe the fast-motion environment in which we evolve. There are obvious limitations to this format – we are well aware of this – but we think that the risk is minimal in comparison to the potential collective gains this experiment can generate. CARTHA is independent, not bound by geographical or ideological borders. It wishes to generate synergies with parallel initiatives and to foster cooperation with others who approach this subject in a similar manner.

The current issue WORTH SHARING is issue number Ø. It aspires to delve into various ways in which we, as builders, engage amongst ourselves and with our built environment. Being at the core of systems of coordination and dependencies, we necessarily share practices, spaces, knowledge, and information. Contributors to the magazine have reflected on this situation according to their interpretations and experiences of what sharing is and how it relates to contemporary architecture and social environments: critical views on our surroundings, whether they be buildings, places, tools, or lasting products of our society.

Working together as a cycle, the next three issues will attempt to further develop our insight into how we perceive relations within architecture's spectrum. Thus, the ways in which architects relate to architects, to workers and to users will be themed under the light of today's reality. These are not uncontroversial or usual topics, and there are many reasons for choosing them. Within this year's timeframe, we aim at attaining a committed, but surely partial, overview of architecture's reality.

Issue Ø marks the inauguration of CARTHA, which we are pleased to share with you.

Francisco Moura Veiga

# Diogo Seixas Lopes

Interview

There is no sign on the door of the building. Actually there is no clue at all to the reality that lies inside. The office occupies what was previously an auto-workshop in one of Lisbon's historical neighbourhoods. The triangular floorplan sets up a two-storey room that has undergone minor interventions, remaining in a typological ambiguity that lends some sort of palpable meaning to the work environment. At one of the edges of the triangle, cornered by two wooden walls, stands a single cubicle, once the mechanic's office and now the small workroom Diogo shares with his wife, Patricia. A wooden desk, smoothed by time and work, stood between Diogo and I. He sat back calmly, smoking at a steady rhythm and invitingly answering the questions posed to him. This was not the first time we had met. I once attended a lecture he gave to a group of Swiss students on a study trip to Lisbon. The topic he had chosen to address was not an obvious choice; hidden historical streets in Lisbon. In the course of his lecture, he drew our attention to the fact that the decayed streets that lay behind and under avenues are, at least, as deserving of a visit as the rest of the city's monuments. The unusual way he presented Lisbon to the students matches his approach to architecture. Diogo studied architecture at the FA-UTL in Lisbon at a time when Porto was at its prime. He focused on acquiring a strong theoretical basis before turning his attention to practical work. He co-authored a book on urban realities[1] shortly after his studies, was co-editor of *Prototypo*, a magazine he co-founded, and is now co-editor of the Portuguese Architectural Guild magazine (J-A) as well as co-curator of the next Lisbon Architecture Triennale. He works with his wife at Barbas Lopes Arquitectos. He shares his work and the results of his work. Diogo is worth sharing.

**Were theoretical production and theoretical contemplation a part of your academic work or did that emerge later?**
The first sign that theoretical production was something that interested me happened during school, because of this professor who asked his students to give presentations about several projects. Flagship projects, in some sense. At that time, access to information was very limited. We were handed several projects under the spectrum of Deconstructivism. I gave a presentation about the Jewish Museum by Daniel Libeskind. This happened during my second year in school, around 1990, and back then I had little knowledge about the theoretical production of architecture, let alone this specific practice, so it was a kind of revelation to me because it was something totally unlike anything I had been exposed to until that time. Even if we do not consider it a theoretical production, we could certainly call it an experimental activity. Eventually, this got me to Berlin and New York, doing internships for Libeskind and Asymptote. Because of this, I had access to the work of other architects hinged between theory and practice. So I developed some interest for that hinge that allowed projects to be vehicles for different subjects besides space, tectonics, or function. This relation between theory and practice would later coalesce with the editorial project of *Prototypo*.[2]

**And how did that move to the editorial world happen?**
*Prototypo* was produced with two other colleagues, one of them the graphic designer of the journal. At some point, we thought that it would be more productive if we created our own project. The first steps date back to 1998, a moment of a certain optimism in Portugal. This made it easier to raise funds to finance the journal as a completely independent venture. The magazine had a structure, an editorial concept that was a success in terms of its scale of operation. Every issue presented a monograph from a foreign architect set side by side with that of a Portuguese architect. A "face-off". There was some criticality in staging contrasts between the work of Portuguese and foreign architects. We tried to play with the interests of different markets, different audiences. *Prototypo* had from the start a mechanism of self-destruction. It was set to end when it reached the ninth issue. P.R.O.T.O.T.Y.P.O.: 9 letters, 9 issues. Along the way we organized a big seminar in 2001, "Performing the City". It was truly a strong event because we had a lot of people coming over to participate as speakers. Not just architects but also researchers, theoreticians and critics. The outcome of those days of discussion was very intense. Our stance towards *Prototypo* was always about the export of contents and the import of knowledge from external agents. When it reached the ninth issue we claimed the right, if not the privilege, to terminate this editorial and critical project the way we wanted to. Afterwards, I made an altogether different kind of move and went abroad. Back then, I was teaching in Lisbon and had been advised to pursue a PhD.

**I developed some interest for that hinge that allowed projects to be vehicles for different subjects besides space, tectonics, or function.**

**Why and how did people advise you?**
I was advised by people outside architectural circles who had experience from other academic areas. Sooner or later you would not be able to teach without a PhD, at least in Portugal. I started to think about this prospect as a "five-year plan". I chose to do it at ETH Zurich, where I already had a small network of contacts via *Prototypo*. During the same period, I established my own architectural practice with my partner and wife Patrícia Barbas: Barbas Lopes Arquitectos.[3] It has been my main activity ever since, even if it happens alongside other projects.

**What about teaching?**
Teaching also, yes. But all of that revolves around my position as a practicing architect, which I consider as strengthening its theoretical dimension. Nevertheless, I see my resolution to pursue a PhD at ETH Zurich, doing research on Aldo Rossi[4], as a major turning point.

**Let me go back to when you were saying that your main occupation is to be an architect, which means building. Built work requires other skills, even if those skills are a little latent. You have criticism, theory, you also teach. I would like to quote you: "References allow us to make choices that are meaningful and, by being meaningful, they are precise." You said that about the Polytechnical Theatre, by Barbas Lopes Arquitectos. My question is a little obvious but I really want you to be clear about it. Do you feel that theory influences your work? If so, do you feel an improvement in your other project faculties regarding your effective work?**
I do. Especially due to these last years of research work in an academic context. I found references on a formal level, but I also became aware of procedures to interpret and transform them. For example, the process of choosing sources. A memory, or an idea, can lead the way of a project. I think there must be an organic process of interaction between all these things. In this sense, to study the legacy of Aldo Rossi was an important contribution to this perception.

**I would like to ask you about two moments that I think are important in your biography. The first moment is the J-A[5], alongside André Tavares. The second would be the Lisbon Triennale, also alongside André. Is J-A's editorial concept, somehow, going to be extended to the Triennale?**
They are different realities in different times. Both came about after several collaborations with André, such as a seminar we organized at the Canadian Centre for Architecture while we were both doing research there. At that seminar, we presented projects that employed strategies to bring Portuguese architecture closer to an international debate. Provokingly, we finished our presentation with a summit organized in a remote corner of the country, which revolved around "powerpoint fights" between a group of colleagues. At the time, we wanted to debunk the proverbial sterility of these meetings using nonsense.

## A memory, or an idea, can lead the way of a project.

**That led to another thing...**
Later that led to CPAM [Concentration of Portuguese Architects in Mação], with a more institutional concept. We hosted these gatherings because the local professional scene lacked a display of critical mass. So we orchestrated our own.

**And what did those gatherings create?**
These gatherings created moments for architects to come together, especially those from younger generations. Thereafter, this led to a series of other initiatives that further highlighted the work of these generations and their new modes of practice. Directing J-A has been a useful manner to chart that activity. It has also been a pretext to engage in teamwork creating a staff of writers, photographers, and graphic designers. Since this series of the periodical started, two years ago, we have walked this path together, developing skills on how to report about architecture. One of our first instincts was to get back to the ethics and aesthetics of a newspaper, because this also had to do with the financial terms of the project and the fact that it had less money. So we decided to make the whole magazine in black and white, with the look and structure of a newspaper. Meaning flawless and factual writing, no footnotes, no ambiguity towards academic production. The first editorial set the tone: "Topics are out. Bring on reality." This happened during times of great hardship in Portugal, also for architects. The first issues express this in terms of the editorials and the topics we chose to discuss.

**Getting back to a point that means a lot to you and that results from my analysis of your work. You gave an interview to *Público*, on January 15 2014, which I shall quote: "We must end our misunderstandings and this turning our back on each other, so that we can better address this crisis that is affecting our occupation." I don't want to talk about the crisis, I would like to focus on "end our misunderstandings and this turning our back on each other"; Is joint authorship something you are aware of as a natural result of different situations in your life?**
I am obviously aware of that pattern since it has been happening for a while. I managed to reinforce these collaborative processes through architectural practice in partnership with my wife. We have established this joint venture under the name of our studio.

Part of this work of shared authorships responds to a critical field of interests that is becoming progressively wider. This allows me to work within an interdisciplinary scope of subjects. I can now favour multinuclear interactions instead of mononuclear ones, like a molecule with different cells moving in all sorts of directions. In our office, we value the individual skills of the collaborators and a sense of diversity that comes from that. It is about appreciating this diversity, but a diversity that is disciplined by work. Furthermore, we do not condone a total separation between life and work. In a way, we live this all the time and it would probably be the same if we were operating in a different field such as politics or the arts. Working under these guidelines is all about creating a core, resulting from a fusion between all these things and how they ultimately converge into architecture and into architectural projects.

> This allows me to work within an interdisciplinary scope of subjects. I can now favour multinuclear interactions instead of mononuclear ones, like a molecule with different cells moving in all sorts of directions.

### NOTES

1. Lopes, Diogo Seixas / Cera, Nuno, Cimêncio, Lisbon: FENDA, 2002.
2. www.prototypo.com
3. www.barbaslopes.com
4. Lopes, Diogo Seixas, Melancholy and Architecture: On Aldo Rossi, 2015, Park Books.
5. www.jornalarquitectos.pt

### IMAGE CREDITS

Photograph by Francisco Nogueira.

Roland Remaa

# Curated Hermit

What we share shapes our society and changes our personal habits. With the increasing number of people living alone in cities, it is worth asking how this solitude shapes our personal identity.

If there is such a thing as an urban hermit, a lone dweller, then what could be the role of his sharing his personal life with others? In order to approach the idea of sharing, let us first explore the very opposite of the seemingly public medium of our social affairs by considering a hermit, the embodiment of a person who lives in seclusion from society.

The very word we use here, hermit, from Latin *ĕrēmīta*, means 'of the desert' and originates from Christian hermits who lived in the Egyptian deserts. It is important to note that the content of the word has various nuances and forms of practices for different cultures and beliefs worldwide. While some forms became institutionalised, such as the desert communities which became the models for Christian monasticism, others remained solely dependent on individuals. Although mostly motivated by religion, the underlying idea during the period of seclusion is to renounce one's daily habits and personal volition in search of a higher consciousness.

Most of Asian Buddhism follows the idea that a person should spend time apart from his everyday, earthly way of living at least once in his lifetime. In some branches of Tibetan Buddhism, it is required of monks to go on a solo retreat for three years and three months. The monks live in caves and forests for deep contemplation. Although they are searching for solitude, they do not necessarily avoid villagers that come their way. Instead, they unconditionally help the inhabitants, if only in return for a piece of bread to eat. The hermit subordinates himself to other living beings through the absence of ego. While committing himself solely to others, he is no longer at the centre of his actions himself, therefore entirely sharing himself with the world. This very absence of ego can be seen as absolute sharing. In order to depart fully from his self, a hermit could, for example, act as a scarecrow in the fields. To abandon one's personal identity within society by living in an absolute absence of self, ultimately leads to identification of the hermit with the forces of nature – like a wind that is felt and is then already gone.

Strangely enough and by way of contrast, hermits who could not hide their traces were immediately wanted as great teachers. Hermits were even followed and sought out. The paradox lies in the fact that after returning from seclusion, the sharing of experiences as great stories only promoted the hermit's new identity as a survivor and therefore reinforced his ego. We might as well say that hermits whom we know today by name as poets or writers are actually failed ones. We can read their curated stories and imagine them without experiencing them in reality. Although this is the beauty of literature, we could also ask if we were supposed to read these stories. The question lies in the beginning – in whether the act of sharing itself was appropriate on the hermit's part.[1]

Social changes such as the rise of the solo dweller, the surge in social networks and peer-to-peer logistics combined with an ageing population, as is common in Western countries, change the way people interact with each other. There is less dependency on the communities where people reside, while there is at the same time an increase in highly individualised control over daily habits, communication being one of them. Events are organised casually, food is delivered, news is read and friends are made without the individuals involved leaving their personal territories. Although people live densely side-by-side and are linked into the urban facilities of services and infrastructure, there is no longer

A    Saint Onuphrius from Egypt – one of the most famous hermits who lived in the Egyptian deserts in 4th or 5th century, who's severe lifestyle became a cult and an inspiration for several monasteries.

any urgent need for sharing heated bathrooms or kitchens. The number of one-person households has increased worldwide.² Living alone is common and it is fair to ask whether modern dwellers are turning into urban hermits. Although solitude is the common ground between hermits and solo urban dwellers, it is important to differentiate how they share themselves with others. Unlike a hermit who aims to lose his ego, a solo dweller finds advantage in solitude in order to customize everything for the ego. Solitude here does not immediately mean loneliness, since great cities are vibrant with intriguing individuals. A hermit can offer help in a village while a solo dweller catches up with friends downtown, but the underlying difference is how the decisions are taken – the first being accidental and the latter organised.

The possibility to switch on and off, to busy and to offline or even to become invisible only reinforces the ego and increases the highly individually curated self, where unwanted topics can simply be avoided. Modern social media have offered us the best means to curate our self-image. The actions taken are increasingly at the centre of personal commitment. Our personal knowledge and visual perception as well as valuable information, and quite often less valuable information, are continuously shared through a neatly personalised filter. In a similar but extreme manner, the very act of sharing can be considered as having also become the means to present a personal image rather than the actual content of the shared information. Sharing becomes the victim of objectification. While it still remains the medium that binds society, it is less accidental and more personalised. Furthermore, gratitude or feedback is expected from the contributor's followers, regardless of whether the real content was even received. The anxious state of waiting for people to 'like' or to respond raises self-awareness and personal identity even more.

What is shared around us can therefore be viewed critically. Was this story just worth sharing? Perhaps the increasing number of urban solo dwellers that live their seemingly customised dream lives, are more like curated hermits that only want to tell their stories. The underlying question of whether we were supposed to read these stories at all still remains.

AUTHOR

Roland Reemaa (1987) studied at the Estonian Academy of Arts and completed his MSc degree in architecture at TU Delft, The Netherlands. He currently holds a guest teacher position at TU Delft for studio In Chicago in chair Complex Projects, exploring the methods to research a city. He is an architect at KAAN Architecten in Rotterdam. Roland works independently on several art, film and research projects, often in collaboration with Laura Linsi. Roland lives and works in Rotterdam, The Netherlands and shares his life with London and Estonia.

NOTES

1  Alari Allik – Eraklusest. Radio show on ERR Radio. Translated from Estonian by author. http://vikerraadio.err.ee/ helid?main_id=1937381
2  Euromonitor International. One person households: Opportunities for consumer goods companies. http://blog.euromonitor.com/2007/09/one-person-households-opportunities-for-consumer-goods-companies.html

IMAGE CREDITS

A  Onuphrius – an icon 17th cent. from Stańkowa, Historic Museum in Sanok, Poland. https://commons.wikimedia.org/wiki/File:MHS_Onufry_Pustelnik_1_po%C5%82_XVII_w_Sta%C5%84kowa_pl._jpg.jpg

Rubén Valdez

# Sharing

A Reflection on
Contemporary Dwelling

"Only if we are capable of dwelling, only then we can build."[1]
Martin Heidegger, Poetry. Language. Thought, 1971.

Basing his remarks on etymology, Heidegger states that *Bauen*, to build, relates to the Old English and Old High German word for the act of building – *buan*, which means "to dwell", to remain or stay in a place. *Bauen*, according to Heidegger, also relates to nearness and neighbourliness, and implies to spare and preserve.[2] For Heidegger, dwelling is the basic character of being, we unconsciously dwell, but only when we are conscious of it can we build; "build out of dwelling and think for the sake of dwelling."[3]

Although the etymologies used by Heidegger apply almost exclusively to the German language, the reflections which emerge from them are somehow of universal value. Influencing many architects who have focused primarily on cultural, historical and emotional values, the ideas of Heidegger have infused the practice of architects to create work that is "richly associative"[4] in terms of everyday life an the way we inhabit space. There is no question that we all have different ways of dwelling and different conceptions of home that may vary depending on respective cultural and social backgrounds. Furthermore, there is no question that a proper understanding of dwelling may lead to a proper understanding of building; however, it is of utmost importance to keep in mind that dwelling is a concept in constant change and that, even if certain cultural, historical and emotional values remain, the dynamics of society change at a faster rate than architecture. Additionally, architecture is usually a consequence of these changes. As Sheller and Urry affirm in their influential paper *The New Mobilities Paradigm*[5], one of the most important changes in societies in the last decades has probably been the fact that constant movement within different entities (cities, countries, or even continents) has

A   Linda Voorwinde, A glimpse of a world that exists beyond the boundaries of everyday life, 2013.

become not only more affordable and frequent but in some cases even necessary. Work, studies, pleasure or forced displacement have driven people to regard several places as 'home' at the same time, as they appropriate and dwell in different spaces in very short periods of time. Seen in this light, the concept of dwelling becomes more complex: how can we define dwelling in a present where a significant percentage of the population lives in a constant state of travel. In a world where more and more individuals dwell simultaneously in multiple locations, how can we define the concept of home?

If we define home as the place we appropriate and regularly dwell in, then home is the apartment we share ten days a month, our parents' house, that charming place we found in *Airbnb*; home is Europe, is America, is the intercontinental flight between them; home are the airports and train stations we know by heart as they become our home for the couple of hours during which we inhabit them every week (if only all of them had free wifi access). Internet devices help to keep us connected to our multiple homes, becoming a key instrument to simultaneous dwelling. We exist, relate and work through them; they link us with all of our different locations, creating a single one that gives us the comfort none of them can give separately. We continue to develop our lives through a long distance dwelling, we leave, stay in contact and come back, trying to re-appropriate places that are not necessarily the same each time we visit them. Our territory is a broad multiplicity of places where we develop our life simultaneously; we dwell in movement, appropriating and re-appropriating a space that is no longer only ours.

Dwelling in several places in short periods of time makes it unaffordable for each of us to cherish and protect all of them. Hence, a new way of dwelling has come, less focused on the house and more on the territory, a territory we all share and constantly inhabit despite distance. With this in mind, we have to question the strategies that are based in a permanent or at least long-term single dwelling for a sedentary life, we need to redefine these strategies either with architecture or with new ways of exchange and appropriation. Sharing comes to mind. Different strategies have already arisen, whether *Airbnb* or *Kraftwerk 1* [6] in Zürich. They have provided a revolutionary basis on which to re-think the concept of dwelling and the economic exchanges around it, thereby involving completely new ways of appropriating space. As many of these kinds of strategies are of an economic and social nature, it is our responsibility as architects to reflect about this new paradigm and understand it in a much deeper way so as to "build out of dwelling and think for the sake of dwelling." [7] Society changes at a faster rate than architecture and the way we dwell is no exception. There is no valid reason to ignore the human and emotional values that compose architecture, but one thing is for sure, the Black forest farmhouse [8] needs to suit the contemporary dweller.

### NOTES

1. Heidegger, Martin. Poetry, Language, Thought. Harper and Row. New York 1971 (pp. 145, 147, 158).
2. Ibid.
3. Ibid.
4. St. John, Peter. The Feeling of Things: Towards an Architecture of Emotion Shaping Earth. Wolver Hampton, UK: MS Associates and the University of Wolver Hampton, 2000 (p. 78).
5. Sheller, Mimi and Urry, John. The New Mobilities Paradigm. Environment and Planning, vol. 38, 2006 (pp. 207 – 226).
6. *Kraftwerk 1* is a housing cooperative in Zürich, that operates under a share scheme, "buying" shares of the apartment one will inhabit together with other flatmates and selling them once one leaves. The housing scheme is composed of apartments that range from 1 room to 13.5 rooms, making sharing a key part of the project. www.kraftwerk1.ch
7. Heidegger, Martin. Poetry, Language, Thought. Harper and Row. New York 1971 (pp. 145, 147, 158).
8. Ibid.

### IMAGE CREDITS

A   Photograph by Linda Voorwinde.

### AUTHOR

Rubén Valdez (Zacatecas, Mexico, 1986) studied architecture at the Accademia di architettura di Mendrisio and contemporary art at ECAL (ècole cantonal d'art de Lausanne). After doing an internship at Miller & Maranta Architekten in Basel and Estudio Toga in Mexico, he worked independently in Guadalajara, México, on several single housing projects. He has been participant of different architecture and art exhibitions such as "Monumental Masonry" at the Sir John Soane's museum (London), "Vertige des correspondances" curated by Julien Fronsacq at ELAC (Lausanne) "Life is a Bed of Roses" curated by Stephanie Moisdon at Fondation Ricard (Paris).

Vera Sacchetti, Juan Palencia

# Towards the Edge of Knowledge

Lessons Learned from Sharing what (we didn't Know) we Know

### Inception

Ten minutes into Stefano Orani's lecture, the room was silent. It was late April 2014 and around twelve people were sitting in a white living room, some on the couch, others on the floor. A side table had snacks and drinks at hand. Stefano stood in front of a projection of a spectacular image, a chronological diagram of the universe's expansion since the Big Bang. A physical cosmologist, Stefano was one of the first guests of TEOK, an informal lecture series founded in Basel in early 2014, and he was sharing what he knew and loved about the first instants of the life of the universe. Guests were silent, absorbed by this larger-than-life topic that expanded way beyond what our brains are used to thinking about during daily life's many menial tasks. The serious atmosphere, however, was quickly interrupted by questions and doubts, in an approach that helped understanding of its complexity and brought it closer to the minds and hearts of all those attending. By the end of the lecture, laughter filled the room – the sunset light was still strong, and a series of equations projected onto the wall lingered on as guests and speaker continued conversation.

A project originally born out of a few drunken nights and whatsapp conversations, TEOK (an acronym for The Edge of Knowledge) is an informal lecture series where uncommon, unexpected topics are presented in someone's living room. Lecturers are encouraged to talk about things they love and know about, but that are not centrally connected to their daytime occupation. Their short presentations are interspersed with snacks and drinks to encourage informality and stimulate conversation, and topics have ranged from food to the cosmos, internet memes and personal obsessions. The events always take place on Tuesday nights, and surprisingly to us at first, leave everyone energized and full of ideas.

The series' inception was sparked by curiosity. As expats living and working in Basel, the TEOK co-founders were genuinely puzzled by the large number of interesting people to be found in the city, not to mention its cultural capital and international aspect. In effect, Basel is, upon careful observation, one of the most international cities any of us has lived in to date; and not only that, but also filled to the brink with early and mid-career professionals with different life and cultural experiences, most of whom are significantly competent and have come here to work, live and achieve something. This makes for an extremely singular combination, and we were fundamentally curious about what moves and intrigues these people other than their day job. The foundation of TEOK hinges on the belief that all of us in this city know more about something than anyone else around them; should they share their knowledge, the lives of those who surround them will become better. The event series advocates the dissemination of knowledge in its most pure incarnation, and no topic is considered unfit for a TEOK lecture. Sharing is caring – and TEOK is the living proof of this assertion.

## Growth

Throughout the following nine months, TEOK grew in scope and complexity. Our speakers proposed new, interactive lecture formats, doing away with the projector at times and delving into more experimental territory. The curation process behind the event showed us that, at times, speakers don't think that what they are interested in can be interesting for a wider audience – it is our challenge to change their perspective, too, and make them see their own interests from an outsider's point of view. Topics and ideas

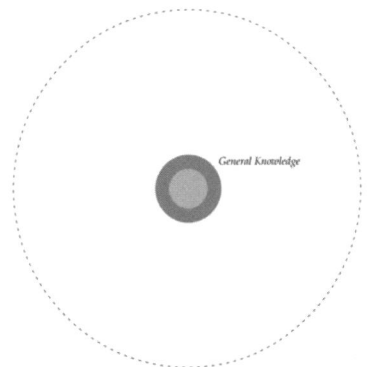

A   General knowledge, as seen within the sphere of knowledge.

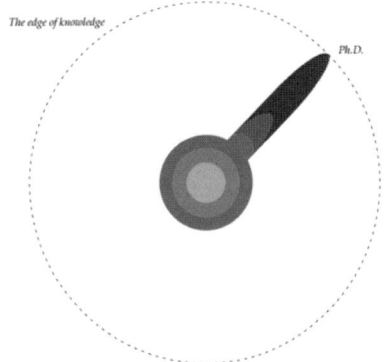

B   Reaching the edge of knowledge in any given field, marked by an exponential departure from the sphere of general knowledge.

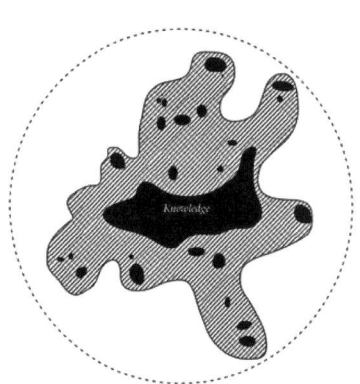 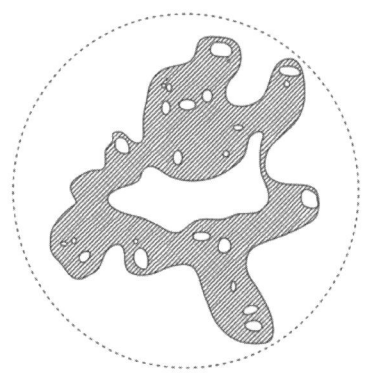

C    A redefinition of the sphere of knowledge: white marks the unknown, and black marks the known aspects within the sphere of knowledge.

D    A redefinition of the sphere of knowledge: the grey areas mark those aspects within the sphere of knowledge which we believe we know or know only fragments of.

discussed in the lectures soon became more interactive and participatory.

Jasmin Albash gave us a singing lesson, introducing TEOK guests to the Complete Vocal Technique and showing that everyone can sing even if they don't really think that they can. David Gregori y Ribes and Brigitte Clements brought unexpected food pairings, proposing combinations that challenged our notion of taste and enhanced our experience of coffee. But the complexity and interaction was not restrained to the mere formal aspect of the lectures; speakers like Tobias Eglauer challenged the core definition of The Edge of Knowledge [Fig. A and B], proposing a redefinition of knowledge [Fig. C] from a clear-cut term to an ambiguous denomination full of grey areas. [Fig. D] Through his lecture, we understood that knowledge is also incremental and questionable, and through unexpected interpretations there can be new ways of looking at the world around us. Similarly, lecturers such as Matylda Krzykowski raised the ante, proposing different ways to look at the world from the point of view of an object or typology. [Fig. E] Matylda chose the sausage as a typological starting point, and took TEOK guests on a fascinating tour that connected the dish to contemporary sculpture and minimalist art. Simultaneously, Mariana Santana also used her core training as an architect to take TEOK guests on a journey through François Schuiten and Benoît Peeters' *Les Cités Obscures* comic series. Her lecture was a typological delight, analyzing architectural influences and echoes in a singular parallel world. With these experiences, we understood that the creative audience that comprises most of the community around TEOK brings a fundamentally different outlook into the unexpected topics on which they choose to share their views. [Fig. F] This is a way of seeing that is fundamentally architectural and artistic, and ultimately changes the perspective of all those attending the event.

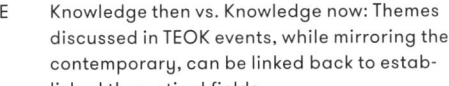

E   Knowledge then vs. Knowledge now: Themes discussed in TEOK events, while mirroring the contemporary, can be linked back to established theoretical fields.

F   The many links between themes presented at TEOK events help create a rhizomatic snapshot of contemporary knowledge production.

We didn't realize this would happen before we started, but slowly, TEOK grew from a mere friends' meet-up to something very different. As the events continued throughout the year of 2014, the community around TEOK grew and expanded exponentially. Drawing initially from the interests and intellectual pursuits of those nearer to us, we ended up getting in touch with several fascinating individuals and institutions, all of which merely confirmed the suspicion that gave rise to TEOK in the first place: we find that what we are actually doing is making a survey of the cultural outputs of the contemporary, creating a window into the fantastic, rich ensemble of people that live and work in this city.

## Expansion

At 7:40 p.m. in early December 2014, the large Depot Basel gallery space was empty. There were benches and chairs scattered around, some blankets on the wooden floor, and an unflinching beam of light projected onto white-painted glass, where the word TEOK floated in mid-air. A long side table harboured a myriad of vessels with small amounts of food inside. The fridge was full of beer. But there was nobody there. Yet, Depot Basel was the first local institution to invite TEOK to partner in one of their specific programs. Before, the event always depended on the generosity of its hosts, members of the TEOK community that offered their living rooms to host the event, determining the intimate scale and scope of each session and the reduced number of guests that could be present. At the end of the year, Depot Basel's invitation came just at the right moment – our 10th edition and one-year anniversary – giving us the opportunity to reflect, for the first time, on the nature and potential impact of TEOK. It also gave us the opportunity to inhabit a larger space and open up the event to the whole city: projecting the lectures onto one of the Depot Basel windows, we created a moving display that could be seen by anyone crossing the surroundings. The structure of the evening was, on this occasion, more ambitious and somewhat more formalized. Adhering to Depot Basel's DISPLAY program, the 10th edition of TEOK was structured around that concept in collaboration with Depot Basel, with lectures delving more or less literally into the topic – ranging from a taxonomy of museum displays to Spanish roundabout "art". Over the next days, many encounters around the city still referenced the evening: people were intrigued, stimulated and curious, had thought about the presentations on their way home, debated them with their partners and friends, taking TEOK outside the time and place of the event, into their brains, their lives, their conversations. The impact continued beyond the physical reality of the event: it had stayed with those who had witnessed it, not just a visual impression, but sparking intangible consequences in thoughts and ideas.

This immaterial impact, intangible and immeasurable, is for us the most rewarding aspect of TEOK. The repeated observation that the events stay in the minds and hearts of people has made us wonder if in contemporary society, where the Taylorist conception of work and production is currently falling into decline and constantly being questioned, there can be new models to inspire and encourage work and production – in our particular case, the production of knowledge. And it has also made us ask ourselves if TEOK is not just an opportunity to disseminate, but to generate knowledge itself, capturing the essence of the contemporary. As we question what the future impact and reach of this initiative promises to be, TEOK has started to expand and evolve, in a rhizomatic manner that has started to escape our control. The original concept of an intimate event is still maintained and continued in Basel. Simultaneously, TEOK has forged partnerships and collaborations, such as the one we initiated with Depot Basel, and generated offshoots in different cities – until now, Madrid and Santiago. The event series has gained a standing in other contexts, reinforcing existing networks and uncovering new possibilities of collaboration, creating new modes of inspiration and spreading what we've come to believe is a good virus.

TEOK was conceived in Basel in 2014 by Marta Colón, Juan Palencia and Vera Sacchetti. See what we're up to at *teok.info*, follow us on social media, subscribe to our mailing list and come to one of our events!

AUTHORS

Juan Palencia (1981) is an architect and designer, co-curator of the TEOK informal lecture series and an avid social media user with a fine eye for internet imagery. Following his training at ETSAM Madrid, Juan developed projects with award winning studios, among them Langarita-Navarro Arquitectos, Estudio Luis Úrculo and HHF Architects, while simultaneously conducting an independent architecture and design activity. Juan is currently based in Basel, Switzerland, where he is an architect at Burkhardt+Partner.

Vera Sacchetti (1983) is a design writer and critic. She is co-curator of TEOK Basel, managing editor at the Barragan Foundation and co-founder of the editorial consultancy Superscript. Originally trained as a communication designer, Vera attended SVA's MFA in Design Criticism as a Fulbright scholar. She was formerly curatorial assistant for the BIO 50 design biennial in Ljubljana, web editor at Domus, co-editor of "The Adhocracy Reader" for the 1st Istanbul Design Biennial, and served as head of international communications at EXD'11/LISBOA. With Superscript, she headed the "Towards a New Avant-Garde" event series at the 2014 Venice Architecture Biennale. Her writing has appeared in Domus, Disegno, Change Observer, The New City Reader and Frame, among others.

IMAGE CREDITS

A–B  Adapted from Matt Might, presented at TEOK #2.1 by Stefano Orani.
C–D  Adapted from the diagram presented at TEOK #6.1 by Tobias Eglauer.
E    Graphics by TEOK.
F    Images courtesy of Stefano Orani (TEOK #2.1), Chrissie Muhr (TEOK #9.1), Giulia Mela (TEOK #3.1) and Matylda Krzykowski (TEOK #8.2).

Mark Minkjan

# How to Move from Architectural Cheerleading to Architecture Criticism

### Not worth sharing: visual snacks

The problem with most architectural media is that the largest share of their content is made up of visual snacks – those smooth renderings and glossy photographs we see flashing by in our social media feeds. Fast food is the quickest and easiest way to satisfy an appetite, while it hardly contains anything substantial. That's why you'll crave for more soon after your first snack, which again won't benefit your health. Architectural media fill a demand for luscious images, but substantial reflection on the social and public relevance of celebrated projects is sparse. This has a detrimental impact on the condition of the architectural profession and what it produces: the built world we live in. If you were to create a live feed of the latest updates from the most-visited architectural websites and blogs – which is child's play with all the great sharing tools available – what you would see is a constant flood of either fantasy renderings that can never become reality or stylized photographs of luxurious design scenery. Both of which have nothing to do with the real lives that most of us live. Call it the 99 percent, if you like.

Indeed, this is already an alarming observation, but what is worse still is that this visual overload is hardly met with suspicion. Architectural projects should be questioned for their actual functioning in reality, for their societal impact, their political meaning or their developers' intentions. These are just a few of the crucial criteria that are often overlooked or ignored. Instead, designs are merely consumed as visual fast food, and architecture seems to have been completely de-politicized and reduced to an aesthetic undertaking for the media that cover it.

The demand for the newest, most spectacular snacks to look at is insatiable. We continually browse the optimistic imaginations of what the future could look like and aren't interested in

A     Rendering by Urban Future Organization (UFO) and CR-design.

what the visual treats say about a culture or mean for a society. What's uploaded today is out-dated tomorrow. There's an endless, vicious cycle in force: if the design is not spectacular enough, it's not published and if it's not published, it's obviously not spectacular enough. To make it even more incestuous, the main consumers of these media are architects or aspiring designers. Who are they designing for? Moreover, what are architects-in-training to expect of their future careers when following the media that cover their desired profession? What are architects to expect their designs to be judged on? The media are contributing to a dumbing down of how we see architecture. Reporting on architecture is less and less about creating better cities in an equitable way, but increasingly describes individual projects without analysing architecture as a larger social project and the separate designs as an articulation of political, economic and social choices. Most design media content only consists of aggregations of blindly republished press releases, renderings and photos that have been sent in by architecture offices, while omitting interpretation. Here, the audience is withheld guidance to understand the world in which the slick projects are constructed or to decipher what they say about the culture that brings them about. Everything has to be easily digestible and instantly satisfying, and people aren't challenged to put things in perspective. By walking down the path of today's visual culture, the media have made their content attractive to both the layman and the architect, but naturally such a crowd-pleasing attitude goes at the expense of intelligent reflection.

### Worth sharing: productive criticism

So that's what I think is not worth sharing. But what is worth sharing? Clearly it's not the architectural cheerleading in a media world where the coverage has become the architects' PR. Architecture does not equal fashion. It is more than just a consumer good that only enhances the appearance of its buyer. Rather, the design of space has a direct effect on the world we live in. Therefore it should not just be talked about for its shapes and materials. Architecture can create value for the entire public, but it can also be exclusive terrain for the happy few, while helping those who use it to dress up their real estate investments making a fortune, leaving the rest empty-handed. Its main objective should not be to be most fashionable. Presenting it as such in the media is anything but constructive if we want to talk about how architecture can contribute to society. Instead, it should be questioned and investigated to the fullest extent. What is worth sharing today is proper architecture criticism that puts design into context, and is not tucked away in obscure magazines or the outskirts of cyberspace.

Although having become increasingly rare in today's media landscape, there are still critics who judge architecture not by its image, but by its public meaning and urban implications. They try to reveal the cracks in the shiny surface, dig out facts about the politics and economics that determine the architectural outcome and their social effect on the city. These practices are the things that deserve more sharing. Architecture is not (just) its image; it is always political. It is also always a social and economic affair. That's where the issues at stake lie. The culture that builds it should be analysed and its effects on the world should be traced back to it. Therefore we need more experts from various fields to evaluate the built environment and broaden the focus on architecture, while letting this analysis feed into the media that scrutinize design. Architecture should be seen as a societal project. The questions that should be asked include: whose interests are served? Who profits? What does it do for a city besides looking spectacular and being expensive? Why do we – the public – need this project? Why did the local government approve of it? Of course, beauty (although a subjective, fluctuating quality) is not something negligible. In fact it should also be promoted as an enriching public value that architecture can bring, but it should be something that everyone can enjoy, not just those who can afford the Pinterest-popular architecture. The renewed serious interest in architecture should take root again in several fields of media. Dedicated architecture media have to pick up the critical magnifying glass again, while other media should reposition architecture at the heart of the societal debate. A prime example of the latter is the British newspaper *The Guardian*, which has developed its 'Architecture and Design Blog' into a more active and committed architecture section over the past few years, currently being one of the go-to online sources for an intelligent contextualization of architecture. Here, architectural projects and urban plans are subjected to serious scrutiny and the appearance of the designs is anything but the main topic. Instead, spatial design is regarded a civic undertaking that is the result of politics and economics and influences the well being of people. Design is only seen as the physical expression that represents dominant ideals and agendas. If more media outlets follow this example, the public attitude towards architecture can become more critical. Simultaneously, design professionals and architecture students will recapture the awareness that they are working on a social project – instead of seeing the job as being vain set-dressers for those that actually decide how cities work – and can eventually take back a central role in urban development.

The twenty-first century architecture critic is less preoccupied with geometry, dramatic light and other visual traits, but rather focuses on what architecture does and where it comes from, analysing not only single buildings but expanding her or his focus to entire cities and cultures: from the political process that led to certain designs or plans being realized, to the effect on the socioeconomic composition of a city, to the public gains and public expenses architecture generates. Sure, no single person can do all of this on his or her own. But with all the available sharing tools, the broad body of architecture criticism can be brought together. Urban space philosophers, hard core planning legislation experts, social critics, architects, economy writers, geographers and others should all contribute to the debate.

And no, this kind of media attention for architecture doesn't have to be boring. It shouldn't be abstract, because it is about places that people can relate to. It's about the world we live in – or want to live in – and for that reason relevant to everyone. We should be talking about the things we see, but shed light on the dark matter behind it. In an age of growing urban development pressure worldwide that crowds our cities, the real issues call for more attention, and hence for real journalism that requires time and skill. But the result is worth it, and absolutely worth sharing. So let's change our architectural media diet from fast food to multi-ingredient slow cooking. Let's shift our focus from visual quantity to urban quality.

AUTHOR

Mark Minkjan is an urban and architectural geographer. He is co-founder of the Failed Architecture Foundation and editor-in-chief at *failedarchitecture.com*. Mark is also part of Amsterdam-based Non-fiction, an office for cultural innovation.

IMAGE CREDITS

A  Courtesy of urban future organization and CR-design. www.designboom.com/architecture/ufo-cr-design-cloud-citizen-shenzhen-super-city-competition-09-15-2014/

Antoine Prokos

# This Changes Everything

Architecture of the Commons

The narrative of architectural history is a powerful tool for theory, if not the authentic form of theory in our discipline. It is of course being continuously analyzed and debated with a huge degree of complexity. Nowadays, 40 years after the reformulation of the context of architectural history by Manfredo Tafuri and his group, merely going into the matter demands an immense amount of theoretical precision in order to avoid repeating common knowledge or worse, contributing to the pile of meaningless pseudo-theoretical alchemy. Nevertheless the debate is far from closed, especially if we consider new urgencies and new concerns which are now more real than ever. The agenda of a hundred, fifty or even ten years ago cannot be taken into account in the same way as before. We need to search for new meaning and for new stories. Below are some thoughts about a possible one.

When the now orthodox debate on operative criticism was still radical and revolutionary, one of the founding principles of architecture as we know it was silently being subjected to scrutiny from a hugely pertinent angle. The Doric temple, the "starting point for European architecture"[1] might have been born through a process which was much less self-referential than has been thought to date. In 1990, Goerd Peschken, German archaeologist and architectural historian, published a text called "Demokratie und Tempel"[2] (Temple and Democracy). Based on the abundant visual material published by Rudofsky[3] and an earlier study by another historian, Hans Soeder[4], he attempts to explain the ancestry of the Doric order within the functional vernacular of granaries. Peschken, following in Soeder's path, observed the similarities between the triglyph-metope sequence and the lateral walls of various types of vernacular granaries ventilated with thin vertical openings in a rhythm of plain parts and regrouped slits. In addition, a picture of such a barn is a pretty self-explanatory statement on the columns and the capitals. To protect the grain from rodents, the construction is placed on top of columns themselves finished with a horizontal plate. According to Peschken, pieces of cloth drenched in repellent (Ionic order) or acanthus leaves (Corinthian order) that are naturally unpleasant to vermin were often added to this capital. Peschken's work has come back to light with the third issue of the French architectural journal "Marnes", which resulted in an initial debate on the implications of the matter. Most notably, in an article published in the same issue, Philippe Villien proposed looking at Peschken's interpretation of the Doric order in line with Banham's pledge for the well-tempered environment.[5] The thick roof and the triglyph as a ventilation apparatus support such an idea, but can we be satisfied with reiterating a well-known and decently understood point where there is room for so much more? Where Villien sees an argument about climate in architecture, there is probably the missed opportunity for symbolism that goes much further than the hierarchy between structure and piping.

While Villen's observations on architecture and the environment do not go very far, he does grasp the most important point that we all need to acknowledge: "Demokratie und Tempel" is an excellent starting point for a very important evolutionary step in the current status quo of architectural theory. Even if they are not a call for the complete reversal of our knowledge, these observations offer a new, stimulating possibility for the whole moral genealogy behind architectural thought. Until now, we thought that a given structure, the temple, invited reflection through its special character on the perfect construction and led to the sublimation of previous construction. Peschken's and Soeder's assumptions link this open question of the language of architecture with the most pure form of collective meaning: the agricultural and territorial organization that is the one and only origin, the unique true subject of common existence as we know it.

It goes without saying that the topic of the commons has always been present. While ancient Greece coped rather simply with the issue, maybe in part thanks to the symbolic power of the temple, the Roman Empire had a pronounced dependency on a much more complex scheme. With its accomplished territorial management and the powerful soldier-slave feedback loop, it achieved a very high level of sophistication in the distribution and transformation of common goods.[6] Although the Doric order had been almost forgotten by the time Rome started its expansion[7], there is evidence for civic architecture with explicit symbolism related to the Commons within the intriguing artefacts left behind by the empire. One of the most significant being the tomb of Eurysaces, the freedman baker.

The symbolism generally attributed to this tomb is that of the freedman.[8] Its foremost significance is understood inclusively within social status, underlining the importance of the family line within the Roman Empire and the struggle of the former slaves, the bourgeois of their age, to elevate themselves and their families into some form of posterity. But the most important symbol might be a different one, that of the baker. The ornamentation of the tomb stems, in fact, from Eurysace's occupation. The round motifs on the façade are alleged to correspond to the measuring units of grain[9], thereby preserving these for posterity, if not for Eurysace's family. The passage from the form of the granary to the rules of bakery is very well suited to schematize the different hierarchies in the handling of resources between the Greek and Roman periods. The question is no longer about the collective capacity to provide

A

B

C

society with grain, as that is taken for granted, but much more about individual capacity to succeed through transformation of a resource that is given. This shift on a vast scale is the same as that which has operated for a couple of centuries. It is at the very centre of our own predicament.

There is an opening here for further discussion of the crisis of the present, the environmental crisis, while refraining of course from theorizing any form of sustainable development. This term in itself has become a label for an anti-theoretical fantasy, a form of wishful thinking already lurking within Banham's technological dream. It is no secret to anyone that the modes of common existence, embodied in their initial purity by the temple, need profound questioning in their current form, 2500 years later. This interpretation is becoming more relevant every day, with the problem of the 21st century rapidly emerging not as a mere problem of technology but also as an inclusive ethical problem, a problem of capacity, of resources and of mere honesty and morality towards the Commons. This naïve speculation on language doesn't offer any solution to the current set of problems, but I hope it is a clear introduction to something worth sharing.

### AUTHOR

Antoine Prokos was born and raised in Athens, Greece. He left the country to undertake his studies in architecture at the Ecole Polytechnique Fédérale of Lausanne. After his undergraduate studies in Lausanne and Delft, Antoine worked with architect Jean-Gilles Décosterd, while also participating in projects by Studio KG and the organization of Lausanne-Jardins 2014. He has also realized freelance projects in Switzerland and Ivory Coast.

NOTES

1. Georg Peschken, Demokratie und Tempel: die Bedeutung der dorischen Architektur, Berlin, Verlag der Beeken, 1990. French translation by Corinne Jacquand in Marnes III, May 2014, p. 289.
2. Peschken, Ibid. pp. 289 – 313.
3. Bernard Rudofsky, Architecture Without Architects, New York, Museum of Modern Art, 1964, illustrations 90-94.
4. Hans Soeder, Urformen der abendländlischen Baukunst, Köln, edited by Carl J. Soeder, M. DuMont Schauberg, 1964, pp.121 – 125.
5. Philippe Villien, Le Dorique Bien Tempéré, published in Marnes III, May 2014, pp. 329 – 341.
6. In this way our own society is not too dissimilar to the Roman one, the soldier/agent of acceleration having been replaced by the consumer and the slave/source of energy having been replaced by fossil fuels. The decrease in resilience as the system stretched and overshot was meant to be the main reason of the decline of the Empire, as it will be for our own empire. See Paolo Fedeli, Ecologie Antique, Paris, inFolio, 2005. and Jared Diamond, Collapse: How societies choose to Fail or Succeed, New York, Penguin Books, 2005.
7. Peschken, Ibidem pp. 289 – 290.
8. On the significations of the tomb see Lauren Hackworth Petersen, The Baker, His Tomb, His Wife and Her Breadbasket: The Monument of Eurysaces in Rome, Art Bulletin Volume 85, Issue 2, 2003 and, by the same author, The Freedman in Roman Art and History, Cambridge, Cambridge University Press, 2006.
9. Samuel Ball Platner & Thomas Ashby, A Topographical Dictionary of Ancient Rome, Oxford Reprints Series, Oxford, Oxbow books, 2002.

IMAGE CREDITS

A. Le Corbusier, Vers une Architecture, p. 16.
B. © Philippe Villien, Marnes III p. 332.
C. Samuel Ball Platner, A Topographical Dictionary of Ancient Rome, p. 412 – 413.

AbdulFatah Adam

# Under Demand

"What is the city today, for us? I believe that I have written something like a last love poem addressed to the city, at a time when it is becoming increasingly difficult to live there."
Italo Calvino on 'Invisible Cities'.

The conception of contemporary architecture relies very much on the ways in which art and culture intervene in the conversations and debates about the modern city. The paradigm of the contemporary African city – in this context, Nairobi and Mogadishu specifically – depends wholly on the ever-changing worldview of what Africa is, what an 'African' is, and most importantly, where Africa seeks to define itself in the context of its constant conflicted reference to the West. African architecture has had a protracted engagement with the natural and material sciences – what it is experiencing now is not an organic transition but rather the constant morphing of the persona of the architect from artist, to draftsman, to cultural consultant and, occasionally, to tradesman. Today in Africa, the architect encounters cities facing the crises of post-war Europe or America. These are cities long deemed incapable of meeting the demands of societies in rapid expansion but still in a constant rush to add to a concrete melee that grows increasingly entangled by the day. Cities ravaged by war and economic crisis which insist on expanding along the grain and which every day continue to attract immigrants worldwide – an engagement forced by multiple circumstances, often urgently and without the foresight that is an urban planner's dent. Government task forces and professional urbanists are constantly engaged in discussions about urban revitalization, while the architect on the ground lays slab after slab to keep up with the demand of cities constantly on the rise.

We observe two cities, growing in tandem but confronting distinct realities. Mogadishu builds

A

B

against the living legacy of a thirty-year war that has ravaged a once beautiful landscape – there the architect is challenged to create an experience of the land that is aesthetically rehabilitative, responding constantly to physically traumatic realities. Nairobi, on the other hand, attempts to erase the heavy memory of apartheid. A city built as the ideal manifestation of racial classification, today the architect has the heady task of creating an environment where the city's denizens are mobilized into a tangible social mobility, contrary to the historic restrictions of their environment. In thinking about the possibility of architecture to profoundly alter the makeup of politics and nations, it is the architect's challenge to seek out new possibilities for architecture in order to move forward from the impositions of the modernist movement on a landscape such as this.

In that respect, the architect is pushed to question the purpose of architecture in the physical context to begin with, and moreover in the metaphysical context – to examine the genesis of movements for which there is often little motivation beyond urgency and necessity.

It is in these that the architect comes to stand precariously on untested ground. He becomes both urban planner and design theorist to a new age of architecture fitted to the social realities of a modern Africa. One where the landscape is advised by both the residue of colonialism – a long and dark legacy – and the neo "Afropolitan" fantasy which merges with a savvy Africa with a returning diaspora that brings new perspectives of the West – perspectives which are no longer heavy with the inheritance of war, drought or hunger.

The architect designs for spaces where trauma is deeply embedded in the physical archive. A 'spatial therapist', his work does not end on his computer screen or on his drafting board. He is challenged to engage with the spaces in which he works in a constant discussion of past disturbances pitted against the promise of a brighter

C

D

future. In every way, he is challenged to recreate the narratives of spaces whose history cannot be determined but yet are hungry to build a future rooted in a glorious past. To these changing realities he is obliged to adapt by using a thoroughly interdisciplinary approach, one that reaches beyond the concept of form in order to include technical, economic, social, and political needs in urban design discussions. In this respect, he is obliged to form collaborative and creative relationships with artists of various disciplines – engaging conversations across mediums to inform what he then manifests in his construction of a lived reality. In engaging multiple disciplines, the architect, as the creator of tangible or literally concrete spaces, becomes in his realm the primary incubator of artistic thought – building the infrastructure in which culture is able to thrive. Here we step away from the utopic fantasy of architecture where the architect designs for a demystified context. Immersed in the chaos of modernity, the architect builds a response, often facing off and challenging business monopolies, politicians and developers. In this respect, utopia becomes a question of engagement – an ethical and social stance or commitment towards creating worlds that respond to the needs of their populations, rather than imposing a physical scope on urbanites and urging them into a reluctant and impractical adjustment.

E

#### AUTHOR

AbdulFatah Adam (Nairobi, 1982) studied architecture at the University of Nairobi. After doing an internship at Herzog & de Meuron (2009) he went back to Nairobi where he worked for DesignARTitude and was involved in design and construction of several projects, notably a mosque and community centre. Thereafter, AbdulFatah founded studio.14, which is based in Nairobi and Mogadishu (Somalia) and is involved in solving design problems, ranging from graphic to architectural.

#### IMAGE CREDITS

Photographs by AbdulFatah Adam.

CARTHA

# Guido Guidi
## A Visual Contribution

Ganko on Guido Guidi

## Living Traces

"Le temps qui passe (mon Histoire) dépose des résidus qui s'empilent : des photos, des dessins, des corps de stylos-feutres depuis longtemps desséchés, des chemises, des verres perdus et des verres consignés, des emballages de cigares, des boîtes, des gommes, des cartes postales, des livres, de la poussière et des bibelots : c'est ce que j'appelle ma fortune."
Georges Perec

"To live is to leave traces."[1]; thus reads one of Walter Benjamin's best-known aphorisms. The statement is not so obvious as to present no difficulties. Above all – and contrary to what one might expect – it is not about melancholy; at least not only so.

We live in a time dominated by the categories of abstraction and indifference, a time of definitive erasure of specificity and ultimate interchangeability: the era of the generic. "Liberated from the straitjacket of identity"[2], everything is reduced to communication flow, is rootlessly free to move from anywhere to anywhere, encountering no resistance, leaving no traces. Through the ubiquity of simulacra and the mass-mediatic conflation of time's three horizons into an indissoluble 'now', we live in a condition of "eternal present"[3], where the possibility to address any sort of permanence seems to be precluded a-priori. In a world pervaded by distrust for the past and disillusion toward the future, the question is how to turn our postmodern nihilism into simultaneously critical and operative tools. Is there any way to exploit our cynicism in order to readdress a proactive and authentic notion of life? Is there any way to use our disillusion? Certainly, since Benjamin's times, to leave traces may have become increasingly difficult. Traces are something ephemeral, a locus of ambivalence suspended in the unstable space between construction and dispersal, presence and absence.[4] Nevertheless, although mostly unintentionally, we still do leave traces in our wake. Beyond the decay to which they bear witness, the mutability to which they testify, traces are also insistence, persistence, survival. No matter how fragile and trifling it might be; a trace is always an index of life.

The pictures by Guido Guidi that inspire these words share a sense of precariousness that is far remote from the mythic aura of timelessness that has enveloped today's world. In all its inertia, the reality they portray is nevertheless provisional; still vulnerable to the vicissitudes of time. With humbleness and discretion, these pictures pay homage to places that hold a strong value for their author, therefore distancing themselves also from local indifference so typical of the globalism of our times. These pictures 'are' the places where he lives and, as we can guess, he loves. They are surely places he has deeply experienced: his native region *Emilia Romagna* and its neighbouring region *Veneto*. Perhaps this autobiographism should discourage perception of them as models for reflection of a general nature, but it is exactly the outdated nature of these images that constitutes a reason of compelling interest. They represent the outmoded insistence of their author on the definition of boundaries – the preliminary limitation of the field of investigation to the well-known and the ordinary, the necessity of a solid anchorage to reality – and are not a contained work ultimately driven by the fear of chaos, but by the act that makes its full exploitation and enjoyment ultimately possible.

With scientific accuracy these pictures follow life and its unfolding, accompanying the patient accumulation of its traces, their vanishing as well as their survival, in order to restitute to us the sedimented history of a place. Combining the apparent detachment of an archive with the impossibility of establishing an emotional distance from the object of their attentions, they subtly unveil a strong meditative charge. The boundaries between intuition and knowledge, analysis and affection, distance and intimacy continuously blur within these images. These pictures do not judge the life they record; they are not a medium conveying their author's opinions, but simply a medium that allows us to share his experiences. Each picture is not only the record of a fleeting impression over the artist's eye, but a thoughtful contribution to the understanding of a context that is plural from the very beginning. A background from which the photographer – as anybody else – can emerge only momentarily, before seamlessly blending into it and ultimately – as dictates the destiny we all share – vanishes. Each of these images is the act of participation in a collective project.

> "I do photographs to see better, with more clarity. Maybe then, the others will also see better."[5]

Although their acute awareness of life's temporal essence can certainly induce a sense of melancholic acceptance, these pictures are pervaded by a force that suggests a less nostalgic and more proactive understanding. After all, nostalgia is nothing but memory projected into the future; life seen through the eyes of those who will come. Like Benjamin's Angel of History, despite looking back, these images are moving forward. Even accepting a certain degree of disenchantment as a constituent part, if these pictures are anyway nostalgic it is not because they recall some idealised past – rather the opposite given their often marginal subjects – but because of the light they shed on the future. Collecting the signs of past and present, these photographs activate our reasoning in the incessant search to answer the perplexity engendered by an increasingly precarious reality. Each image is not only an act of archaeological documentation prompted by the necessity to preserve memory, but an invitation to actively engage in the eternal process of accumulation of traces that is life. Deeply aware of their own impermanence, these images stand for a perpetually open, yet to be determined – and defended – future. In the moment when they expose us to the impersonal and anonymous spectacles of history – the more silent and unpretentious as well as the more traumatic and monumental – they remind us of our collective responsibility toward the future we share, the traces we leave.

### AUTHOR

Ganko produces architecture. Ganko was established in 2011 by Guido Tesio (1984) and Nicola Munaretto (1984) following previous experiences with Baukuh (Milan) and OFFICE kgdvs (Brussels). After three years spent between Milan and Beijing, in 2014 Ganko has relocated to Basel and Lausanne, Switzerland. In 2013 Ganko was invited to contribute to the book "Pure Hardcore Icons: A Manifesto for Pure Form in Architecture" edited by WAI Think Tank for Artifice Books, London. Since 2014 Ganko has been guest editor for the catalogues of Beijing-based art gallery Intelligentsia. Recent works by Ganko have been featured in Domusweb, StudioMagazine and SanRocco.

### NOTES

1 Walter Benjamin, "Paris, Capital of the Nineteenth Century", in Reflections: Essays, Aphorisms, Autobiographical Writings, New York, 1986.
2 Rem Koolhaas, The Generic City, in S,M,L,XL, 1995.
3 Fredric Jameson, "Postmodernism, or, the Cultural Logic of Late Capitalism."
4 Rye Dag Holmboe, "Gabriel Orozco: Cosmetic Matter and Other Leftovers", in The White Review, Online Issue, march 2011.
5 Guido Guidi, La Figura dell' Orante. Appunti per una Lezione 1, Ed. del Bradipo, Ravenna 2012 (English translation by the authors).

### IMAGE CREDITS

Photographs gently shared by Guido Guidi through Galeria Pedro Alfacinha.

# I
# CONFRÈRES

| | | | |
|---|---|---|---|
| 66 | **CARTHA**<br>Editorial | 99 | **Maria Barreiros**<br>Hierarchy and Process in Architectural Working Structures |
| 70 | **Matilde Girão, Interview**<br>Grafton Architects | 116 | **Atelier Angular**<br>Bridging the Gaps |
| 78 | **Andrew Mackintosh**<br>Sharing without Dialogue | 120 | **Migrant Garden**<br>40 Architects Making 40 Birdnests |
| 82 | **Benjamin Krüger**<br>My Eyes Are not Our Eyes | 124 | **Victoria Collar Ocampo**<br>Shared Concerns – Inquietudes Compartidas |
| 90 | **Luis Pedro Pinto**<br>A Letter to RG | 128 | **Visual Contribution**<br>Rasmus Norlander |
| 94 | **Whoodstudio**<br>Les Garages – We, Ourselves and I; New Spaces for Modern Nomads | 135 | **S.A. Bramble on Rasmus Norlander**<br>Enclosed Moments |

I CONFRÈRES

## Confrère: "fellow member of a profession"

How do architects relate to each other nowadays? Before trying to address this question, it is pertinent to make a clarification, to distinguish between types of relations and ways of communication. Although they inform each other, they are not necessarily the same. Relations amongst architects is a very intriguing and inclusive map of these three elements: architectural representations, balance between "I" and "we", and time. When we talk about ways of communication, we are referring to ways of experiencing architecture. Hence, we could say that the only impartial way of doing this is by visiting buildings and cities. By contrast, partial ways of experimentation are representational media such as texts, drawings, floor plans, sections, elevations, perspectives, renderings, images, as well as representations of built architecture such as photographs or videos. All these ways of communication present a partial or edited view by the person who produces them.

What are the types of relations amongst colleagues? Historically, we could mention a number of professional relationships: the master-apprentice relationship with its transmission of knowledge within a hierarchical system which has evolved in complexity over time; the arena of public competitions and public and published debates; schools; professional associations and manifestos or groups.

However, what is of utmost relevance here is that these types of relations or any others are governed by the timeless conflict of the binomial "I" versus "we", or the creator-author versus group-collaboration. Our present world allows for unconscious or non-orchestrated global relations nurtured by an increase in exposure to architectural representations and designs as well as the consequent impact on projects by architects who are often geographically and culturally far apart. Accordingly, communications and means of travel also allow for collaborations which are no longer restricted by geographical limits. This prompts a revision of the figure of the journeyman. Nowadays, we all find ourserlves in an intensified and perpetuated journeyman state.

Competitions – As with all other service providers linked into the capitalist system, architects have two paths from which to choose when approaching the acquisition of a job: present better quality or present a cheaper price than their competitors. The issue of quality is not always clear-cut; it remains, from a certain point onwards, open to interpretation. Prices are figures, and as such, are easy to compare.

This seemingly democratic system of acquiring/appointing a job through open competition can raise the general quality of architecture and allow young architects to compete with established ones on neutral ground. On the other hand, it can also create situations of precariousness when the prices paid for architectural services are reduced in the desperate struggle to obtain "work". In which situation do we find ourselves in?

School and professional associations – It would be pertinent to ask whether they are carrying out their job of being platforms for communication and exchange amongst architects as well as fulfilling their role towards society for the dissemination of architectural knowledge. We could question whether the number and size of schools in each country truly facilitates those goals. Are these institutions succeeding or failing in supporting the profession?

Manifestos – Do they make sense nowadays? Are they becoming more frequent? This is the cyclic connotation of Time. Will we soon witness a revival of manifestos? Or maybe they never really left us.

Where is the focus in the binomial "I" versus "we"? Is it on current relations amongst architects particularly affected by the idea of collaboration and a social agenda? Is the focus coming back to the "we", to a broader social-politic dimension of architecture?

2008 – 2015, we could list Madrid, London, New York, Hong Kong, the Arab Spring: the beats of these manifestations continue to resonate. The precariousness in the profession due to the imbalance between the number of architects and the size of the market, as well as to the unsolved adaptation of architecture to new professional scenarios where the architect has very limited control over the cities and the construction processes, is silently eroding the professional scenario in more than a few countries.

Today we are at the dawn of a new age and we have just witnessed the decline of an era characterized by the celebration of excess to different extents. On the one hand, the excess of construction with a dramatic impact on the number of built properties, the housing market collapse, and the use of the territory; on the other hand, the excessive celebration of the "I" that gave rise to the late 20th century architectural star system and marked a certain period. Nowadays, it seems that this is not the way to go. This phenomenon was in part the reverse side of large public expenditures on iconic buildings that no longer enjoy the acceptance of citizens. In addition, ecological concerns are growing rapidly. Ecology understood as something collective, social and energetically efficient. The new generations, and by new generation we mean practicing architects regardless of their age, are affected by an increased awareness of this concept of community.

We believe this to be the global scenario that consciously or unconsciously informs the experiences of our contributors. Indeed, such a perfect cocktail results, as stated, not only in a major awareness of ecological and collective issues, but also in greater interest in collaboration as a strategy to face challenging times.

Matilde Girão

# Grafton Architects

Interview

Living in a network culture, where communication travels at a speed of a link, we position ourselves to stay one station away from a destination. Plugging in/out; switching on/off; signing in/out is our response to a working agenda. There is no address to where the interview took place. There is a common virtual space of communication.

> "(...) supermodernity produces non-places, meaning spaces which are not themselves anthropological places and which, unlike Baudelairean modernity, do not integrate the earlier places: instead these are listed, classified, promoted to the status of 'places of memory', and assigned to a circumscribed and specific position"
>
> Marc Augé, Non-Places:
> Introduction to an Anthropology of Supermodernity, 1995, p. 77 – 78.

It was both 4 p.m. local time, in Dublin and in Lisbon. Our distance was as far as logging in; entering our username and accepting the invitation to establish a virtual space connection via Skype – a telecommunication video chat. And that's that. Proving right our condition in today's society, from that moment on, we were both conditionally framed in each other's screen. There was no place of reference, but an ephemeral transitional entity.

Sharing common grounds since 1970, Shelley Mc Namara and Yvonne Farrell, both graduates of UCD – University Collegue Dublin – established Grafton Architects in 1978 (*graftonarchitects.ie*). They are Fellows of the RIAI (Royal Institute of the Architects of Ireland); International Honorary Fellows of the RIBA (Royal Institute of British Architects) and are elected members of Aosdána, the eminent Irish Art organization. They have recently won the fourth annual Jane Drew Prize.

Yvonne Farrell & Shelley McNamara, Grafton Architects

**What is the meaning of *confrère* to you?**
By *confrère* you mean collaboration?

**Exactly. As a form of engagement between architects.**
Right. I think architecture is a collaborative endeavour. Whether it's within the studio or beyond the studio. In one of your questions, from the review you sent previously, you ask about Group 91 and how the collaboration worked. Maybe I'll speak about that first and then come back to the meaning of the word. So, in Ireland, I think without us realizing, three generation of architects had been teaching together ever since being students together. And, what happens when you are teaching together is that you develop very long conversations and again maybe without us realizing, we were developing a common ground. Our common ground for Group 91. We felt, especially in Ireland, that there was an architectural culture to be built. We were conscious that in other countries there was a much stronger culture of contemporary 20th century architecture and this is to do with the fact that we were a young country in terms of our independence. And there were a lot of issues, I suppose, regarding identity and many other things. So, Group 91 happened because this was in the air. And when Dublin was City of Culture

> We were against all the big commercial offices, including some international commercial offices – SOM. So a group of seven small practices came together to take part in this competition and we won.

in 1991, we knew it was time to react and do something. We came together to make a project, which was about developing new typologies based on the eighteenth century houses in Dublin – eighteenth century Dublin is a city of houses – and because at that time it was quite derelict in the city centre, we felt that it needed its streets rebuilt with new house types. So that was our first reason for setting up Group 91, to make this exhibition. Then because this group was already formed, when a competition was announced for the regeneration of a very large quarter in Dublin, called Temple Bar, we were shortlisted to be one of the practices to enter this competition. We were against all the big commercial offices, including some international commercial offices – SOM. So a group of seven small practices came together to take part in this competition and we won.

**And did you have a sort of group manifesto?**
We had an unspoken manifesto that we had developed over time. We believed in the repair of the city. We believed in the idea of city as a series of layers not needing the tabula rasa approach and so we adopted – not knowing the word at the time, which Manuel de Sola Morales coined – an urban acupuncture philosophy. That was what we were doing – repairing and stitching back this piece of city together. So it was a very exciting and important time for us. For seven offices to come together was not an easy task and what was good was that each practice came to make one project.

**Ok, so this was the starting point?**
Yes, this was the starting point. And going back to your question about *confrères*, in general, I think there is a strong connection between teaching and practice in architecture. We find this a very fruitful relationship. We try to make our office feel like a studio. We absolutely believe in collaboration as the very core and basic idea in the practice of architecture.

**I imagine this also links to the number of collaborators you have in your studio.**
Yes, we keep our studio quite small. The largest we have ever been is 21, maybe 22. This is probably the limit we would like to oparate

as in order to maintain very direct and personal relationship with each project and with each group. This allows for a cross-fertilization between groups, so that sometimes a group of people working on one project jumps to reinforce another, which we believe to be one of the most important resources as a practice. For instance, recently we were doing two competitions wherein our instinct was to break down the practice into two teams, but we decided not to do that. Instead, we decided to group ourselves together in a melting pot, so to speak, for a short stage and only divide for the final production. We believe in the chemistry and the accident that happens when you ask a diverse group, with diverse talents, to think about one thing. Sometimes it's the outsider that makes a comment or a proposal that acts as the catalyst.

**In one of your lectures you explain your *Diagrams of Intent* as "secret enigmatic symbols that form a part of the DNA of each project". Do they appear at the beginning or are they the result of something achieved during the process, after all due procedures?**
It is always different. Sometimes it happens early on, where a sketch captures something and because we know there is something in there, we try to translate it into architecture. And other times, it comes from after a lot of struggle, where everything seems foggy and confusing and we question ourselves a lot until arriving at this sketch, this kind of hieroglyph that captures the core of each project. It is amazing how essential these sketches can be, as a form of communication between us, and between outsiders.

**Are these sketches produced by both you and Yvonne?**
Yvonne and myself produce them but other people in the office also produce them. The ones that are published and credited to us are our sketches. So many of them come from us but very often a sketch that someone in the office draws also becomes part of the process.

**Going back to Group 91, how did it end?**
It is very interesting. I remember young architects saying to me – you really failed because Group 91 finished – but we had never thought about it as being something that would go on. We felt that it was something magical that came together and was completed because everybody made a project. I suppose things happen naturally.

**A built project?**
Well, not everybody actually. One of the architects, McGarry Ni Eanaigh, unfortunately didn't because they were doing a bridge across the river Liffey and that project stopped. It was a tragedy. But effectively, people made their projects and when the project was done, everybody went their own way. Although we have spoken about collaboration, and some people within the group have collaborated since, I think if there were certain opportunities it could work. Again, I suppose you have to believe that things happen naturally. It's hard to force collaboration. And in fact, we tried once or twice to collaborate with people with whom we thought we had common ground, and we do, but then the chemistry of working together was quite difficult. So it doesn't always work so easily. It depends on how big the project is and how independent you can be while respecting egos.

**And boundaries, I suppose. Understanding where those boundaries touch and distance themselves. How was the working space of Group 91 organized? Was there a physical space or did each practice work independently?**
We worked closely together, meeting once a week. We divided the area into different parts and each practice had to make proposals for those areas and then we worked on how to stitch them together. We reviewed each other's work. Which was very painful, at times, because you know your peers; you respect your peers and so criticism from your peers is painful and some people are more fluent than others and make beautiful drawings whereas other people are slower and make not so beautiful drawings. There was always this balance to be held. In the end, a number of collaborators undertook the mission of bringing together our proposal in terms of format and graphical representation. It was important that it looked like one project.

**Exactly. So here we reach the issue of authorship. How was this preserved?**
I don't think, at the time of the competition, authorship was an issue because everybody had made a huge contribution and, we really did feel everybody owned that project. No one individual or no-one's office owned that project. There was a very strong sense of it being a team project. Everybody invested their energy at the

same level and everybody made a very important contribution. So, there was no issue of authorship, really. Well, I certainly didn't feel it. It was Group 91 project and that was it. And then of course, when the projects were completed, the authorship became very clear. Here, we were dealing with individual projects after the competition phase.

**Do you feel it would make sense to go back to a Group 91 collaboration?**
Absolutely, if the combination is right and if the scale is right. We are always open to collaboration; it's just that there hasn't been that many of those opportunities in Ireland, in terms of a whole urban quarter being regenerated by one company. See, the Temple Bar project was effectively administered by the state. Many of the collaborative projects are now run by commercial developers that are not so interested in us.

**You describe the role of an architect as "the translator of need into built work, into the silent language of space". This is, in every dimension, a simple yet complex explanation of what architects do. What if the need is questioned?**
We always question the need, actually, the need in terms of the brief; the ambition of the client. For instance, in educational buildings, which we are lucky to work on often, the need is questioned in terms of: what is ethos, what is the hidden ambition that the client wants but can't always express. Consider the Bocconi University in Milan, in some ways you could say that the brief, the ambition, or the perception of Bocconi, may have been that it's quite a conservative university of economics. However in reality, because of our belief in the role of education in the city, we thought beyond that and felt that the university is a place of exchange, as a marketplace, that it has an urban and a social role to play. We perceive the university as a very important institution in any city, hence the idea of opening the university up to the city was part of our philosophy. Allowing a clear relationship between the university and the city. In this sense, you could say we were questioning the need in terms of architectural values. I think an architect brings a set of values to a project as a

> We always question the need, actually, the need in terms of the brief; the ambition of the client.

form of reaction to a very precise analysis. We enter a project with a precise analysis, like a detective or psychiatrist, and question ourselves – what does the client want and what is our translation of that need into space or into architecture. The discussion and the answer are very different. For instance, in Lima it was a completely different situation, because of our understanding of the culture and of the climate. Then there are times that you question need. For instance, if a commercial developer is trying to make too much profit and is pushing the architects in a compromising direction, one has to resist that, even at the risk of walking away.

**You give a great example of how architects should collaborate with contemporaneity and its tools – "With regard to computers and technology, it's the way you direct technology and the techniques of architecture that matter" – and then you mention the pavilion of Siza and Souto Moura for the Serpentine Gallery of 2005 in Hyde Park as a piece of traditional timber construction, beautifully crafted and highly sophisticated, made by computers. Each piece and each shape was different, cut with a laser. The process was computerized but the result felt like craft.**

Well, we felt that very strongly. A year ago, maybe two years ago, we were going to an exhibition in Verona and we saw the most beautiful staircase made by the building workshop of the university of Syracusa, in Sicily. They made this fantastic stone spiral stair with cantilever steps. They were combining solid stone with post-tensioning. So again it is the combination of a new technology with the historic craft. There is nothing more exciting than to be able to hold onto both and not lose the presence of one because of the sophistication of the other. To be able to hold those two things together is wonderful and important. Then you are not afraid because you can place a value on the ancient and bring it together with the highest of technology. This however requires that one has to orchestrate.

**How would you describe the daily meaning of the relation between master and apprentice?**
The way that we feel is that we are always apprentices. We are always learning from younger architects, from architects that are alive, from architects that have passed away and from younger

colleagues. I think we are always apprentices and that is wonderful because we are always being challenged and always learning.

**You once also said, "Something fantastic about architecture is that, still at the age of 95, you are still realizing you are learning. Architecture is an amazing discipline."**
Yes, and it is. Alejandro de la Sota said a wonderful thing about teaching, which I can't remember exactly but was something like "The only difference between the teacher and the student is that the teacher has more experience, and the thing that they both share is doubt." This is really interesting and really important because nobody is sure in the making of the project. Nobody has the answer. It's not because you are older that you have the answer. I mean, very often the younger architect finds the answer much more quickly than the architect with more experience. Or experience gets in the way of being able to see clearly. It's very interesting. There is no certainty.

**I also believe there is something very positive about teaching. Shifting from academic approaches to office projects allows one to open the spectrum of reality. Finally, did you have a master figure, a reference?**
We did, for sure. Le Corbusier was our master. We apprenticed ourselves to Le Corbusier almost fully, as the nature of our education. We still go back to that work because of the fantastic range. Of course, you have a master when you are young and then you put the master aside and you go off and find many other things that enthuse you because you are free and open, but I would say the solid ground is still that initial deep exploration of the work of Le Corbusier.

IMAGE CREDITS

Courtesy of Grafton Architects.

Andrew Mackintosh

# Sharing without Dialogue

In architecture we are in a position in which we can share our work and thoughts without the need for the written or spoken word. Through drawings we have the ability to communicate with one another on a common basis and exchange on an agreed method of representation. With plan, elevation and cross section, we share all the facts required to construct a building and explain its use. This is an extremely clear and concise method of sharing information; one could say it is similarly found in mathematics – through working almost exclusively with numbers and symbols, ideas are able to be exchanged and understood universally.

During this process of translating thoughts into an accessible format, we gain the skills necessary to later analyse them. It is fruitful that in the experience and knowledge we gain through producing drawings, we expand our own vocabulary in reading drawings.

### Analysts learning by doing

Let's take an escape stair as an example. This is an area usually completely reduced to its minimum legal and functional requirements and is one of the most easily identifiable objects in our catalogue. Once you have had to design and move around a fire stair in a couple of different projects, you begin to understand the requirements and rationale which lead to that element being placed in that exact position within a building. In this way we can think of drawings as a kind of pictogram, a symbol on a plan which you can almost immediately visualise and comprehend. With more time we continue to consciously record our experiences and define categorisations for architecture. You can't put architecture in boxes, but you can recognise through analysis that what you're looking at is a hotel for example. Through our everyday working with the basic architectural elements such as door, window, stairs, we can not only directly get an idea of size, scale and proportion from a drawing but then formulate educated assumptions as to its function.

## Fantasies in the undefined

Of course, in this act of sharing through drawing, we lack key parts of an architecture which we require to allow us build a real picture in our minds. In most cases, materials are lost and the reader must begin to speculate on what sort of finish would be in this space, how would it be treated, what colour would it be? These are critical points in helping construct a complete understanding of what someone is trying to share. However, one can look at these lapses of information as an opportunity to romanticise about what we would like to envisage. What one can conceive as a strong solid space of white concrete with a light green marble floor and dark oak doors, might in reality just be plasterboard walls with a carpet floor and plastic doors. This possibility to fantasise through the missing pieces creates an internal dialogue in which we begin to expand our own wishes and thoughts within the context of what somebody else is providing us.

## Stranger than fiction

The way we can communicate with one another about fictional architectural ideas without the need to produce a physical building is a very cathartic experience. From the freedom of the drawing board, one can propose and express the radical and take it no further than a pulse of expression with no commitments. Nevertheless, we must then ask the question whether a drawing will ever become a piece of architecture if it does not go through the

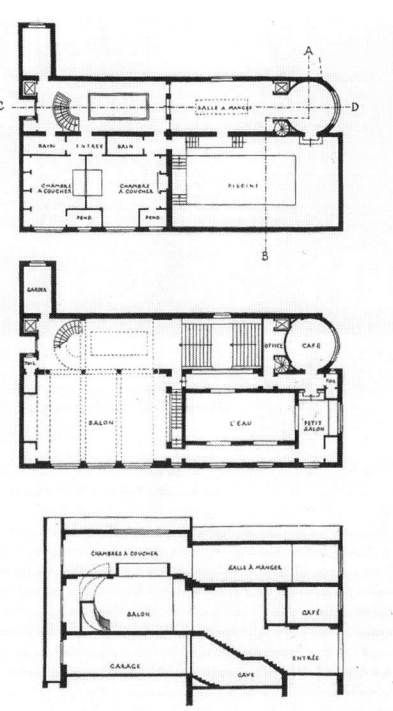

A     Josephine Baker House by Adolf Loos.

B    Rialto Bridge by Andrea Palladio.

final obstacle of being built. Think of the Baker house by Loos.[Fig. A] In this unbuilt masterpiece, through its drawings alone, we are provided with all that we require to distinguish it as piece of architecture. We can picture what lifestyle would exist in this palace for the glitterati, the champagne-fuelled parties of the voyeurs and how one would inhabit the spaces, walk around and swim in the pool. Similar to Palladio's design for a Rialto bridge in Venice [Fig. B], which appeared in his third book of architecture, the project was never realised but had been so widely published that it represents the Palladian Bridges as a building type.

## Hereafter

The ability for a piece of work to continue through the medium of drawing even after its physical destruction is reassuring for its capability to carry on participation in architecture.

Perhaps one of the most recognisable and overused references for this is the floor plan for the Bank of England by Soane.[Fig. C] It is intriguing by its complex arrangements and legendary by its destruction. Nearly 100 years after its demolition, all we are left with today is a mere outer wall and the drawings with which to analyse this architecture which used to exist. However, perhaps this interest and trust only works for projects of a not so distant past. If we had no accurate record of the floor plan from Soane, would we still be so enticed by it? The lack of hard evidence could, in this case, destroy any truth we hold on to such a project and reduce it to an indeterminable study and piece of mythology.

## A Monochrome Manifesto

Through the accessibility of communicating by drawing, ideas are able to continuously resonate

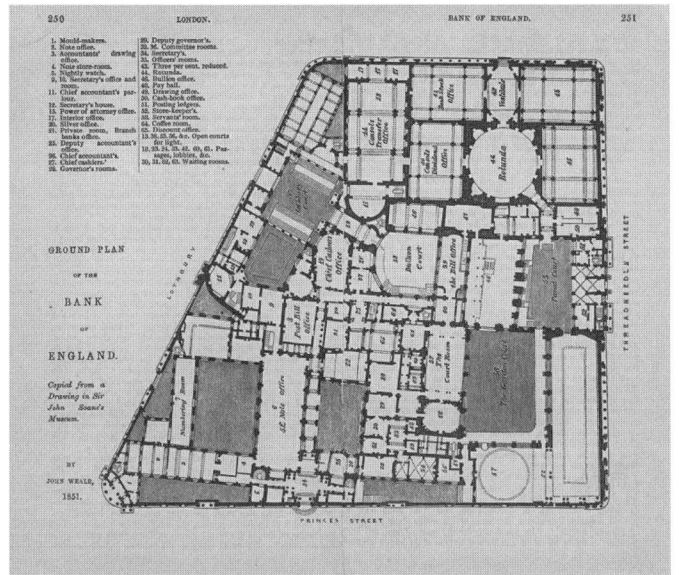

C  Ground plan of the Bank of England by John Soane.

in our discourse of architecture and to enable borderless debates without the need to be physically present. While this is certainly in our consensual approach of sharing at the moment, drawing will always remain completely undemocratic. In this way we have a particularly eccentric medium; we define enough of a common language by consensus to understand each other while allowing ourselves enough space to define our own attitude and position within the established frame. The "It's not what you say that's important; it's how you say it" approach of representing one's self. This inevitably produces mixed results, some in which representing is more important than content and vice versa. By creating these wordless manifestos we put ourselves in the best position for being read in the future, we define everything and nothing, all at the same time. Without writing we give no solid explanation for our reasoning, no guidebook or precise statement to be adhered to. Instead, we use a mixture of common values and individual attitudes to share our positions with one another.

AUTHOR

Andrew Mackintosh studied architecture at the Scott Sutherland School of Architecture in Aberdeen and is presently an architect at Christ & Gantenbein in Basel, having previously worked for Sou Fujimoto in Tokyo and Christian Kerez in Zurich. He was awarded the 2010 Norman Foster travel scholarship for his research entitled "In search of cold spaces", a global study of northern public spaces. Prior to this, he had participated in the student exhibition for the London Architecture Biennale 2006 and the Six Cities design festival, Scotland 2007, both in collaboration with Jonathan Woolf.

IMAGE CREDITS

A  Paul Groenendijk and Piet Vollaard, Adolf Loos. House for Josephine Baker, Rotterdam, 1985.
B  Schumann-Bacia, Eva, John Soane and The Bank of England, Essex, Longman Group UK, 1991, p. 132.
C  Ground plan of the Bank of England by John Weale from an original at the Soane Museum, 1851.

Benjamin Krüger

# My Eyes Are not Our Eyes

Images of the same places, buildings and details are taken over and over again. For the most part taken without consciousness, just as marks of footprints on a map, which creates an endless, fatigued stream of architectural photography. The work *My eyes are not our eyes* wants the viewer to look at known architecture of our collective memory again in order to ask the question: why did that building become a masterpiece? At the same time, the consciously blurred photographs reduce architecture to the most basic shape in order to provoke a discovery of new traces and meanings.

AUTHOR

Benjamin Krüger was born into a young family in 1982. He had a strong interest in clouds in his youth. In 2002, he started to study industrial design but switched to architecture at the Bauhaus University in Weimar. After a semester in Sweden, he graduated and started working with Herzog & de Meuron, where he remained for three years. At the moment, he is an associate at HHF Architects and interested in cloud studies again.

IMAGE CREDITS

Photographs by Benjamin Krüger.

Teshima Art Museum by Ryue Nishizawa, Photograph 2012.

Pestana Casino by Oscar Niemeyer, Photograph 2012.

I CONFRÈRES

Palazzo della Civiltà Italiana by Ernesto Lapadula, Giovanni Guerrini and Mario Romano, Photograph 2014.

Villa Müller by Adolf Loos, Photograph 2007.

I CONFRÈRES

Chiesa di Santa Maria Annunziata by Donato Bramante, Photograph 2014.

Katsura Imperial Villa, Photograph 2012.

Solomon R. Guggenheim Museum by Frank Lloyd Wright, Photograph 2011.

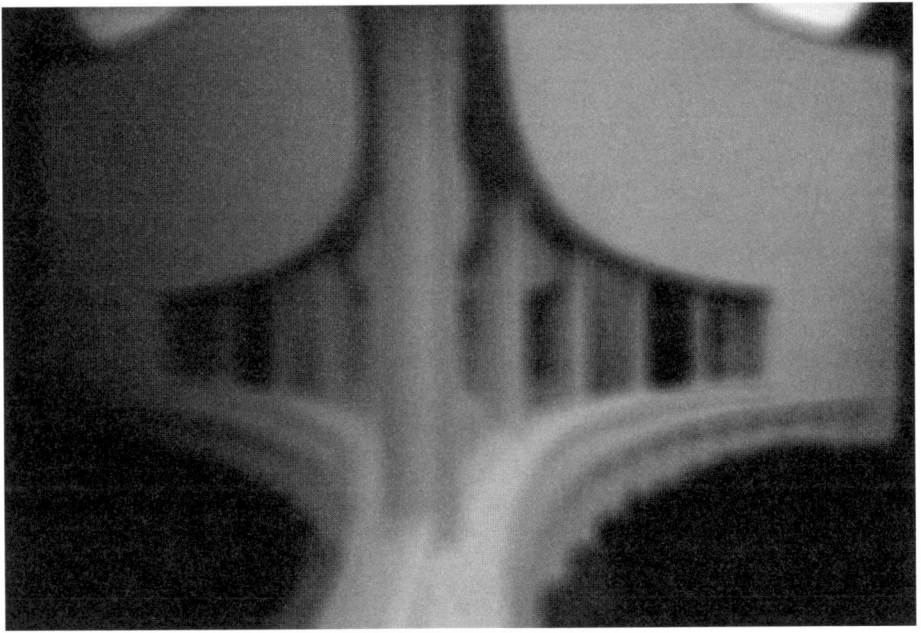

Studio Aalto by Alvar Aalto, Photograph 2006.

Rusakov Club by Konstantin Stepanovich Melnikov, Photograph 2012.

Collection Goetz by Herzog & de Meuron, Photograph 2009.

Maison du verre by Pierre Chareau, Photograph 2015.

Skogskyrkogården by Gunnar Asplund and Sigurd Lewerentz, Photograph 2006.

Luis Pedro Pinto

# A Letter to RG

At the time of the events reported, my employment contract with the architecture studio in Lisbon where I was working was non-existent or, actually, I was an "independent worker".[1] In this situation it was not specified if working outside the studio was illicit or not, although I have always questioned myself about the republican idea that ethics only exist within the law.

Lisbon, May 2015

Dear RG

The story I wish to tell you goes back about ten years. For a number of reasons I never shared this neither with you or anyone else, and so this story has become a secret. A secret that I am now sharing with you.

When I started to work in your studio in 2001 I was twenty-two, and although I often seemed to appear very certain, I had great doubts about the world, about work and architecture. University had taught me some theoretical concepts, little practice and a great deal of illusion. Working for you was the beginning.

The beginning was marked with a project and a client. Such an extraordinary client, PCR himself! Unlike that saying, "when you sign a contract with the client you get to know your enemy", this was totally untrue in this particular case. PCR triggered the story of a friend, the story of a house, the story of how to build a house and how to develop a project, many projects. No gimmicks, no recipes, no bullshit.

During that time, while I was doing the Portuguese Architectural Association internship and I was a wage earner at your studio, I got an invitation through my father, who knew one of the administrators, to present a fee and cost proposal for a building for washing facilities for Valorsul.[2] I confess I don't quite remember what went through my mind in that moment. I remember a tremendous amount of happiness, almost childish.

90

A

That project could facilitate my being on the road towards my own built project! But I also remember being afraid and having real doubts about whether I could do it alone. After all, it was natural that I felt that way, considering that I hadn't even finished the Portuguese Architectural Association internship. I was not even officially an architect.

Three possibilities emerged in that situation. The first one was to decline the invitation by referring to my intern status. The second was to bring this project to your studio. Finally, the third possibility was to present the mentioned financial proposal and do the potential project by myself.

The first option was never really an option because it meant quitting, and I had already learned with you not to do that. So the doubt remained between the other two options. Bringing this project to your studio would certainly result in a real structure and in negotiation leverage with the client, and it would also gain, an undoubtedly level of quality. On the other hand, although this would reduce the level of risk, I would waste a real opportunity to work by myself, which probably would never be repeated again and I would also lose access to the entire profit of my work. Oh mercenary spirit!

I chose the third possibility. I presented my proposal, elaborated according to the current established financial and covenant logic and I didn't tell this to anyone, especially not to you. And my proposal was accepted! From one moment to another, I had my first commission. I was about to design a proper building, with a time schedule, a real location and a client to work with. If projects weren't already easy to execute at the studio together with you, imagine this one alone! Working between the kitchen table and the desk of my room, models, preliminary studies, execution drawings, budgeting, billing, and all the necessary tasks which we very much enjoy doing, came into being. Everything was done during the night,

B

after dinner and through entire weekends at my parent's house, where I had just recently finished the final project for the university.

Beyond my enormous doubts about what I was architecturally offering, constantly accompanied by my favourite Herzog & de Meuron monograph, and beyond the difficult task of fitting 250 lockers and I don't know how many toilets from that program, time management was the hardest and most complex task at that point. Especially during the construction period, when weekly technical meetings and construction visits had to take place during the day. I strategically scheduled them for 8 a.m. so that I could be fresh at the studio at 10.30 a.m. at the latest, as if nothing had happened. All of this for one entire year.

I remember passionately defending the option of using Viúva Lamego's tiles on the restroom walls during a construction meeting. The contractor wanted to change for a cheaper option, claiming that it was a misuse the tiles in restroom facilities. I couldn't have disagreed more with him! For me there is no such a thing as first or second-class work. The tiles stayed. I also managed to keep the exposed concrete. And the same goes for the U-glass on the main facade, the white crushed stone in the garden, and everything which I had thought about at home, alone.

Considering the circumstances, things didn't go that badly. I guess some sort of innocent luck accompanied me during the whole process, beginner's luck maybe. Added to this was the willingness of the client to forgive some extra work and dubious choices.

So many times I wanted to tell you. I wanted to share with you my anguishes and architectural doubts. I am sure that you would have helped me greatly. That you would have said "change this, do this instead of that, son!", that you would have told me to come to work later and that I could have skipped some work in order to go the site. But I didn't! At a certain point, I thought it was

C

too late and that you would be upset with me for not having told you about the project from the beginning. I thought that you would have considered that as a disloyalty, a breach in our friendship, which was long-standing by then.

And this is it. The construction was finished. There was even an opening ceremony, which I did not attend because it coincided with my working schedule at your studio. Likewise, I never photographed the building. In fact, I never went back there. This was probably my way of keeping it a secret.

AUTHOR

Luís Pedro Pinto was born in 1978, in Lisbon. Fascinated by cities, he graduated in architecture at Universidade Lusíada de Lisboa. For over a decade he worked enthusiastically on projects and constructions at Bak Gordon Architects. In the spring of 2015, as a consequence of a natural state of restlessness, he thought it was about time to continue… solo.

NOTES

1  Independent worker are workers of a company but are not their employees, at least regarding a legal point of view.
2  Valorsul is the company responsible for the treatment and recovery of urban waste in the area of Great Lisbon.

IMAGE CREDITS

Photographs by Daniel Malhão.

# Les Garages

We, Ourselves and I;
New Spaces for Modern Nomads

Four months ago, in November 2014, we started a project entitled *Les Garages*: a collection of experimental living units inside a former exhibition space for second-hand cars. There are two important things to say about the project.

Firstly, it deals with a socio demographic transformation that we are experiencing and that I would like to call: the modern nomads. Young people in particular have become increasingly mobile, geographically, socially and professionally. For many people I know, only few things are stable. I think it might be that an overwhelming amount of opportunity leads to an increasing difficulty in taking decisions. I myself am, at this very moment, sitting on the train with my laptop, reading the slogan of the CFF, the Swiss train service: "Unterwegs zuhause", at home on the go. Architecture as an economic process which forms the built environment rather than as an academic discipline, still has a way to go to address this phenomenon, as well as other demographic socio-economic developments. There are more and more projects that are sensibly addressing these issues, but they usually depend on very strong organisational structures to really achieve their goals, as these initiatives still go against the current market dynamics. *Les Garages* is situated somewhere among these initiatives that are slowly finding their way into our built environment.

Another point worth mentioning in the context of this article is the exact organisational structure that evolved from the specific condition from which *Les Garages* originated. In this project, over 30 people collaborated on the production of what are now six prototypes for mobile sleeping units inside an open space. Modules that in principle, allow empty spaces to be quickly transformed into rudimentary living spaces which serve as a landing platform for the intermediate situation that so many young people find themselves in.

These modules are part of a design series that we are developing for the modern nomad.

A series of modules that are specifically designed for people who have their home inside a backpack and their work inside a laptop. If you want to take this further, for argument's sake, a building could be reduced to a skeleton of concrete slabs and façades. The interior constantly evolves, lightweight structures would be perpetually replaced and recycled, adapting to the ever faster, ever changing demands of society and the market. The true domino house and some evolved type of furniture, nothing else. But that is another story.

## Let's start at the beginning

Many people who arrive in Lausanne as students from abroad, or even from other parts of Switzerland, have great difficulty in finding accommodation. Students often camp on the camp-site near the universities, or sleep in dormitories at the youth hostel. The local housing situation in general is very difficult due to the steady economic growth of the Lemanic Arc, the densely populated zone along Lac de Leman stretching from Montreux to Geneva. An average amount of 1.5% of housing should be vacant for a well functioning housing market that allows for necessary mobility. In the case of Lausanne, vacancy was down to 0.6% in 2012. Students are the last ones served in these conditions, creating the inevitable situation described above. But it was 27 years ago, not in 2012, that students took the initiative from their personal need for affordable housing, occupying abandoned apartments in Lausanne. The 1980s were a favourable period for squatters, and Geneva was, surprisingly, the city with the highest percentage of occupied buildings in Europe at the time. An association in Lausanne called ALJF (Association pour le Logement des Jeunes en Formation) evolved from this heritage in 1988. It houses students in buildings that are temporarily empty prior to renovation or destruction. The concept is known, especially in Holland, as anti-squat, because of the benefits that the owner of the building has. Empty buildings are problematic for a number of reasons but, most importantly, they can still be used, even if only for short periods.

As young, recently graduated architects, we are interested in the topic of housing and temporary use of empty spaces not only due to our individual experience, but also due to larger issues such as the issue of student and professional mobility within a European context, a mobility that we like to categorize as modern nomadism. These people break free from their original social environment on an individualist quest for fulfilment, success or escapism. Of course the story of the journeyman is as old as history itself, but the acceleration of the phenomenon that has been witnessed in the last decade due to transport and communication technologies, as well as political and social transformation, justifies the affix modern. During our studies, we were lucky enough to become members of the ALJF, and Christoph Holz has now become a member of the committee, managing housing for over 200 students in Lausanne in otherwise empty buildings.

Our recently founded office *Whoodstudio* was not created with the aim of completing the largest number of projects possible, but is rather an open structure allowing us to explore multidisciplinary issues in which we are interested. Our studio is one of a number of young, emerging architectural collectives in the French part of Switzerland with a similar work ethic. Even though there is no real structure connecting the individual studios, there seems to be some sort of cohesion in attitude amongst them. The intention to not to work for an already established office,

A

B

but to find one's own path, often original and paired with multidisciplinary activities and design research, is clearly evident.

## Les Garages

*Les Garages* was initiated by Christoph Holz, but he is far from being a solo act. In September 2014, the ALJF received a space formerly used as a showroom for a second-hand car dealer. This is not the typical place for student housing proposed to the ALJF and a transformation into real apartments was not a worthwhile option. However, the issue of temporarily transforming industrial and commercial property into housing is very relevant. It recently caused a controversy in Geneva, where a proposition to change the LDTR (Loi sur les démolitions, transformations et rénovations de maisons d'habitation) was discussed and almost put to a vote. The current vacancy of available office space in Geneva was about 240 000 m$^2$, or 5.9 % of the total available surface in 2015 (source: DTZ). We find similar statistics for the entire Lemanic Arc.

The idea of temporary transformation combined with a space that is ideal for showing car-sized objects produced the proposal for an exhibition of prototypes for mobile housing units. These could be tested as part of a real-life experiment. The ALJF mailing list is littered with emails from people looking for a couch or a room for a few weeks or months. The concept was developed by Christoph Holz, Gabriel Gonzalez and Mattia Pretolani, the latter two also being members of ALJF, forming a research group called 'habitat minimal' with the aim of exploring alternative possibilities for cheap and simple housing. The ALJF, with its origins in the squat movement, still signs contracts entitled *Contrats de Prêt à Usage* with the building owners (usually public institutions) that govern the use of the building

c

without the payment of rent, with repairs and running costs only having to be covered. This situation has generated a benefit, and thus the *Garage* project received 5500 Swiss francs of funding from the association.

The work group then circulated an invitation for participation in the project, asking young architects or designers to design a module for a maximum of 1000 Swiss francs, with at least one bed and a maximum surface area of 7 m². Another criterion was that the structure had to be transportable and pass through an opening of 1.6m by 2m (which is based on the fire exit door sizes in most commercial and industrial buildings). It is fair to mention that *Le Repaire Fantastique*, one of the young architectural collectives in Lausanne already proposed a type of *cadavre exquis* collaboration between young architects. The project never saw the light of day, but LRF invited all collaborators and friends to a meeting where the ideas for the project were presented.

The *Garage* project was also proposed at this meeting. After this meeting and the circulation of the idea amongst the network, six teams confirmed their participation:

PSHHH (Guay Antoine/Reverdin Gaspar/Reymond Aurélien) are recent graduates in interior architecture from the HEAD[1] in Geneva. They proposed a structure based on a collage of several types of primitive huts, all based around a central fireplace.

Gabriel Gonzalez, sociologist and member of the ALJF and the "habitat minimale" work group, conducted a workshop with students from Athenaeum, a private architecture school in Lausanne. The proposition by Eric Essa was adapted and became a cube space consisting of several stackable elements.

*Whoodstudio* (Holz Georg-Christoph/Wéry Jeanne in collaboration with Widmer Regis) are recent EPFL graduates. The project KASA is an envelope made of recycled cardboard that places second-hand furniture around a bed in the middle.

The Project *Diogenes Grid* was conceived by Pretolani Mattia (member of the ALJF and 'habitat minimal', student in architecture at EPFL) and Guex-Crosier Grégoire (also student in architecture at EPFL). The module hides a bed within a bookshelf made up of OSB panels and has insulation made of crushed glass and wax.

*La Bifanas* was conceived by Renens Breitling Lawrence in collaboration with Le Pommelet Nicolas from the Creative collective *Le Sapin* in Renens, near Lausanne and uses only 3 × 5 m timber slats and rope for the A-frame structure.

Laurent Chassot (LRF), Agathe Mignon (currently PHD doctorate at EPFL) and Victoire Paternault joined forces to build *One Sheep to Sleep*; a very finely detailed indoor tent made of real wool felt.

## Conclusion

All the participants in the project, however diverse, are locally based. The place, the location is important. Any link must be supported by a network and a physical place where this network can find some form of manifestation. Through the rapid spread of information, everybody can be a part of a project, by deciding to come and participate or just have a look. Everything is quicker but is then quickly forgotten too. The heart of a project has to be strong to stay in the memories of those who, somehow, come in contact with it. This, at least, has not changed. In French-speaking Switzerland, the architectural community, or the people actively participating in events and the generation of ideas, feels like a village. And a really small one at that, when compared to the villages that we find in much larger countries such as Germany and England. In the end, the people who took part in this experiment all knew each other through some connection from before; they all agreed on a common method, idea, and basis for working, without ever agreeing on it. There is a manifesto because there is none. In the case of *Les Garages*, we see that choosing six groups of architects to collaborate, but still letting them choose and interpret the theme (microhabitat in this case) was a good way to proceed. Doing this, we let the small group practice the "I" under a theme of a "We". Everybody felt attached to a cause, but was free to create as they wanted. There is something very efficient in the structure of smaller groups that follow a specific structure, but are otherwise free to evolve within its boundaries. It has a much less complicated organisational structure; it is more bottom-up. The original form of collaboration, the "We" is a top down, hierarchical system. The "I" generation is strong and needs to prove itself, to succeed or fail, and then learn from the consequences. A new way of collaborating is emerging and, maybe in a few years, we will be able to call it dogma, but dogma as a large signification, more open and extendable.

NOTES

1  HEAD Geneva: Geneva University of Art and Design.

IMAGE CREDITS

Photographs by Whoodstudio.

# Hierarchy and Process in Architectural Working Structures

### Painting

Over the last years I have worked in two different architecture practices. Similar in size and type of work, they are however opposites in their working processes, and as a consequence, in their workload. At first glance, the hierarchical structure looks similar, however the presence of a non-architect as the manager in charge of the design process as well as the construction work for the entire architecture office, changes the office complexity completely. This is reflected in the map of relationships created through the entire process, the extent of responsibilities assumed over the design process by the entire team, and the quantity of support material produced.

### Type A

In Portugal, the typical author-workshop seems to persist, where one figure and one figure only – the architect – is at the centre of the search for clients, potential investors, team management, and the pursuit of design decisions and solutions. Plus, and quite frequently, these tasks are overlapped with a teaching position in an architectural school.

Here, the creative process, as well as the team coordination, is usually open to input from all the team members. Normally, one or more architects (depending on the practice size and amount of work), adopts the position of project manager and assumes a higher position in the hierarchical pyramid. Thus taking on more responsibilities, but not exactly more decision-making power. The project manager works closely with the architect in the development of the entire design process. Following the architect's first ideas and input, he or she develops a complete design proposal, from the conceptual to the detailing stage, co-ordinating the required and specified phases of the design process as well as contact with all the workers, specialists and suppliers involved. The collaborators and/or interns of the architectural practice answer directly to the project manager and the architect and usually produce support material in relation to each and every phase of the design process.

When contacting an architectural practice of this kind, the client is in search of a specific design made by a specific author. Here, one buys a piece from an author. In this sense, the cost of the work cannot easily be compared to current market indicators and negotiable parameters. A higher starting price is assumed by default and defined by an a priori cost classification. After the design process, the relationship with the client moves forward to the construction phase. But, by this time, the main responsibility shifts from the architect to the contractor, which reduces the architect's position to a consulting role.

## Type B

When the managing figure of a practice is a non-architect, the office seems to open up and pursue a more entrepreneurial structure. The manager concentrates on the search for clients, potential investors, team management, and above all on the control of all budget ceilings and production timings among contractors, workers and suppliers.

Here, the creative process, as well as the team coordination, is mainly supported from the team members with little input from the manager but a high level of co-ordination from the project manager. This person coordinates the development of the entire design process, distributes work accordingly to each team member, ensures compliance with scheduled times and costs controls, contacts and handles the dynamics between all the workers, specialists and suppliers involved. The collaborators and/or interns of the architectural practice answer directly to the project manager and the manager, and usually produce support material in relation to each and every phase of the design process. Depending on their capacity, and due to their workload, they see their responsibilities quickly increased.

When in contact with this practice, the client is in search of a service. Here, one buys a product. This is especially relevant when the practice not only offers an architectural service, but complete control of all the subsequent phases of the process. The practice not only suggests and comments on the contractor's proposals and monitors construction work, but assumes entire responsibility for the construction phases, including contact with every contractor and its workers, the handling of all legal issues, negotiations with suppliers, the control of time and costs involved, and all the unpredicted events that occur during the construction process.

This obviously augments the responsibility of the architectural practice, overloading the workers' availability and time, but at the same time increasing the practice's margin for economic profit. By controlling the entire process, every choice of worker, supplier and material, is revised time and time again in search of a better price. The building process is deconstructed and reorganized in small packages to allow the negotiation of each and every phase and /or required piece of work. The same thing happens to all the materials required and the suppliers of equipment. This process demands a huge capacity for negotiation from the practice manager. Since the client budget has been discussed at the beginning, this continuous negotiation allows the income of the practice to be increased, and leaves a margin for the definition of extra components not considered in the previously negotiated budget.

The negotiation of construction work phase by phase also allows for phased payment. After the completion of each construction phase, a chart with the quantities, measurements and percentage of work done is issued, and payment is made according to what has actually been completed on the construction site.

However, even though it has economic advantages, this continuous negotiation demands a tremendous ability on the part of the architecture professionals in the practice to juggle and be flexible. Since the choice of suppliers and materials is under constant negotiation, the design proposal also needs to be constantly adapted. To assure quality and the utmost respect to the architectural proposal, the team needs to be one move ahead to prevent mistakes and errors from modifications to previously selected solutions.

## Carving

By enlarging the work spectrum and responsibility of a practice to include the construction process, one may find a path to stability in a profession that is, in its current state, not economically viable. In this sense, the difference lies not in whether management is performed by an architect or a non-architect, but mainly in the chosen attitude towards the current market and service provided. At the same time, this position allows for greater responsibility from the architecture professionals, which goes hand in hand with an increase in training by way of 'learning by doing'. Here, the autonomy of the discipline is maintained and even improved by the exchange of know-how and information between the entire team, workers, suppliers and other parties involved in the project. Would then be every professional positioned at a correct and fair place in the decision and responsibility hierarchy and in the productive process. With this, not only does the entire working structure take on an increased dynamic, but it also allows for individual members tend to feel and be more involved in the complete working process.

However, even if a positive view can be carved out with regard to the work process and experience from this type of practice, something is lacking. At this point, we are left again with the ghost of the author-architect. The idea of the future of a practice built together with the collaborators' support never appears as a concrete possibility. The openness of the employer-employee structure to alternatives such as partnership or limited liability company is never considered.

A closer, partial, and sequential involvement of the collaborators in the company structure would allow for the sharing of responsibilities, and as a long term solution, for maintaining a sustainability practice and team maintenance. The sharing of responsibilities would extend not only to work production but also to the financial and organizational model of the practice. Investments, partnerships, customer acquisition and selection, payments, contracts, budget control and negotiations, would be done with a more professional approach. The finances of the practice would not be turned into a mixture of the manager's private expenses and those of the company, as frequently happens in Portuguese companies. Staff hiring and management, scheduling, timing and wages would be discussed effectively and well provided for, avoiding burn-out collaborators as well as precarious and badly-paid working positions with scarce quality free time.

If this kind of practice, conduct and structure is not unusual in many countries, it seems to be a distant idea from most Portuguese architectural practices. Treatment of the architectural practice not as an author workshop, but as a profitable and regular service which still aims to reach a high quality standard guaranteeing a social, urban and aesthetic commitment and a sense of respect for the entire working team, seems to be the logical approach for a discipline which, like many others, strives to function in the current market economy.

AUTHOR

Maria Manuel Barreiros (Coimbra, 1986) graduated as an architect from the Department of Architecture of the University of Coimbra. She was an editor of Revista NU from 2005 to 2012 and maintains regular collaboration with different architectural publications. In the last 5 years, she has collaborated as an architect in two different offices in Lisbon and Oporto. She currently works as an architect in Bak Gordon Arquitectos.

IMAGE CREDITS

Graphics by Maria Manuel Barreiros.

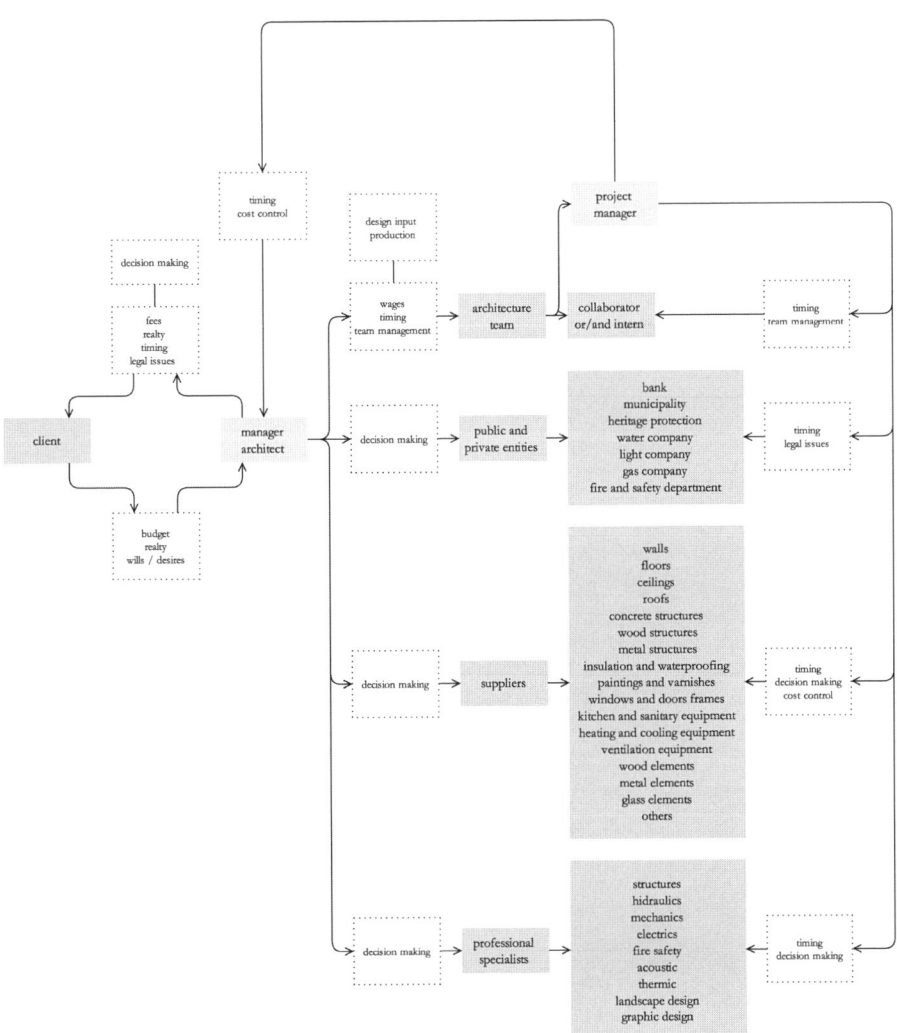

A     Relationships Map – Type A

Diagram of the interactions created in a typical authorworkshop office, here named type A. As the architect concentrates in himself the decision power, his responsibility towards the end product increases, while diminishing the project manager's autonomy. At the same time, the project manager's workload persistently increases and with it comes his responsibility towards team management. A weaker control over the project costs is evident.

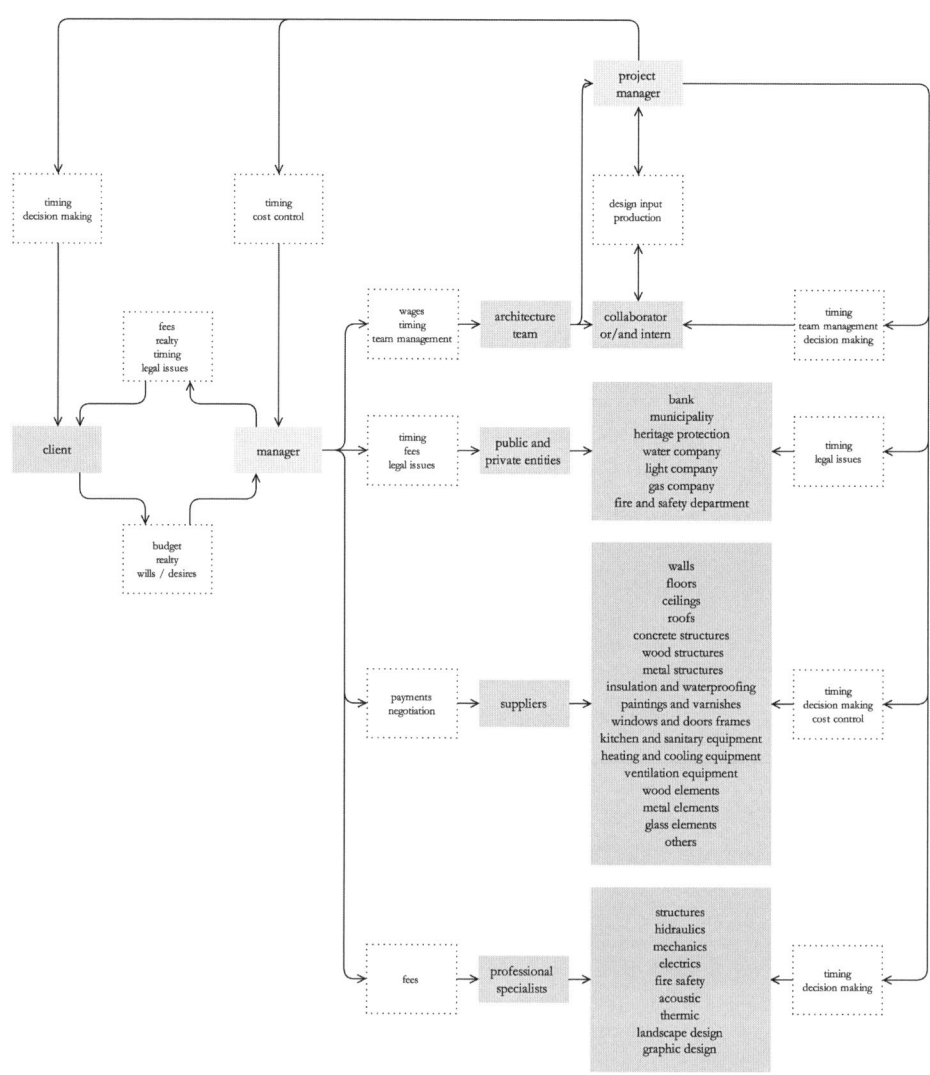

B     Relationships Map – Type B

Diagram of the interactions created in a type B office. As the influence of the manager in the design process decreases, it augments his investment in the office negotiation capacity. At the same time, responsibility is divided with the project manager, which in turn divides the large workload with the entire team.
A bigger pressure by the manager on the project manager is evident.

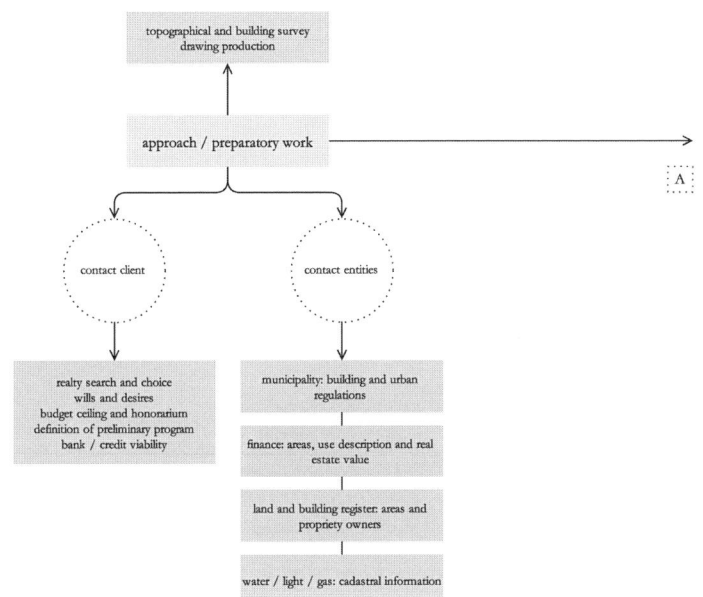

C   Work and Responsabilities Map – Type A and B

Diagram of the amount of work involved in both type offices (A and B), specifying the most common phases of the development of an architectural design project. Also specified are the responsibilities concerning this same development and the relationships which those responsibilities entail. (pp. 105-109)

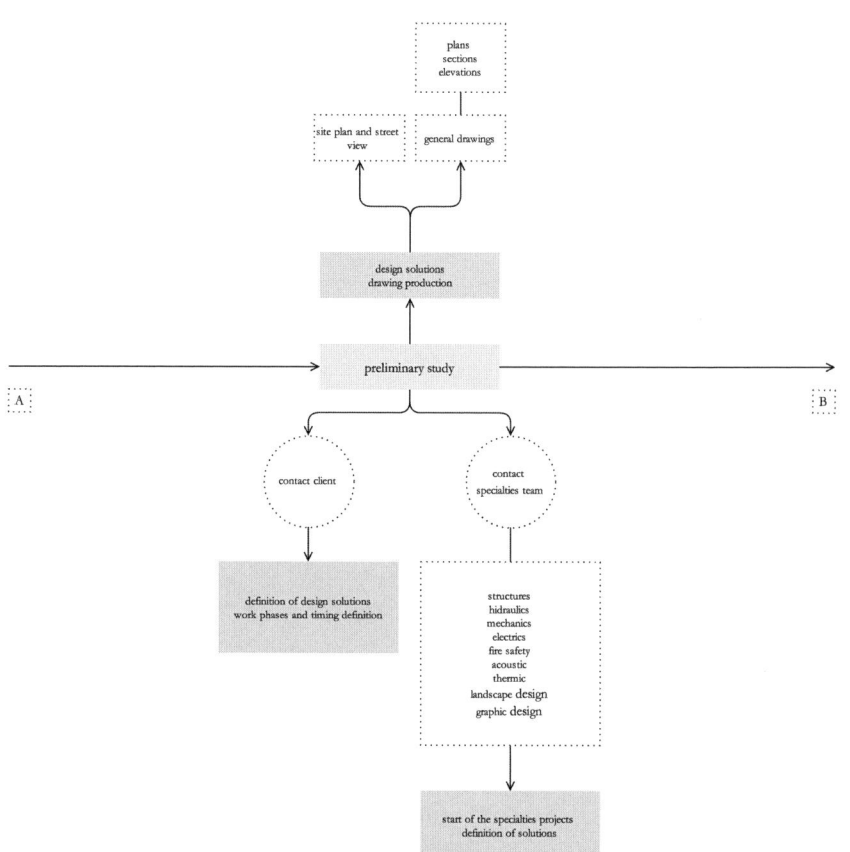

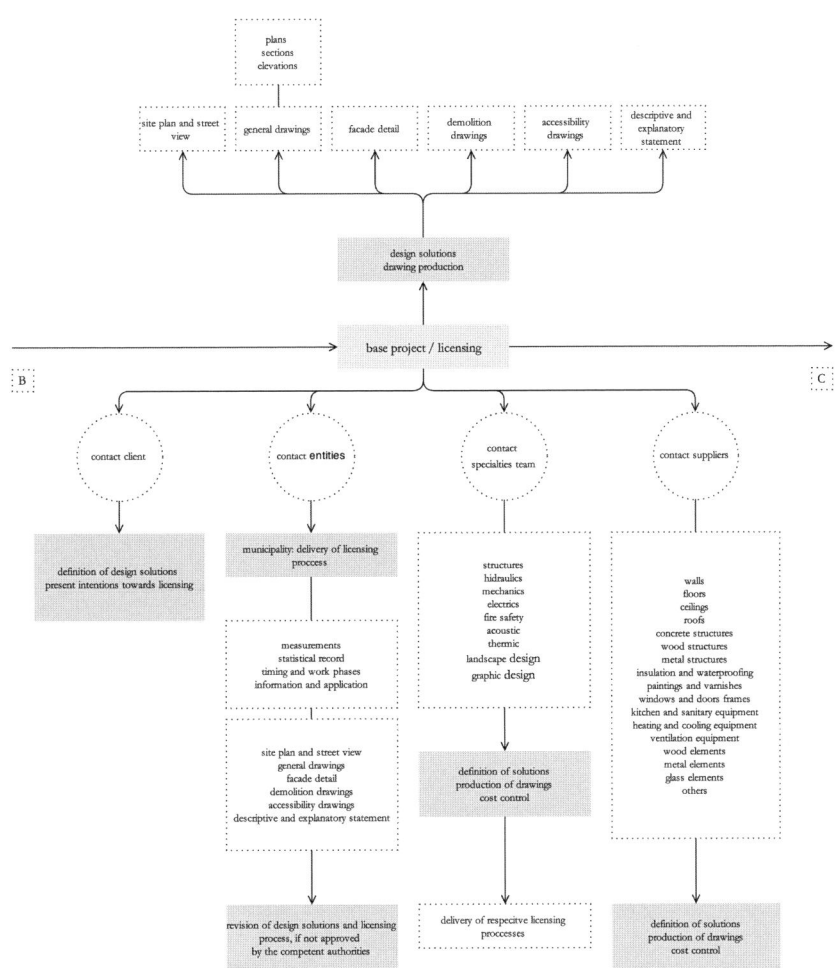

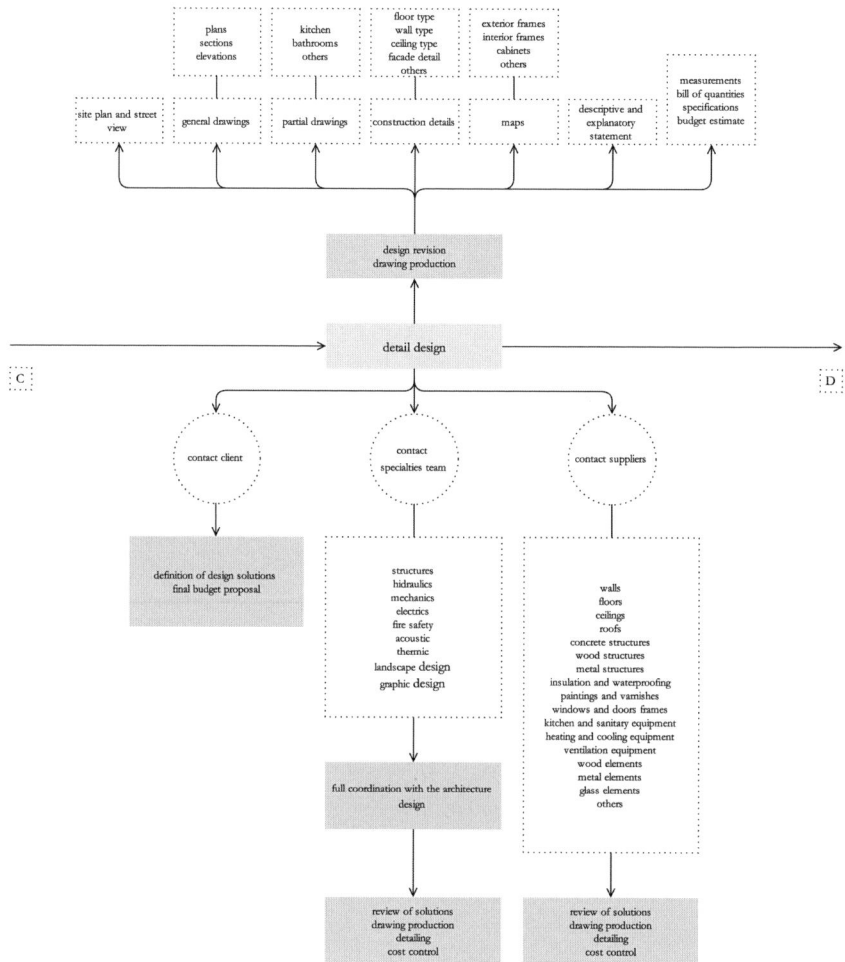

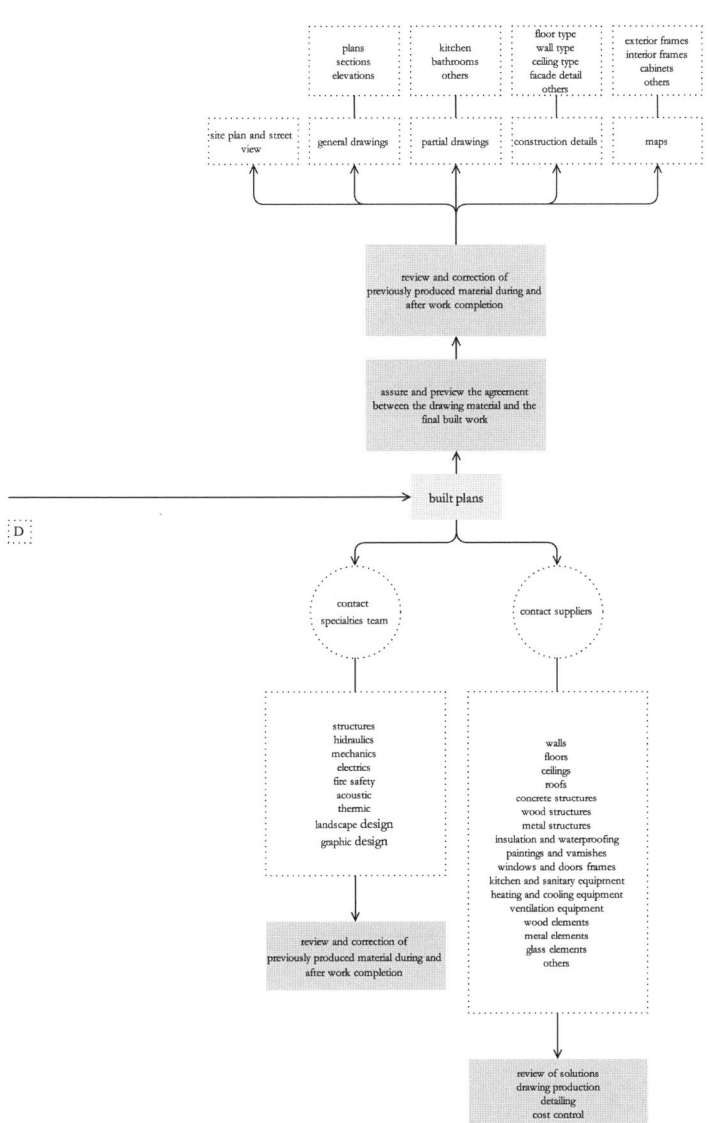

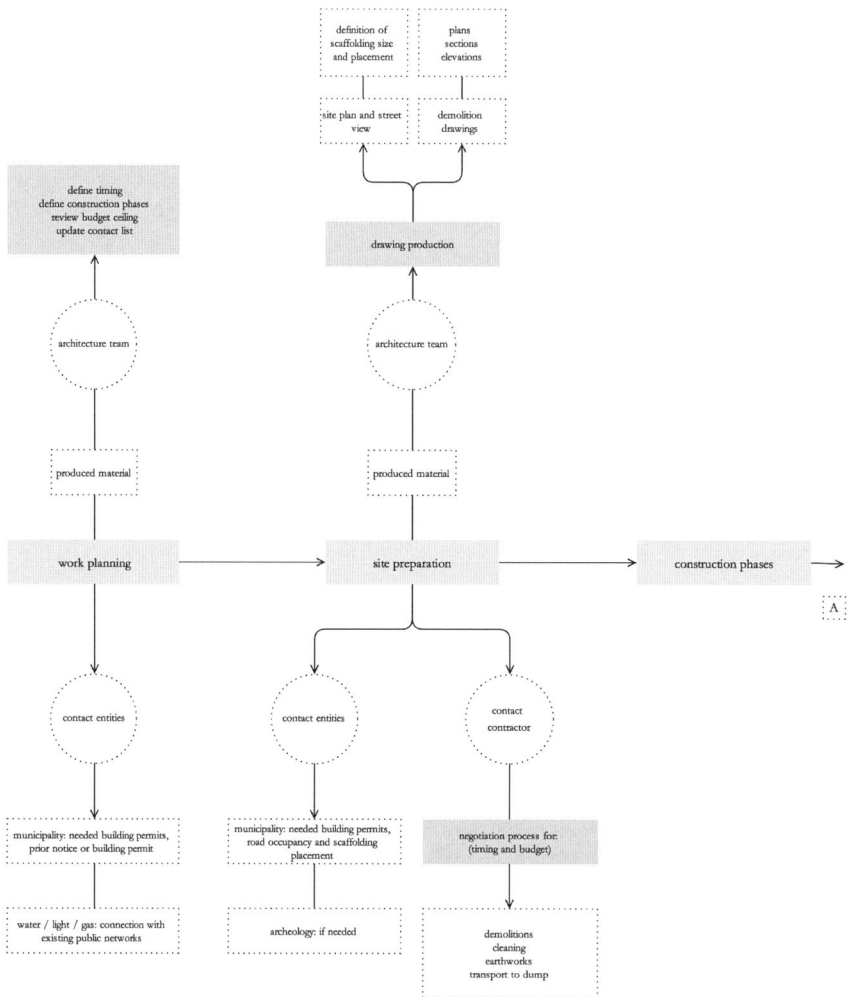

D  Work an Negotiations Map – Type B

Diagram of the construction phase developed in a type B office, specifying the most common phases of a construction work. Time is divided between producing drawings, establishing contacts and making negotiations. In every construction phase the cycle is reinitiated, and time is consumed. (pp. 110-115)

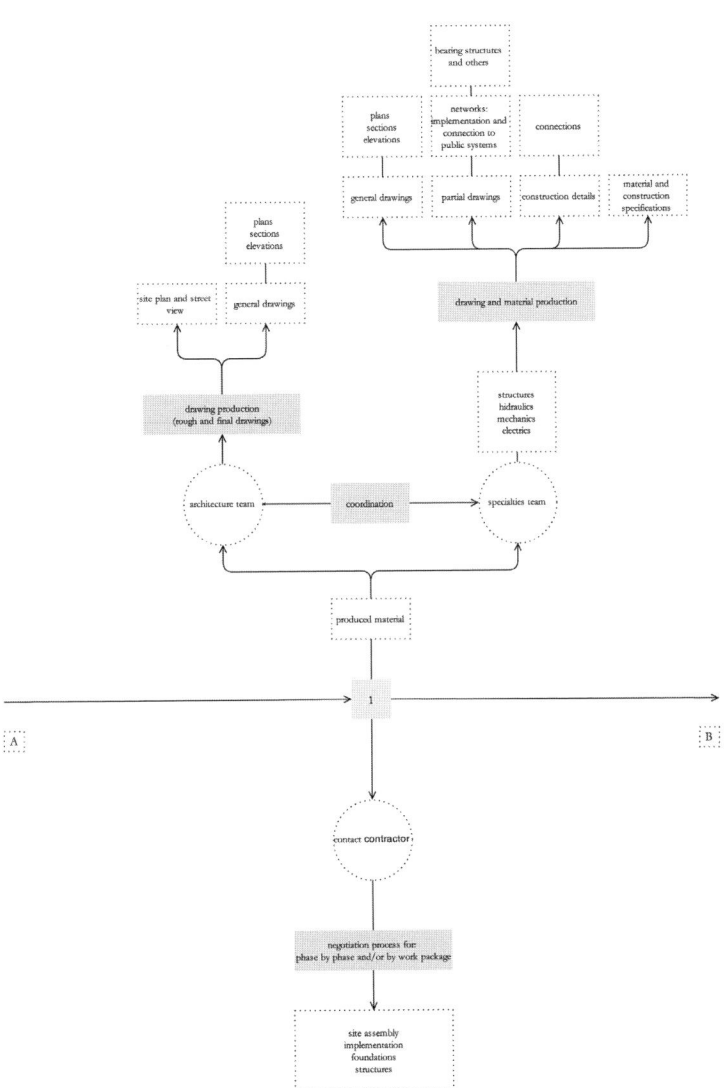

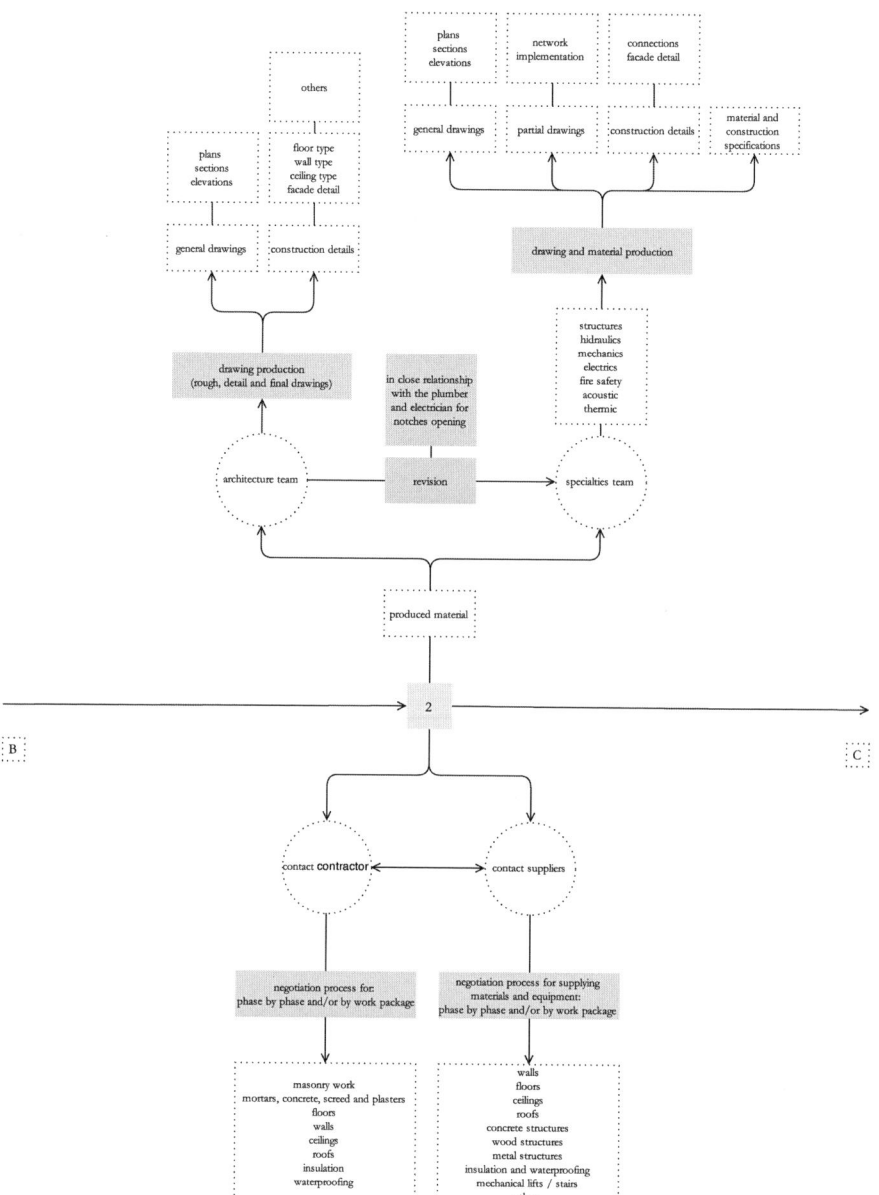

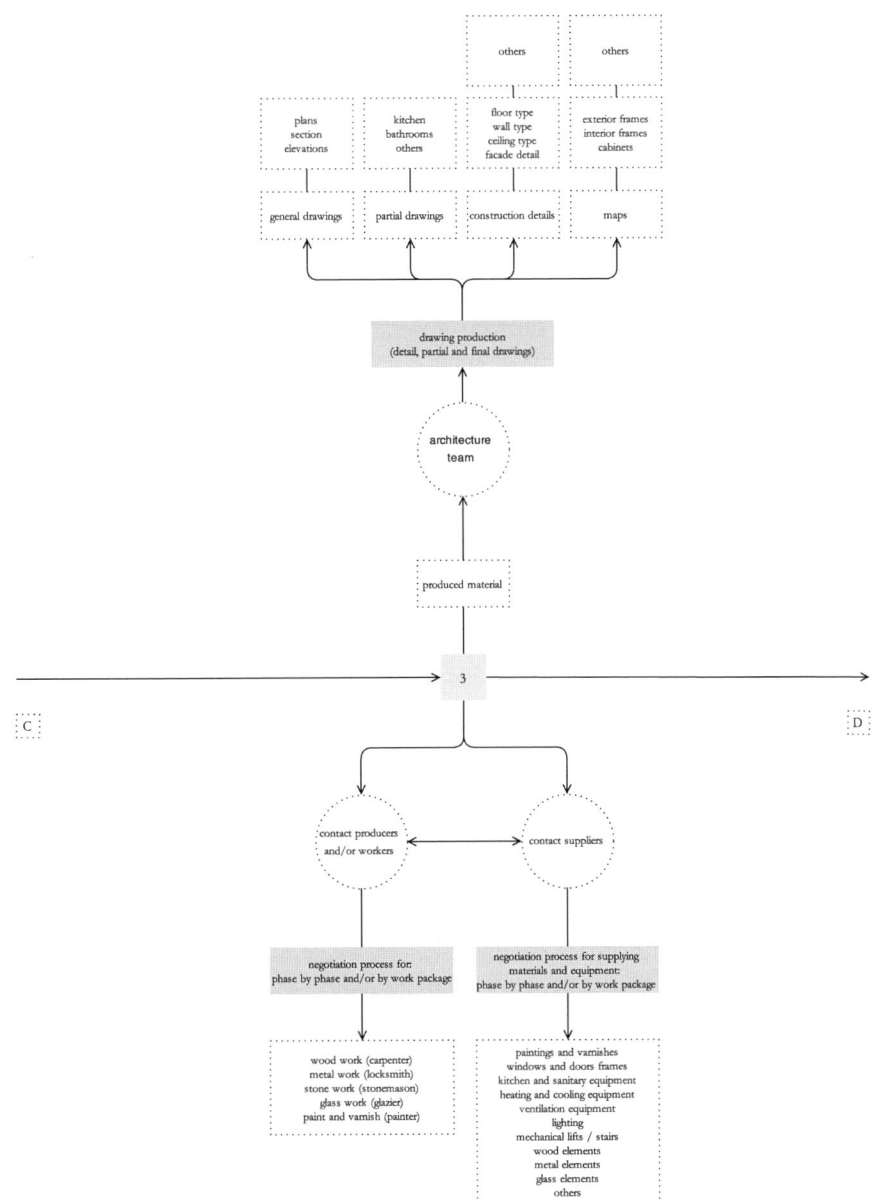

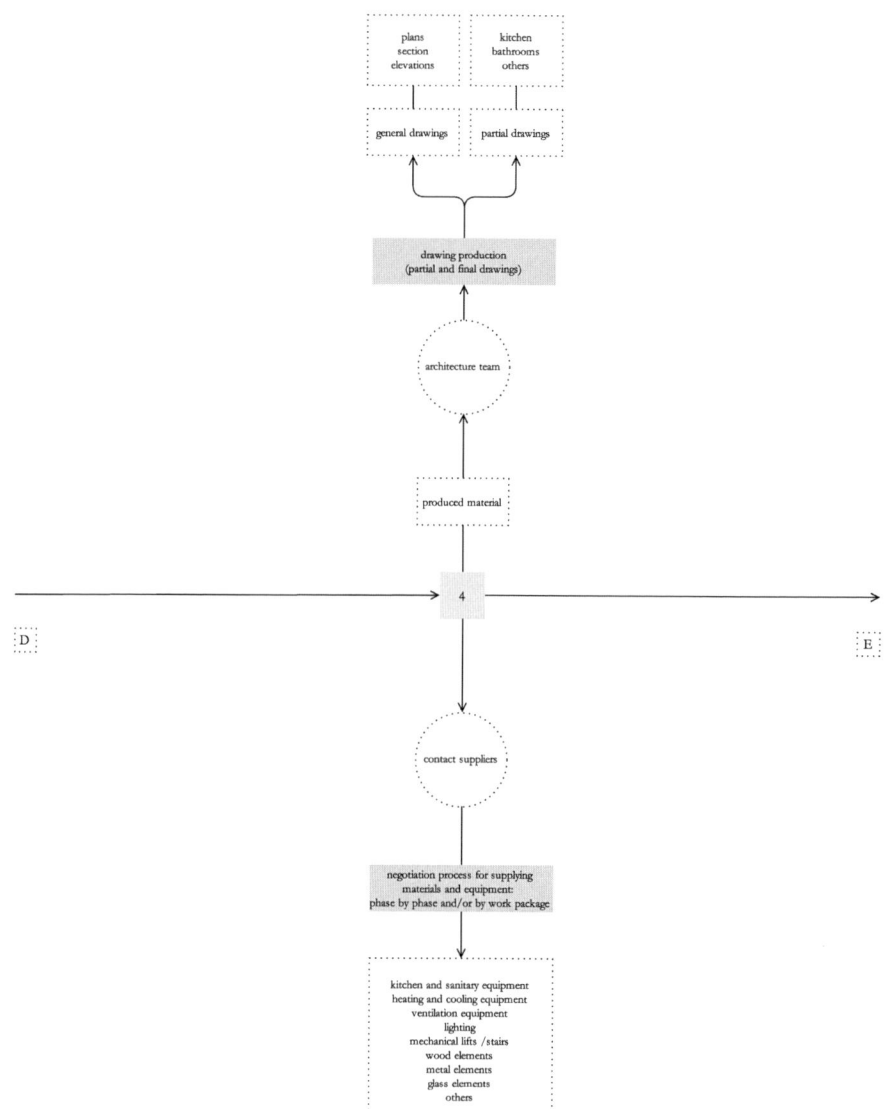

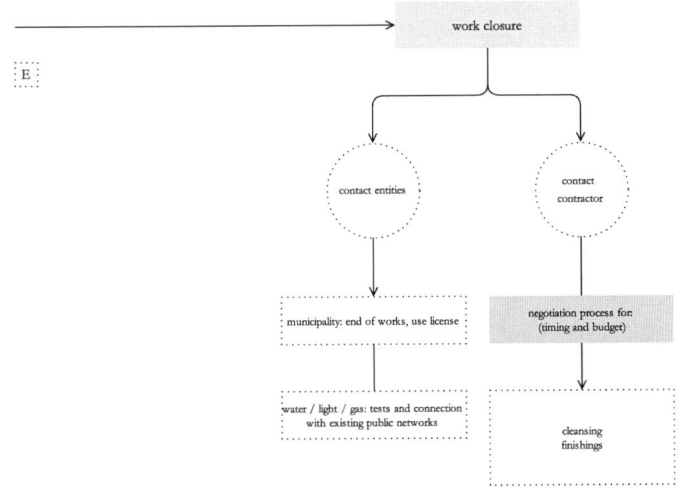

Atelier Angular

# Bridging the Gaps

### Context

Any social, cultural, and academic intervention needs a context in order to be well understood. The context of what we are developing is our own background; it lies within our society.

In our country, we are facing a fast-shifting scenario marked by a decrease in quality. There is a clear constant process of decline in the population's labour conditions, a reduction in our families' economic capacity, and a general decrease in quality of life. We are watching 'live' the collapsing of many of our state systems, such as the judicial, educational structures and health care, the bankruptcy of some of our institutions, and an enormous loss in political reputation. We are witnessing the death of the middle class and the fall of the social state. Our young population and new graduates face harsh employment conditions that lead to the migration of a qualified workforce. Additionally, there is a strong decline in birth rates as well as a steady aging of the population. This is the general picture.

In the environment in which we have chosen to place ourselves, we notice the lack of support and promotion of the cultural and artistic worlds; the depreciation of the individual as a thinker, a creator, someone gifted with sensorial, sensitive and creative capacities, and as a being that expresses its condition through all forms of art. Considering education, we see a generalized program, a process which homogenizes qualification. We observe an inadequacy of the educational system with respect to this new generation and, almost contradictorily, an increasingly overspecialized population. We also feel the absence of a more global, eclectic and holistic way of observing, of thinking, of perceiving things. In the backdrop to this situation, we face an alienation of the population and a lack of critical capacity and response, the absence of the desire for change, which leads to a scarcity of alternatives to the status quo.

A

B

## Genesis

*Angular* started as a group of seven architecture students who came together to create a young collective, aiming to develop practical skills and teamwork experience through participation in competitions, as well as the development of cultural and architectural projects. Before we met, we had already discussed some theoretical architectural themes and consequently also focused on society and how it perceives architecture. Coming together at ENEA (National Architecture Students Meeting) in Porto, we realised that, besides these preoccupations, we shared some thoughts about the insufficient dynamics in our actions at our universities. We came together because we believe that group reflection and debate can lead to more productive and complete conclusions. They allow us to have a more accurate and wider range of action. We started seeing architecture as a very interesting tool for social change. The field of architecture is of course closely related to our capacities and areas of interest, but it has this very peculiar characteristic of being broad and extended to almost all fields of knowledge. Architecture somehow has the capability of bonding scientific, social and artistic areas within its own field, revealing itself as a product of this eclectic combination. However, this potentially wide scope of architecture gets reduced by the path we have come to expect from our architecture students and by the actual professional activity in our country, both of them insufficiently open to these other areas of knowledge. Thus, if we first started as a group of students that enjoyed working together and debating architecture with each other, we soon concluded that we should define our stance facing the major problems we detected, starting with those which were closest at hand.

C

## Zoom-In

Contextualized by the Bologna Process, our architecture course at Faculdade de Arquitectura da Universidade de Lisboa suffered a great compression of working hours, project classes, and a constriction of programmatic content. These factors, combined with the lack of proactivity and motivation by students and professors due to salary cuts, resulted in the almost complete abandonment of complementary activities and actions.

We deem these "extra-curricular" activities to be absolutely necessary to the health of our school: students' work exhibitions, interdisciplinary contests, visits to architecture offices and buildings, travelling and getting to know other realities. For us formation is more than what you absorb during classes. It is what surrounds you and the creative environment that can push you further. Additionally, we noticed a non-existent connection between all six Lisbon's schools of architecture, a great handicap in what could, or should, be a Lisbon School of Architecture. Maybe this way, with a consortium of the Lisbon schools, we could get more diverse architectural thoughts and conceptions and we would be able to treat this new potential diversity as an advantage, pushing for positive communication between these conceptions. Thus, facing these problems as potential opportunities for change, in addition to concern at overspecialization and the holistic mindset, we made an effort to generate structures that would allow us to approach the task of closing these gaps in our learning system in a proactive way.

## Past-Present / Reactions

We joined NAVE, a student association of about thirty students, in which we produce a regular program for the academic community. With this initiative we intend to promote events such as conferences, debates, competitions, exhibitions, and to shake up our school status quo. Encouraging students to attend events outside the classroom, creating a critical mindset not only between students but also among professors, promoting contact between them, developing opportunities for students to show their work, to see each other's work, to work together and to get to know other disciplines: we believe this to be a good way of starting to practice a new education dynamic. The *mesa redonda com belas artes* (round table with fine arts) project proportioned interaction between architecture and students of the visual arts, trying to recover their long time relationship. This interdisciplinary development produced an exhibition, hosted at Lisbon Architecture Triennale's headquarters, which showed very good results from this thought-sharing experience.

### Intentions / Future

Keeping the same course, we intend to work on the *Ponte* (bridge) project throughout next year. This venture aims at stimulating strong bonds amongst all six architecture schools in Lisbon and other schools from artistic, technical and social areas. The project will thus generate a broad intellectual platform of critical and well-informed reactions to our panorama.

#### AUTHORS

*angular collective* is a group of architecture students from Faculdade de Arquitectura da Universidade de Lisboa, who are currently completing the third year of the Integrated Master Degree in Architecture. All members share interests in areas such as music, fine arts, literature, photography, cinema, education, and, of course, architecture and urban design. The collective begun in 2014 and it was one of the seven selected projects on the contest for the Creative Hub of Lisbon's Architecture Triennale. During 2014/15 academic year we started NAVE – students' cultural core of lisbon's school of architecture – and we've created *mesa redonda com belas artes* (round table with fine arts) project.

Catarina Mateus, Madalena Caiado, Henrique Pintão, João Romão, Manuel Santos, Pedro Mendes, Ruben Silva.

#### IMAGE CREDITS

Photographs by *angular collective*.

# 40 Architects Making 40 Birdnests

*Migrant Garden* is an experiment about architectural manifestos.

Camilo Rebelo, Rudy Ricciottì, Point Supreme, Atelier Branco, Emilio Marin, Atelier Fala, Michele De Lucchi, Go Hasegawa, Anna Barbara, Gonzalo Del Val, Francesco Librizzi, Miniatura, Juan Carlos Dall'Asta, Perry Kulper, Cini Boeri, Matilde Cassani, Buildin Building, Fosbury Architcture, Pezo Von Ellrichausen, FormaFantasma, Amunt, Filippo Orsini, UNULAUNU, Eduardo Castillo, MoBo Architects, Nieto Sobejano, Marcio Kogan, Fabio Alessandro Fusco, Altiplano, NETWERCH ARCHITEKTUR DESIGN GRUNDSÄTZLICHES, Mio Tsuneyama, Fuminori Nousaku, Bureau A, MVRDV, Italo Rota, A12, Beniamino Servino, Sergio Crotti, Luca Molinari, Purini Thermes.

*Migrant Garden* called on a heterogeneous panorama of 40 architects, offices and designers to investigate "architectural manifestos". Each architect was requested to design and conceive a birdhouse by hand, starting from a house-shaped block of Acell foam and respecting a series of defined rules.

40 designs, 40 different ages, 40 different formations, 40 offices, 40 cultures, 3 different generations, 15 countries, 4 continents, organized in a temporary travelling architecture exhibition.

What happened to the architectural manifesto? Why should manifestos exist? Are they still meaningful in a globalized panorama of cultures and influences or does a geographical, cultural, economic and substantial difference between architectural languages of design still persist? Are they no longer necessary in a job that does not see itself in terms of the 'lone genius' but, on the contrary, to a set of anti-heroic gestures, as stated by Felicity Scott in 2011? Is it true that the manifesto has been tamed, losing in inventiveness, in its capacity for investigation

A

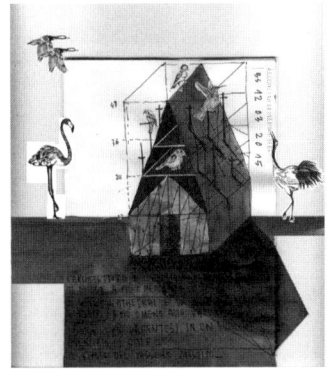

B

C

and interpretation?[1] Numbering between 1 and 100 collaborators, each office has its own different approach to the practice of architecture. Sometimes that approach is based on an image and sometimes on a methodology. Sometimes the same approach is characterized by a shallow pragmatism of solving and creating problems, sometimes it reveals a strong and deep stance. This is what manifestos are dealing with. Manifesto comes from the Latin *Manifestus*; *manus* the hand and *fest*: taken in hand. We draw, we sketch, we express ideas and we shape the future with the same hand. A manifesto can be considered as the way in which someone aims at declaring their critical perspective on the world in order to improve it. A manifesto can be found in many disciplines, from arts and design, to poetry, literature, architecture and more. Different approaches have to be considered under three main contexts: [1] generational, [2] geographical and [3] cultural.

[1] In the last fifteen years, due to the Internet and the economic revolution, we have been taking part in a major change. The way of experiencing the world has changed drastically. Today, a flight ticket costs less then a T-shirt, and this economic issue has resulted in totally different ways of perceiving the world among younger generations of students and architects. This situation has created an environment of hybridization, with new cultures coming into contact with each other and, in turn, influencing new approaches to architecture.

[2] *Genius loci* has always been a central question in the debate about architecture, and it can be considered as the whole kaleidoscope of cultural and architectural characteristics, of languages, of customs that characterize a place, an environment and a city. If society is somehow moving towards globalization, belonging to a territory still persists as a fundamental component for an architect's formation. The place

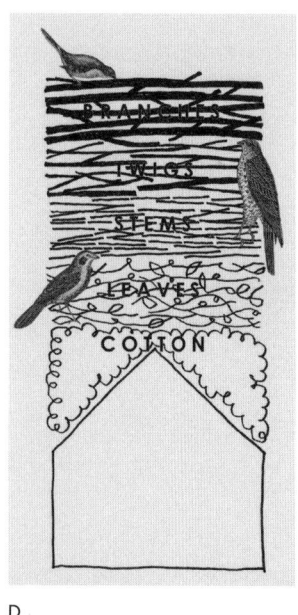

D

E

F

in which we live unintentionally influences our aesthetics, and since it is common nowadays to travel between numerous places, this fact has determined a different perception of the world and of architecture.

[3] "Human cultures are more numerous than human races."[2] Each culture, some more than others, has its own strength to determine a sensitivity and human customs that directly influence architecture. History, like architecture, is something cumulative, and today we cannot say that Japanese architecture is made by Japanese people only. There is a sort of hybridization of references and formations. Today we are living in the age of travel and it is common for lots of people to travel around the globe and live in several nations, mixing their cultures with the new ones they find themselves in. These stratifications of cultures composed by differences and similarities are necessary for the formation of new cultural identities and, in that sense, strongly influence architectural production.

*Migrant Garden* started in May 2014 thanks to a team of seven architects with a common passion for architecture. The project was immediately accepted and supported by the Politecnico di Milano and by Acelltec Industries and was displayed in a temporary preview installation for one year. It has been published in many national and international magazines and has collected numerous positive reviews from architects and the general population.

*Migrant Garden* promotes culture as a horizontal value. Nowadays, older age is commonly synonymous with higher knowledge, but, if we consider that Michelangelo Buonarroti carved the Centauromachia at the young age of 17, this postulate does not make sense. Formal hierarchies no longer have importance. The focus is on the quality of the ideas and not on the label. Forty architects have enthusiastically decided to accept the challenge: the design of a birdhouse. Every house will be an architectural manifesto. Each participant has the same rules, the same possibilities and the same starting point: a house-shaped block of Acell foam. Each architect has been chosen according to three parameters:

–Geography;

–Age;

–Size of the office.

The result is a heterogeneous panorama of 40 architects belonging to 15 different nations, from 3 different generations with a number of collaborators ranging from 1 to 100.

*Migrant Garden's* "Architecture zoo" was inaugurated on 19.06.2015 at the Politecnico di Milano in Piacenza. After the 1.0 inaugural exhibition, *Migrant Garden* moved to other art galleries, institutions and museums in order to spread these 40 visions of architecture throughout the territory. At the end of the project, the birdhouses were sold and the money raised given to charity. These are *Migrant Garden's* untouchable landscapes.

migrantgarden.com

NOTES

1 "What Happened to the Architectural Manifesto?", Columbia University's GSAPP, 18.11.2011.
2 Claude Levi Strauss, "Races and History", 1952.

IMAGE CREDITS

A   Beniamino Servino.
B   Beniamino Servino, Bird's cathedral.
C   Beniamino Servino, Gold signet.
D   Mio Tsuneyama & Fuminori Nousaku, Ashedas Resources for Birds Nests.
E   Perry Kulper.
F   Altiplano, Rigogolo.

Victoria Collar Ocampo

# Shared Concerns

Inquietudes Compartidas

### Prologue

This is a fictitious conversation between two "confrères" sharing their opinion about contemporary relations between architects. Establishing a conversation about the current ways we behave and relate to each other might enable us to understand the importance of processes, of valuing the information we deal with and of always trying to go beyond the image. One could maybe go so far as to conclude that one's attitudes towards similar situations with which we, as architects, are confronted, could act as new common guidelines to follow.

### Dialogue

*@arch88*: Do you think that the relations between architects still exist at all? By relations I mean the will to really see and understand each other, to truly collaborate.

*@iamnotanartist74*: Nowadays there does not seem to be direct relations between architects, at least not as we understood these in the past. Apparently, the straight lines that we used to follow throughout the last decades have turned into more complex architectural approaches. There is not just a one "truth" anymore. In fact, there are so many lines that we no longer meet to discuss future guidelines as we used to. We do not establish the basis for the way to proceed. There are no CIAM, manifestos, rules or styles anymore.

*@arch88*: But then, do you think that there is no longer a common way of thinking? We are still dealing with similar elements and often use common procedures or find similar solutions. Where then, do architects diverge? Why do they differ? Where is the inflection point?

*@iamnotanartist74*: I guess the answer could be related to the new media. Today we receive much more information than a few years ago. Until now, when we needed a reference we had

A  Diptych of the Duchess and Duke of Urbino, Piero della Francesca, 1472.

to search for it, whereas today we have an overdose of information, which comes to us even if we make no effort whatsoever to reach it. Social networks, blogs and so on have a lot to do with this situation. The risk with this volume of information and images is that there is no filter applied; no attention is paid to what lies behind it.

@arch88: I see your point. However, I find it more relevant to say that architects behave in an increasingly multidisciplinary manner and, as we open broader fields, we receive and produce even more information.

@iamnotanartist74: Certainly, this is very important. The tools that we use for working nowadays such as computer programs, parametrical design, 3D printing and modelling machines, are increasing in number and complexity. We have access to far more resources than a few years ago, mainly thanks to the Internet providing us with a huge database, blogs or sharing platforms. As you said, we are getting into a much more multidisciplinary system; one in which different "professions" are mixed up and limits get blurry. We can no longer get a satisfying result simply by applying direct rules. We need to try to understand the different processes and similitudes between different disciplines in order to interiorize them.

@arch88: As Balenciaga used to say: "A couturier must be an architect for design, a sculptor for shape, a painter for colour, a musician for harmony, and a philosopher for temperance." Likewise, architecture covers several fields including sociology, politics, cinema, photography and design.

@iamnotanartist74: So then, could we say that the process is as important as the result? When somebody explains the process behind an image, much like the concept of the project, we start to give more value to the object. By knowing and understanding these processes, we discover new interests in formerly unknown subjects and therefore widen our scopes.

B    Metropolitan Opera House in Taichung, Toyo Ito.

C    Cross rail underground infrastructure in London.

*@arch88*: Therefore, it is worth when sharing an image to describe why it attracts our attention as well as to reveal the processes behind the object or the concept itself.

*@iamnotanartist74*: I agree with you, and would even argue that, for instance, we should not only be amazed by a hydraulic floor tile because we find it "beautiful" but rather because we have understood its process of fabrication and have interiorized the value of its craftsmanship. This critical thought could be applied to textiles as well. For instance, we like to touch a fabric, we like its texture and its colour, but only when we have truly understood the complexities of the process can we really admire the product.

*@arch88*: Exactly. Another example could be the way we find relations and similarities in the proceedings of very different projects, such as an architectural project like the Metropolitan Opera House in Taichung and an engineering one like the Cross rail underground infrastructure in London. [Fig. B, C] It is often in the details or even in the anomalies that we discover the intricacies of a project. But we should be mindful to share our findings with care. Instead of sharing our ideas as absolute truth, we should emphasize our interests or concerns.

*@iamnotanartist74*: Then we both agree that there is still a line, a common relation.

*@arch88*: Well, is this not just a way of behaving towards different situations? This way of observing should be considered not solely towards different processes, objects or images, as mentioned before, but as a lifestyle, whereby we develop our critical minds as architects and make decisions by analyzing what is behind what we see. Perhaps we do not need more rules. Perhaps this could be the relationship between architects: sharing concerns.

AUTHOR

Victoria Collar Ocampo was born in Zaragoza and graduated as an architect from the University of Barcelona ETSAB, having also studied at the ETH Zürich. She currently works at Herzog & de Meuron in Basel after having gained experience in offices like Josep Ferrando in Barcelona, EM2N and Wolfgang Rossbauer Architekten, both based in Zürich. In 2014 she founded Ochentay-doskilometros (www.82km.tumblr.com) together with Jon Garbizu Etxaide, where they share their concerns as explored in this dialogue.

IMAGE CREDITS

A   Diptych of the Duchess and Duke of Urbino, Piero della Francesca, 1472. Image taken from Wikipedia.
B   Metropolitan Opera House in Taichung, Toyo Ito. Image taken from 82km.
C   Cross rail underground infrastructure in London. Image taken from 82km.

CARTHA

# Rasmus Norlander

A Visual Contribution

A. S. Bramble on Rasmus Norlander

## Enclosed Moments

"Need one point out that (...) the gentle warmth of enclosed regions is the first indication of intimacy? This warm intimacy is the root of all images."
Bachelard, Gaston, "The poetics of Space", 1969, p. 154.

Rasmus Norlander produces still images, not movies, not shouting photos, not unsettling dynamic pictures.

As an architectural photographer, Rasmus has a bold stance regarding his profession. His photographs do not try to reproduce the buildings they depict; they do not try to replace the actual experience of the space. They are two dimensional representations of the reality of a certain building, in a certain place at a certain time.

This honesty and humbleness is extremely valuable in architectural photography. Distancing his work from a noisy spectacularity, Norlander allows the projects to be enticing and suggestive in a very subtle way, denying the need for fast readability of the architecture's dynamics and spatiality.

Spaces are shown in a generic way, open wide to be read and interpreted, almost without scale in their cool nudity. Warmth is scarce in his photos but comfort is still, somehow, a constant. People are, most of the time, absent from his frames and, when present, they acknowledge the camera in a technical interaction, gazing into the lens. Rooms are flattened into the bi-dimensional plane of the image, bringing to our attention the materialisation of the spaces. There is a peaceful stillness to these works. Shapes and colours seem to retreat to a quieter place within the frame. They are still present, still dynamic and full of meaning, yet toned down to a balanced warm whisper, allowing us to discover our own path into the beauty of the still image.

In his *Zürich West* series, he manages to isolate the quiet roughness out of the ever-growing, hectic, ambitious, constant construction site that Zurich has become in the last decade. The playground of numerous architects, where they interact with each other in a multitude of ways, is shown here in a fair manner, with a complete absence of favouritism in the way buildings are pictured, giving us the rare chance to read their intentions and presence as they were intended to be read. A part of the city that lives and acts as a beehive, full of movement and noise, presents itself frozen in the calm frames of the series. Details are allowed enough time to appear to our eyes, are allowed the needed significant presence to act as markers on the evolution of the cityscape. The diffuse treatment of light lays a thin tissue over the scene, enabling the abrupt verticality of the pictured new buildings to smooth into the blurred horizon.

IMAGE CREDITS

Photographs by Rasmus Norlander.

I CONFRÈRES

# II
# MANNSCHAFT

140 **CARTHA**
Editorial

142 **Francisco Moura Veiga, Interview**
Samuel Schultze

150 **Joanne Pouzenc**
Womannschaft

154 **Fabrizio Ballabio**
Role Module – Zanuso's Participatory Design or the Architect as Manager

162 **Mio Tsuneyama**
Towards "Build the House"

167 **Alan-Miguel and Rubén Valdez**
Technocentric Neoliberalism and Okness – The Shaping of the City

170 **Cristina García Baeza**
Architecture Construction Process – A Molecule

176 **Vicente Nequinha**
Fernand Pouillon – The Modern Master Builder

180 **Walter Achermann**
The Team Captain – Notes on a Life of Building

184 **Visual Contribution**
Joël Tettamanti

191 **Mathieu Bujnowskyj on Joël Tettamanti**
The Photographic Ambiguity and the Artification of Architectural Communications

II MANNSCHAFT

## There's no "I" in Team

One can say that "knowledge" has been growing at an unprecedented pace since the first industrial revolution. As with any other field of knowledge, architecture is no exception. Where architecture differs is in its assimilating character; architecture tends to integrate innovations from other fields, or even whole new fields, into its processes. This has a direct influence on the depth and range of comprehension that is now requested from the architect.

Although we can still agree with the Vitruvian view of the architect as a "generalist specialist", the idea of the architect as a "master builder" is something we cannot conceive of at this moment. When the role of the architect must be one of an overseer, how can she/he deepen her/his knowledge of all necessary aspects of the process to the point of mastering them, above all if they keep on multiplying at an exponential rate? For one person to take upon herself/himself the responsibility for all the subparts of the process is not just egotistical but also reckless.

Architects should act as coordinators, attaining a position of overview by acknowledging the necessary work of other "players" during different phases of the process, not by proclaiming themselves as having sole responsibility for the built environment. As we see it, the built environment is as much a consequence of the conceptual work of the architect as it is of the quality of the construction industry, of the engineer's ingenuity or of the nature of local laws.

With this issue, we want to pay homage to all the other entities that play an active part in the act of building, thereby viewing these teammates from the perspective of the architect, from our perspective, by discoursing on our reality and by understanding how intertwined it is with that of those who build with us. To the rest of the team, our most honest thank you.

Francisco Moura Veiga

# Samuel Schultze

Interview

It is easy to sit across from Samuel Schultze. Leaning back on the chairs inside one of the meeting rooms in the freshly renovated Basel office, overlooking the fig trees in the interior courtyard, one can't help but feel comfortable. The room I am in is one of the few enclosed spaces in the huge office. Samuel shares the open-office space with all the other workers that make up the Basel office of Burckhardt + Partner; no private office, no wall between him and his employees. This is quite something when we remember that he is CEO of one of the largest architecture offices in Switzerland, with around 350 employees and a history that started in the early 1950s, and that he was part of the Basel Cityscape commission for 15 years and is currently President of the Board of Trustees of the Swiss Architecture Museum. Still he is no star, no Ronaldo or Messi, more of a Phillip Lahm; a polyvalent figure that holds the team in place through his overview of the game and his understanding of each position's functions. Just before starting the interview, I tell him that we don't want to hear what the CEO of B+P has to say about MANNSCHAFT, we want to hear what he, Samuel, has to say. He then leaned back too and we started talking.

**How would you define the architect's role in a project now, today, at this precise moment?**
Nowadays the architect doesn't have the same role as he did in the past. He used to be not only an architect but also a master-builder, and that worked perfectly back then. His fields of knowledge were vast; he was therefore able to implement his artistic ideas backed by a comprehensive amount of information. He would complete an apprenticeship, he would learn from his master and further develop his skills. The trade he learned enabled him to look at a task in its entirety – he had the overview. With the separation of design and execution, the architect's role changed. He draws the plans, he is still versed in construction matters, but he does not implement his ideas himself anymore. This task has been taken over by the "new" specialized master-builder.

**When did this separation between design and execution happen?**
At the beginning of the 20th century, when architecture crystallised into a separate discipline. In the last century, the architect missed out on strengthening his position as leader of the planning and execution phases and was gradually displaced by the general contractor. The general contractor was better in all matters of

**With the separation of design and execution, the architect's role changed.** accounting and timing, and the architect didn't deal with that part of the process because he concentrated more and more on the design part. Nowadays, this kind of specialization has reached a new level: today we have planners, estimators, acoustic engineers, i.e. we have specialists for everything.

**These specialists for everything, how do you relate to them? For instance, the office you head works for companies (such as Roche or Novartis) that request that an enormous number of specialists and consultants should be involved in their projects. Do these specialists give you the information you need for your work or do they limit you in terms of the design process?**
I think that our relationship towards specialists is rather ambivalent. On the one hand, I'm convinced that we need expertise in order to deal with the complexity of the tasks that we are given today. On the other hand, we have to consider the fact that this expertise also greatly restrains us if we do not question it. Therefore, it is very important that we challenge the expertise they are adding to the project and that we extract what we need to know in order to implement their knowledge in an intelligent way. We have to learn to work with the information the experts are giving us and trust their experience without adopting their inputs one to one. This is a crucial task. Experts often have a very clear idea of how something has to be done. The job of the architect is to bring together different aspects of a project in an intelligent way. He is supposed to oversee the whole process and the entirety of the task. In this sense the architect needs to reconquer his position, which was once held by the "master-builder-architect".

**In this sense the architect needs to reconquer his position, which was once held by the "master-builder-architect".**

**And who holds this position nowadays?**
This position has been taken over by construction managers, people who primarily organize and structure. They are used to making logical decisions but have no affinity with architecture. They are trustees, guiders, schedulers... We should not allow our demotion from our position of overview in the project, otherwise the architect becomes just another expert who is supposed to bring inputs.

**As CEO of B+P, you have already been in the position of working as a local architect by executing a project for a design architect. I'm thinking of the work you did for Renzo Piano, Chipperfield or Libeskind. How was it for you to hold that position? At the end, were you then also "just another expert"?**

In a way it is a thankless job when you have been given the task of guiding the "design architect". You act as the go-between who has to fulfil the needs of two parties, the client and the design architect. The client doesn't dare to give instructions to the design architect, afraid of interfering with the architecture. The design architect, on the other hand, is often struggling with deadlines and financial specifications he does not fully understand. The local architect/project manager is the middleman, the mediator, because he speaks both languages. It is of great importance that he knows the design architect's point of view well and is able to represent it to the client, the same way that he has to represent the interests of the client to the design architect. It is a very demanding job, because you run the risk of being ground down between the two positions. And, at the end, your contribution to the project's realisation is substantial but you are not benefiting from it. The design architect is the one who gets the credit and is published. The client is happy and proud of the result whereas you are not getting recognized for the indispensable job you did. This can be quite frustrating. There was a time when B+P worked in this function for Libeskind, Renzo Piano and Tadao Ando, amongst others. It was extremely educational in the sense that we got privileged insights into their working methods and ways of thinking, but, even with this conceptual and theoretical compensation, we are not putting ourselves in that position anymore. We withdrew from this kind of business because we are convinced that we are good enough to realise projects like that by ourselves.

**As you mentioned already, the job description of the architect has changed. In the design phase too, we are gradually turning away from tasks that have always been at the core of the architect's work (visualizations, layout, graphic conception of the plans) and outsourcing them to specialists. Do you see this as a natural development or should the design process stay in the architect's hands?**

I am against excessive specialization. I believe that the architect needs to handle the devices himself in order to design, plan and communicate his ideas. Certainly there is a kind of specialization, like budgeting or logistics, for example, where, due to the increasing complexity of projects, the architect couldn't possibly manage everything by himself. Still, we would like to keep that kind of knowledge within the company in order to be able to cover all aspects of the project, during all phases, including concept and design.

**As president of the *Ortsbildkommission* (Townscape Commission) in Riehen and a member of the *Stadtbildkomission* (Cityscape Commission) in Basel, you had the chance to sit on the other side of the table and decide how the city's districts should develop. How did you feel, taking this position?**
To work for the municipal authorities was a significant and essential experience for me. But you shouldn't feel too important and get presumptuous. The committee's first goal is to push the good and outstanding projects forward. Often, these good and outstanding projects do not conform to the law. So if you manage to convince the authorities and find solutions with them to realize projects because they are above-average, then you have done a good job. The second goal is to prevent below-average projects being realized. And the third goal is to partially improve a great deal of all the other projects. The city as an organism gains life not just from the outstanding projects but also from those which are average. Average is sufficient, as long as you have highlights in between. But obviously there are limits: A *Stadtbildkommission* cannot lift average quality to a high level, because the project leaders are not able to do so. It's not like at university, where you can tell the students what to do in order to get a better grade; it is much more difficult than that. In Switzerland for example, the profession of the architect is not protected (by law). It means that practically anybody can be an architect and hand in a building application. If you talk to these kinds of people the way you talk to your students, they won't understand a word. Actually this job is much more about interpersonal relations, comprehension and communication.

**What are your views on the future of the building industry, and the role of the architect as one of the many players in it?**
The architects need to make sure that they still can do normal projects (small-scale residential, medium-scale housing developments)

146

in the future. More and more people want to do their project by themselves because it's cheaper. For instance, if one wants to build a house for one family, one can just go to the construction material market and do it oneself. Or small companies can directly address general contractors and tell them "Build me something. We don't need an architect who just brings expenses". For these small-scale projects you have pre-fabricated structures, modular structures and general contractors that displace the architect, making him redundant. It is important that the architect can strengthen his position and show that he is needed. Nowadays, architects tend to be judged by "spectacular" large-scale projects like airports, museums or projects for companies that use architecture as a marketing tool. That's all good but the architect has to make sure to not only take on these large-scale specific projects but also smaller-scale projects. Otherwise "the cookie will only get smaller". I think the building industry in Switzerland is doing well, and will do well in the future because the current building stock is, and will continue to be, in need of rehabilitation. In general we have to stimulate the building culture. Architects should not only be considered for spectacular projects but for normal residential projects of high usability and good quality.

> They need to be the spider in the web, to stand where everything merges in order to have more influence on the design part.

**What do the words *ecology*, *flexibility*, *standardization* and *typology* mean to you regarding the future prospects mentioned before?**

Usually architecture is particular; you always have prototypes. Architecture is consistently reinvented. On the one hand, that is important because we need to come up with site-specific and customized solutions and to carefully analyse the given situation. Now the question is whether this is going to work as well in the future and whether architecture can sustain all these prototypes? And whether, in the future, our society can still afford this kind of architecture or will rather turn to standardisation? Generally the architect does not like the concept of standardisation because he does not have the same kind of freedom of expression. On the other hand, we have to face economic pressures and see that it absolutely makes sense to force standardisation. This is a challenge and it certainly can be an interesting topic. For example, we have to find solutions to provide affordable housing space. Housing space is getting more and more expensive if built as new. This is a never-ending process. In order to provide new affordable housing space, we have to find intelligent solutions and standardisation makes absolute sense in this context. Therefore we have to work with flexible typologies. There was a time where, for every problem, you would come up with an individual and fixed solution. Then the needs changed and the house was not usable anymore. Only old houses with very simple structure survived. They were former office buildings, then residential buildings and are still functioning today. They are flexible enough to fill new needs. Of course the individual house will always exist. Nevertheless, we have to consider both sides and it is important that we develop typologies based on ecological and economical considerations and which can fulfil future needs in a sustainable way.

**Finally, what position should architects adopt when facing the future?**
Architects need to become all-rounders again; they have to broaden their horizons. They need to be curious and interested in all the different aspects of a project. They do not have to be experts, but they need to know how to integrate the experts' input in a clever way and to use it in their favour. They need to be the spider in the web, to stand where everything merges in order to have more influence on the design part. They shouldn't become a pawn at the hands of the client, they should rule the game.

IMAGE CREDITS

Courtesy of Burckhardt + Partner Architekten.

II MANNSCHAFT

Joanne Pouzenc

# Womannschaft

### Feminine thinking

A couple of weeks ago, I received an impromptu invitation to a fabulous dinner. Based on an original idea from Niche Berlin with Rosario Talevi and supported by Perspektive – a programme from the Institut Français in Berlin – the hosts gathered some 20 special guests around the table to think about the production of space from a feminine point of view. The guests were all space-related, mainly architects, and were all women apart from two males. But whereas architecture was our common point, almost none of us was still a practitioner: all of our career paths had caused us to broaden our horizons and to diversify our practices into the cultural, artistic, curatorial or teaching fields.

Why was that? Had we made a step forward on our individual pathways or had we intended to flee from our architectural fates?

Before that occasion presented itself, I hadn't really embarrassed myself with feminist thoughts.

My experiences had taught me not to dissociate males from females and certainly not to claim any difference. I had always accepted as law that women who decide to do a man's job should be aware that the same qualities will be expected of them. Whereas around the table, some very strong characters preferred to defend the idea that women need to fight to get their own way in a man's world, I'd rather argue that women need to adapt and that the dichotomy between men and women should just be ignored. But that dinner blew my mind: of course this distinction exists and is extremely present. Furthermore, to what exactly should women adapt? Very often if not daily, women suffer from untold masochistic rules in their work environment. And if those rules don't apply, for cultural or societal reasons, it's sometimes the woman alone who is forcing herself to be as efficient and as productive in every field in which men excel, if not better.

A, B  Berlin Unlimited, Festival for Arts, Architecture and Urban Research, Oct. 2014.

B

## A woman's style

I was still a student the first time I visited a building site. As part of "on the ground" training, I had chosen a woman architect in order to follow one of her projects undergoing construction. The project was relatively small – a couple of houses in an urban environment – but was already very impressive for the future architect-to-be that I was back then. Actually, any project was truly impressive: as a student, I was constantly asking myself how the shift between the drawing on the paper and the built reality is managed. I was frightened by the amount of information I would still need to become an architect – hopefully, a good one. As I was waiting for that lady architect to come, I was surprised to see her arriving in her "lady" style: heels she could exchange for the non-safety but "at least closed" ballerinas she had in her bag, a normal formal skirt and jacket, and her dog on a leash. It seemed pretty relaxed.

After five minutes of courteous handshakes and smiles, she asked one of the workers to hold the dog for her so that meanwhile she could climb a ladder and go check the first floor with another guy. I didn't think this was truly efficient but I felt relieved. Efficiency might not always be the only measurement tool. As anything else, "efficiency" measured as a productive factor should also be considered from the short-term and long-term perspectives. What I observed back then was maybe the reassurance that the architect/worker relationship did in fact work quite well. It helped me understand that there was a possibility to express and assume femininity anywhere, and also – of course – within an architectural practice.

## 21st century and popular beliefs

When I finally graduated, I was very proud to bring my architect title into conversation, at least the first few times. There is always a moment when people ask you, "What do you do for a living?" and this question often comes right after, "What's your name/ Where do you come from?", usually within the first five minutes.

Depending on the milieu or where I was when asked this question, I often – very often! – faced a strange reaction after I had proudly produced the "I'm an architect" answer. Immediately, as a reflex, people would ask: "Do you mean interior designer?", i.e. choosing the carpets, the colours of the pillows, the fabric of the curtains and the framed pictures to be hung on the wall. The worst bit, however, would come from the fact that women also had that question-reaction. I apparently didn't fit in with their image of "the architect" and if falling into such clichés is a widespread practice, let me take a risk myself in bringing some more stereotypes.

### Different techniques, same results

When they become conflict-laden and involve opposing interests, men-to-men relations are often based on force, strength or pressure. Threats, anger or loud voices are current issues on construction sites. I'm not saying that construction sites necessarily entail conflicts and I have also seen some which operate very smoothly… but conflicts appear and men and women seem to have very different approaches to them. Of course, the architect always has that same threatening tool that doesn't depend on gender: money. But the way deals or negotiations are done definitely differs from one gender to the other. I've seen workmen on construction sites spending the first minutes testing the competence of the woman architect. On arriving, the woman architect will be asked a series of tricky technical questions to which maybe even a male architect would not have any answer. Her competence will then be established in front of the group according to the answer she gives.

I wondered for a long time what the good answers were: I tried several techniques before finding the most suitable one, the one that would give me the green light to lead the construction site and gain the initial respect from the group of people with whom I would be working over the next months. I've faked a "good" answer that appeared to be the wrong one, I've tried to change the topic by pointing out another more urgent matter, I've initiated some sexists jokes or jumped at the occasion to laugh at some, I've tried the "I don't know – I'll ask my boss and give you an answer (once he has enlightened my dark ignorance)", I've made it evolve into "I don't know – I'll do some research and I'll give you an answer", and that was the closest possible answer to gaining respect I could find. Until one day, I just decided to be honest and stop caring: there are things I know, some I don't, some I'm good at, some I'm not good at. And it can be gender related – or not at all. Within the construction process too, I've experienced that gentleness, politeness and understanding can also be used to obtain good results. Moreover, when these modes of behaviour are combined with an already acquired respect, the general mood in the construction process becomes smoother and the whole team works together to fulfil a common goal: making it happen and doing it well.

### Building content

The process of gaining respect may get faster with more experience, but, one undoubtedly has to go through the exact same power-testing at the beginning. But feminine presence seems to be much more accepted in the cultural-architectural sector. Furthermore, in Berlin, women seem to be the leaders of architectural content: the cultural teams of architectural curatorial practices are often built under the leadership of well-connected women who are entitled to put back on paper – and into exhibition spaces – what one has been building and putting into concrete form somewhere else.

I've been working with and within a team of women over the last year: not that being a female was a requirement for getting the job. Being a bit worried at first and aware of the hard level of competition that women apply between same-gender individuals, I quickly observed how women communities can work efficiently together, whatever tasks are given. As such, within Berlin Unlimited (which consisted of a team of 15, of which only two were male latecomers), women designed, organized, estimated, negotiated and built up the entire structure – literally and metaphorically – for a seven-day festival about Arts, Architecture and Urban Research. While I was stuck on office duties, my collaborators sent me a video of the construction site. The short video featured a couple of beautiful women mastering the art of loud power drills and screwdrivers, singing some famous jazzy ballads over the music in the background, covering the noise of their tools while assembling the structures. I wondered quite a lot why no men had joined in this adventure. Perhaps men were just more pragmatic and not willing to give their competence for free to a cultural cause. But the more I receive new applications for future projects, the more I have to face it: they mainly keep coming from the feminine sphere. Women may just need "more" to fulfil their satisfaction ratio. More challenges, more overviews, more domains of expertise, more diversity, more contacts, more adaptability... Unless, once again it's purely coincidental. Sure, the places I've chosen to live in might influence and/or enhance these tendencies: in France, I've had more balanced experiences, in New York, I was the only girl in a 90% gay firm (funnily and naturally, they actually interpreted that I was a boy due to the lack of picture on my resume), in the Bauhaus in Dessau, we were 20 women in a research team of 24. I deliberately choose to exclude from my considerations the parts of the world where men/women differences are, in fact, the most pronounced: I simply have absolutely no idea about those parallel realities and it is unlikely that I would be the right person to depict them. I will just keep my eyes and feminine high-sensitive receptors wide open: maybe there is a lot to learn from those differences in order to finally reach a real balance.

### AUTHOR

Joanne Pouzenc (joannepouzenc.com) is a French architect, curator, teacher and urban researcher based in Berlin. After eight years of architectural practice between France, Germany and New York, she started her curatorial career within the Bauhaus Dessau Foundation programme in 2010. This led to Europe-wide exhibitions (Bauhaus Dessau Foundation, S AM Basel, House of Arts - Brno). She co-founded CollageLab with Philine Schneider in 2012. In 2014, she coordinated and curated Berlin Unlimited (berlinunlimited.org), the first international festival for Arts, Architecture and Urban Research in Berlin.

### IMAGE CREDITS

Photographs by Tanja Katharina Lindner.

Fabrizio Ballabio

# Role Module

Zanuso's Participatory Design
or the Architect as Manager

A concrete pad approximately five metres in area sits below a concrete deck. The pad accommodates a column which is secured within a slot. On two such columns sits an inverted Y beam spanning 12 metres in length. The trylith is then offset at approximately 18 metres distance and connected via 4 hollow V beams laid at regular intervals between them. To a certain extent, this bare and almost rudimentary assemblage of prefabricated elements amounts to the entirety of the architectural process deployed by industrial designer and architect Marco Zanuso in his project for the Olivetti Factory in Scarmagno, begun in 1968 – no definitive form, no fixed internal layout.

Part of a second wave of plants the Italian typewriter manufacturer had inaugurated at the end of the 1960s[1], the project also sits within a broader range of works carried out by Zanuso in flourishing post-war Italy, in which the attempt was made to achieve the complete industrialisation of the architectural project. As one might sense, the system described above denotes a module of the building, and were it not for the refined, faceted forms in which the elements had been cast, it would probably, at first glance, seem no different from any standard application of pre-fab, post-lintel concrete structures the last century has seen. And yet, it is precisely in the intricacy of its tectonic resolution that one can gauge the project's relevance – both in its mirroring of the circumstances in which it came into existence and in the context of more recent debates around collaborative design processes. If, in fact, Zanuso's factory in Scarmagno stands as a testament to exquisitely "Olivettian" value systems, whereby the myths of social collaboration and interdisciplinarity would permeate the most dispersed aspects of civic life, it is interestingly also an incarnation *ante litteram* of what Mario Carpo would have referred to as an "architecture of many hands".[2] One where the managerial nature of the design processes is made entirely visible through the concrete disposition of architectural form.

I

Zanuso first came in contact with Adriano Olivetti around 1954, when the company was undertaking a vast programme of expansion which would result in the construction of a number of new factories both in Italy and abroad. Strengthened by international funding and by an unprecedented wealth in sales, Olivetti was seeking for opportunities to decentralise its production activities towards the underdeveloped regions of Southern Italy (Campania, Basilicata, Puglia) whilst investing in new foreign markets in South America, Africa and the US. In this context, Zanuso's first commissions consisted in the design of two production units in Brazil and Argentina, adding to what Manfredo Tafuri would ironically describe as Olivetti's personal architectural showcase.

The factories were portrayed as the spatial embodiment of the company's excellence, providing a tangible image of it to be showcased globally. If this form of architectural marketing is extremely common in contemporary corporate environments[3], the case in question was in actual fact part of a broader strategy devised by Adriano Olivetti himself after he had first joined his father's company on return from his American studies. Creating the firm's publicity office in 1928 and running it over the course of 30 years, the young heir had attempted to reinvent Olivetti's image claiming the factory as a crucial locus for social, cultural and political reform.

To this objective, architects and planners came to be involved within much larger interdisciplinary exchanges involving not only industrial and graphic designers but also social scientists and doctors among others. Under the tuneful banner of *Comunità*, a movement and editorial project which promoted technological development and social cooperation within a quasi-federalist concept of the State, Olivetti and his comrades presented cohesive studies for new societal models informed by participatory practices and a renewed, "humanitarian" ethos.

If the majority of these propositions was doomed to remain on paper, a concrete implementation of Adriano Olivetti's ideas found its place in the Canavese district (the geographical area of which the main town is Ivrea) around the 1950s. Contingent to the expansion of the company's headquarters in Via Jervis were, in fact, a number of initiatives in the surrounding area which nurtured distributed production strategies as well as concrete forms of social assistance. In 1954 and 1955 respectively, Adriano Olivetti founded I-RUR, the institute for urban and agricultural renovation[4], and the League of Municipalities of the Canavese (*Lega dei Comuni del Canavese*) – two organisms which catered for the construction of smaller craft-oriented production facilities, training centers, social services and more – all of which pertained to the factory and its "community". Approximately 15km south of Ivrea, the factory in Scarmagno was arguably one of the last realisations of this pervasive regional scheme. Commissioned to Zanuso by Adriano Olivetti himself prior to his mysterious disappearance in February of 1960[5], the plant was intended, on the one hand, to consolidate the district as an industrial complex on a regional scale – integrated into and overlaid on the previous agricultural substructure of the area and, on the other, to explore the possibilities arising from the introduction of electrical apparatuses into production processes.[6]

This latter aspect in particular rendered the project a significant opportunity for Zanuso to put into practice ideas which he would later gather under the architectural mantra of "participatory design". The sheer complexity of the mechanical and electrical servicing, coupled with the ever-increasing fluctuating demands of the market, called for a strategic spatial diagram where distinct systems (the production line, the services and the built matter) could be modulated to the highest levels of performance. Effectively, what this led to was an escalation in the forms of expertise involved in the design process, each with its own requirements and operational parameters.[7] If this collaborative model may seem common (or even clichéd) in the current multi-layered nature of design processes – after all, the building industry has taught us that the number of subcontractors and stakeholders involved increases as technology moves forward – there are at least two aspects which make the case an unusually significant one. On the one hand, there is its ideological ancestry in Olivetti's *Comunità* – in ascribing to the cults of interdisciplinarity and collaboration, the project reproduced the company's complex managerial dynamics as an architectural resolution on the scale of territorial governance.[8] On the other hand, there is the literalness with which the model informed the actual design strategy; here, architectural elements, technological circuitry and mechanical production are integrated into a single isotropic system.

II

In broad terms, the project can be understood as the sophisticated application of a series of basic, yet effective, architectural principles determining the factory's overall layout as well as much as its finer detailing. Responding to demands for high levels of spatial and operational flexibility[9], the whole site was structured to follow a rectangular grid of 18 by 12 metres – a curious reminder of the ubiquitous presence of the productive process within the surrounding land. Correspondingly, the grid defined a modular unit composed of 4 pillars, 2 primary beams and 4 secondary beams, all made of pre-stressed concrete and easily assembled. As explained at the beginning, the vertical elements would be slotted in the foundation plinths tapering from a square foot at the base to a rectangular plane at the top. Primary beams were then laid on half of the upper rectangle, leaving space for the next module to develop on the vacant side. If this detail allowed for the building to be expanded in all four directions with the simple addition of supplementary components, it also embedded an element of incompleteness in the peripheral columns which Zanuso eloquently exploited as a means of expression. The tectonic qualities of this junction, where the mismatch between the elements resulted in a greater legibility of the overall system, evokes the syntactic character pertaining to classical architecture divested of its figurative and symbolic motifs. This analogy is made even more relevant when considering how the single module would inform the make-up of the entire system.

Rather than relying on proportional rules, the part/whole relationship here is determined by the mechanical capacity of the ventilation ducts, the terminal channels of which are duly integrated into V-shaped secondary beams. Far from a continuum, the factory was in fact parcelled into four interconnected plants, each equipped with its own powering mechanisms and cluster of auxiliary facilities (changing rooms, offices, a cafeteria and so forth), thus denoting a larger productive module which could be governed independently

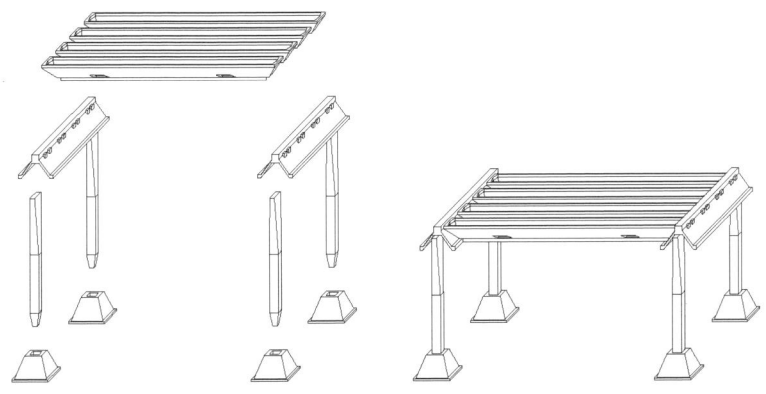

A    Marco Zanuso, Olivetti Factory in Scarmagno (1968). Assembly of prefabricated concrete elements after a drawing by Marco Zanuso.

and repeated at will. In closer detail, the intricacy of the internal infrastructure found its apt resolution in the stratigraphic organisation of the factory's flows in each section. It is here that the project took on the vertical complexity of a city-fragment, bringing in the managerial methods and design criteria typically pertaining to urban planning. Ensuring a maximal degree of operational independence, the multiple vectors running through the space (at this point it is questionable whether we can even call it a building) were assigned autonomous horizontal planes, each at its own height – starting from the ground where the indefinite circulation of humans and goods took place[10], moving to the electric system which was hung below the secondary beams, continuing further into the ventilation ducts and ending in the power supply systems (mechanical and electrical) which were brought into the space via a much larger and sparsely distributed grid of square-sectioned "tunnels". This complex network of human activity, assembly chains, cement, air supplies and electrical circuitry assumed the vertical semblance of an architectural *mille-feuille* where the multiple voices involved in the design process would act on distinct points connected at different levels.

Zanuso's "module-object" (the precise name with which the architect refers to it) can be understood here as the witty managerial tool which denoted the respective distribution of the collaborative processes within the system, while at the same time portioning it into easily quantifiable units.

III

In 1945, Adriano Olivetti published *L'ordine politico delle Comunità*, a compendium of thoughts formulated during his "exile" in Switzerland, which in many ways can be considered as

B, C  Marco Zanuso, Olivetti Factory in Scarmagno (1968).

a manifesto of his "communitarian" thinking. More than that, the book was a thorough proposal for social reform in which material interests were invested with highly moral concerns. Imbued with evangelical spiritualism and socialist hankering, in many ways it ironically anticipated the political turncoats of the later Christian Democrats who would alternately take sides with both Socialists and Communists as suited their needs. Central to Olivetti's thesis was the organisation of society in discrete territorial units of roughly 100 000 citizens gathered around localised administrative organs and highly integrated productive processes (agriculture and industry). This decentralised and distributed entity would act as an easily manageable interface between the individual and the region which, in turn, would respond to the larger body of the Federal State. If, in Olivetti's treatise, the proposed downscaling of administrative bodies to defined geographic areas was deeply rooted in a romantic sense of fraternity amongst men, the ethos behind this model could in fact be better grasped through the entrepreneurial jargons of optimisation and quantifiability. It is in correlation to these that a feedback loop can be established between Zanuso's modular constructions and the company's post-political initiatives in the broader Canavese district. In capitalist frameworks, management is commonly understood as the ability to put reason into practice. It is an instrument intended to legitimise decision-making on the basis of quantifiable bits of information, ultimately driven towards an increase in productivity. Writing at the dawn of the 20th century, manager-engineer Henri Fayol described management as the ability to forecast and plan, to organise, to command, to coordinate and to control.[11] In architectural terms, such are the actions facilitated by modular organisation like that implemented in the construction of the Olivetti Factory in Scarmagno, where building timelines (construction to

c

maintenance)¹², material resources, servicing and operational parameters but also human behaviour were made easily measurable for strategic decision-making. Architecture here took on the character of a vast three-dimensional spreadsheet in which complex data could be analysed/processed in basic tabular form. If Keller Easterling has recently advanced that "the projects of Cedric Price and Christopher Alexander are on the threshold of designing an architecture that has become information", one may wonder whether the project under discussion here did not in actual fact succeed in the surpassing this.¹³

Amorphous, flexible, scalable, quantifiable and multi-layered – Zanuso himself described the outcome as no more than the convergence of data stemming from disparate disciplinary fields. At a time when cybernetic thinking permeated the most distinct branches of intellectual production, the choreographic nature of Zanuso's work as planner in mediating the relationship between commissioners, consultants, and the users of the building (namely the workers) is a heroic attempt to reduce architecture to a purely organisational matter where productivity and pragmatism become the only valuable assets. It comes as no surprise that the architect as a producer of "Objects" became an incongruous figure in the very same years during which Italian historian Manfredo Tafuri asserted that,

> "In the face of modernised production techniques and the expansion and rationalisation of the market, it was no longer a question of giving form to single elements of the urban fabric, nor even to simple prototypes. Once the true unity of the production cycle had been identified in the city, the only task the architect can have is to organise that cycle."¹⁴

With hindsight, we can of course deem the project as a whimsical pursuit. It is by now common knowledge that the integration of services into architectural elements has proven itself to be a shortsighted design solution. This pattern makes itself visible in the tyranny of the drop ceiling in contemporary work environments which, in a way, is but a step towards the complete schism between architectural form and the myriad of technological apparatuses facilitating contemporary life. Yet it remains a somewhat heroic failure, where strategies of embedment take on an almost military role, allowing architecture to retain an agency of sorts in the definition of the end-product. Although only partial, Zanuso's "module-object" contained the whole of the project's architectural DNA within a single unit – its anatomical qualities as much as its technical capacities. It is from instances such as these that new lessons can be learned in order to confront the imminent questions posed to the architectural profession by collaborative frameworks such as *Revit*, *Archicad* or any other *BIM CAD* software.[15] If as Mario Carpo maintains in his book *The Alphabet and the Algorithm*[16], the times are ripe for a complete re-assessment of architects' authority and authorship within design processes, Zanuso's factory in Scarmagno provides an interesting way forward.

AUTHOR

Fabrizio Ballabio (born in Italy) is an architect and educator based in London. He graduated in Switzerland from the Academy of Architecture in Mendrisio (AAM) and received his Master's with Distinction at the Architectural Association in London (AA), where he currently teaches as a Studio Master in Architectural Design and in History and Theories Studies. Ballabio is a co-founder of åyr (formerly AIRBNB Pavilion), an art collective reflecting on contemporary forms of domesticity, and part of the online research platform Factory Futures. A guest critic and lecturer in a number of universities in the UK and abroad, his current research focuses on late baroque architecture in early modern Italy.

NOTES

1   Zanuso alone had received three commissions to design plants in Scarmagno, Crema and Marcianise yet it is also worth mentioning Luis Kahn's design for a factory in Harrisburg, Pennsylvania (U.S., 1966-70), Kenzo Tange's Olivetti Technical Centre and Warehouse in Yokoama, Tokyo (Japan, 1970) and James Stirling's Olivetti Training Centre in Haslemere, Surrey (U.K., 1973). Not to mention the never realised projects for Olivetti factories drafted by Le Corbusier between '61 and '62.

2   For more on this subject see Mario Carpo, The Alphabet and the Algorithm (Cambridge: MIT Press, 2011).

3   One need only to consider how Facebook or Google make use of architecture to corroborate their brands although the list could easily go on for pages. A thorough analysis of this process dealing with Apple's new headquarters in Cupertino can be found in CLOG : APPLE (2012).

4   The objective of I-RUR was to study and execute programmes on a communal and inter-communal basis, devoted to the improvement of social and economical conditions and to the reduction of unemployment. It is important to take into account that this was ultimately a political manoeuvre campaigned by a private company which, humanitarian claims aside, had a firm interest in making the population of the region participate in the productive process.

5   In an interview published in L'Architettura Cronaca e Storia N.3 (1982): 194 – 7, Zanuso himself tells

us it's the last disposition Olivetti had signed before passing away.

6   Throughout the 50s and 60s, Olivetti developed some of the first transistorised mainframe computer systems leading to the 1965 release of Programma 101, often quoted as the first commercial personal computer.

7   Already upon appointment, Zanuso had been coupled with Neapolitan architect Edoardo Vittoria (who had himself worked with Olivetti since early in the 1950s) and Olivetti's own in-house engineer Roberto Guiducci which, in actual fact, both hold a share on the buildings attribution.

8   It doesn't surprise in this respect how, as early as 1962, Edoardo Vittoria himself asserted that architectural design had to break free from the traditional confines of the finite 'building', to absorb the methodologies and practices adopted in urban planning.

9   If in previous plants, elaborate spatial organisations would embody the logics of the production chain, the exigency was now to shape indefinite, climatised ensembles wherein the process of production could at any moment respond to the sovereign requirements of the market.

10  A seminal account on how the new technologies mentioned earlier affected labour dynamics within the factory can be found in Matteo Pasquinelli, 'Italian Operaismo and the Information Machine', in Theory, Culture & Society Vol. 32(3) (2014): 49 – 68. Here the author revives a 'militant inquiry' undertaken by Italian operaist Romano Alquati in Olivetti's computer factories in Ivrea. "The paradigms of mass intellectuality, immaterial labour and cognitive capitalism" are described by Pasquinelli as the latest incarnation of power mechanisms in societies of control.

11  Daniel Wren and Arthur G. Bedeian, The Evolution of Management Thought (Hoboken: John Wiley & Sons, Inc., 2009), 211 – 27.

12  In an interview published on L'Architettura Cronaca e Storia N.3 (1982): 197, Zanuso tells us how in one day three pillars, three primary beams, twelve secondary beams could be built covering an average of 500 sqm per day.

13  cf. Keller Easterling, The Action Is the Form. Victor Hugo's TED Talk (Moscow: Strelka Press, 2012). Zanuso's design is also interestingly correlated to Easterling's definition of 'disposition' as a potential architectural stance in the age of information, as described on pp. 13 – 14.

14  M. Tafuri, "Toward a Critique of Architectural Ideology", 1969, in Architecture Theory since 1968, Ed. K. Michael Hays (Cambridge: MIT Press, 2000): 26.

15  For more on Building Information Modeling and the way it is changing the architectural profession, see Richard Garber, "Optimisation Stories: The impact of Building Information Modeling on Contemporary Design Practice," Architectural Design Vol 79 (2009), 6-13.

16  For more on this subject see Mario Carpo, The Alphabet and the Algorithm (Cambridge: MIT Press, 2011).

IMAGE CREDITS

A   Courtesy of Fabrizio Ballabio.
B   Courtesy of Fondazione Archivio del Moderno.
C   Courtesy of Fondazione Archivio del Moderno.

# Towards "Build the House"

In early spring of 2015, I went to Frank Lloyd Wright's Jiyu Gakuen Myonichikan along with two professors. After attending the meeting that had brought us there, the manager showed us the construction site of the restoration of the auditorium on the southern part of the site. This timber structure was originally built by Arata Endo[1] in 1927, just after the 1923 Great Kanto earthquake.

## Arata Endo

After breaking the "Sakoku"[2] in 1875, the Japanese government invited foreign teachers to come and teach Western technology, culture, philosophy and also architecture. This was the very first moment the "architect" as a professional was recognized in Japan. Traditionally, the "architect" had not existed in Japan; in his place, the "Toryo"[3], the master carpenter, planned, built and managed the construction site.

The manager of Jiyu Gakuen told us that they had found a lot of experimental traces of Arata Endo during the restoration. For example, when the wall and ceiling finishes of the main space were removed for structural reinforcement, they found that the structure did not look as if it had been built by the "Toryo", who generally directed the construction sites of timber structures at the time. An unusual construction had been used: a 2 × 4 roof construction brought in by F. L. Wright, carried by only four pillars and high beams in the longitudinal direction, which seemed to be an influence from Japanese conventional wood framing to gain stability against horizontal forces, making it indispensable after the earthquake. This unusual structure system makes the main hall unprecedented in respect of its construction.

At the time of post-earthquake rehabilitation, when budget and materials were limited, the Jiyu Gakuen needed the space for classes as soon as possible. In order to overcome the shortage of time and funds, Endo hired normal carpenters without so-called "Toryo". These carpenters were open to new ways of construction and detailing, not bound by preconceived ideas, and could also take time to consider and try things repeatedly with the architect. Endo made this experiment possible by taking responsibility for the budget and by hiring and managing the workers.

## FUDOMAE House

We are currently facing poverty that could be compared to that felt in Arata Endo's day after the Great Kanto earthquake. This poverty does not equate to starvation or a shortage of materials, but lack of quality of life. People have to work hard from day to night just to earn enough to cover their basic needs in modern urban society. To break free from this state of being the "working poor", people are shifting their lifestyles and style of work too, trying to cut costs in new ways. The prevalence of the "share house" model is one of the phenomena caused by this situation. People prefer to share apartments or houses with other people in order to be able to "have" larger spaces without having to spend large amounts of money on the rent in the middle of city.

In spring of 2013, I was invited to renovate the house of a former school friend. She had bought a 1970s two-storey detached house together with her partner. The house had a large storeroom on the ground floor and they planned to turn it into a house for seven people who would live together, sharing a living room, a kitchen and a bathroom – a so-called "share house".[4] In order to fit the new uses into the share house with seven bedrooms, we needed to re-organize the plan. The budget was limited, so the clients and I decided to paint the walls, floors and ceilings ourselves, helping to reduce the construction fee.

At the end of the construction process, the client, the client's parents and myself painted the house for a period of ten days in total. I was very pleased to join in with the painting as a friend, to spend time with my clients and to get to know their parents. On the other hand, I ended up not being able to check on the other work still being carried out on the construction site. To have missed these inspections caused misunderstandings with the workers, who had to do things again. This imposed a burden on them and could, in the end, have created an additional fee for the client. The aim was to make the cost lower but this process was reversing the seemingly logical order.

## DO IT YOURSELF

The house has become charming and seems to be a happy place for its inhabitants now. It has also gained some architectural interest by the creation of several shared spaces for them. But the experience on the site at the end of construction process made me think about the role of the architect. By inserting myself into the construction process as a "construction worker", I may have lost the real workers' confidence in me and, what is worse, they may have seen me as an intruder. I asked myself whether my act of painting had been just because of my egotism as an architect to achieve my "ideal space"...

We increasingly see young architects performing "do it yourself" with their client in order to realize their design, professing it as part of their design concept or working attitude as an architect. The reason might be that the client's budget is not large enough and/or that to pay for an architect has not yet become instilled in

A    Jiyu Gakuen Myonichikan Auditorium.

Japanese culture. With this kind of DIY approach towards construction, the quality is clearly not the same as when the construction is done by workers who have trained for years to master a specific technique. I am not sceptical towards "do it yourself", because it might be the trigger for clients to decide that a house is something not to be bought, but to be built. But if the architect joins in, it might mean that unprofessional detailing or construction is accepted. This in turn ignores the workers' value and prevents the passing on of the knowledge and high-quality techniques in Japanese construction of which we can be proud.

### Versus "Buying the house"

A year and half after the completion of the FUDOMAE House, the construction manager was declared bankrupt. He was an independent contractor and worked as such: he received his orders from the architects, arranged all the workers and managed all the costs; this is the general situation of construction in Japan. The quality of the construction therefore greatly depends on the building contractors.

The architects who worked with him were admired and were pleased when they understood that the construction manager was very conscious of design issues and had a really good network of all different kinds of qualified professional workers. Also in the FUDOMAE House, the workers were concerned not only with their tasks, but with the whole construction, allowing them to help each other and discuss details and possible solutions to unexpected situations. This created a good team, which also included the architect and the client. I do not think that it was purely the FUDOMAE House's construction that brought financial problems for the construction manager, but it is not difficult to imagine that the

B   FUDOMAE House (House for seven people), mnm 2013.

architect's amateur attitude, like the one I had, gradually affected his budget.

This incident indicates that the existing system we have in Japan does not suit small projects with small budgets. It would probably have worked well if the clients had been able to spend more money on the construction process, and this would have allowed the contractors to pool some money for covering unforeseen trials and tribulations during the construction process.

But using this system is impractical as we are facing the problem of a "lack of budget". If architects do not break through the existing system and do not work out how to manage the construction site, we will not be able to support the small networks of workers such as those of the construction manager of FUDOMAE House – they will never be able to prove the quality of their work. It will be cheaper and easier to use a product which is embedded into industrialization. If the architect does not find the quality of experimental construction and manage to convince the client of this added value, the client will go for the easier solution, which is to buy a ready-made house. Then clients will tend to "buy the house" and not "build the house". A direct consequence of this, from my point of view, would be that architecture could be completely absorbed by the system of industrialization.

## Experimental Field

The working environment that Endo tried to create with the Jiyu Gakuen Auditorium made experimental construction possible with a small budget. But the way he did it, investing time in trying and thinking together with carpenters, looking for solutions for the structure's system or detailing, was only possible in Endo's time, when labour was not as expensive as it is today. Or is this the case? How can we recreate this kind of experimental construction site without going into DIY or exploding the available budgets?

As a young architect who has small scale projects with small budgets, I struggle with the fatal effects of industrialization. DIY is a possible stand against this situation, but it does not necessarily lead to an improvement in the architectural realm. Our role as architects is not only to design, but also to care for the inheritance and development of the quality of workers' skills. To build a network of qualified workers that will then in turn ensure the quality of the work of the architect. Maybe then, we will get the chance to attain a high level of quality in our built environment, from the design phase to handcraft detailing, despite our small budgets, despite the industrial system, despite our own egos.

AUTHOR

Mio Tsuneyama was born in Yokohama, Japan, in 1983. After completing her Bachelor's degree at Tokyo University of Science in 2005, she moved to Switzerland, where she did an internship at Bonhôte et Zapata Architectes in Geneva, attaining her Master's degree at the ETH Lausanne in 2008. She then worked at HHF Architects in Basel between 2006 and 2008. She moved back to Tokyo, where she founded "mnm". She has worked as an assistant at the Tokyo University of Science and is currently an Assistant Professor at the same institution. She has had her work featured in architectural magazines and is one of the architects taking part in the "Migrant Garden" exhibition.

NOTES

1 Arata Ento (1886-1951): Japanese architect who was chief assistant to Frank Lloyd Wright on the construction site for Tokyo Imperial hotel.
2 Sakoku, "Locking country": In the Edo Era Japan refused to have any relationship with other countries, except for China, Portugal and Netherlands.
3 Toryo is the master of carpenter who leads the construction site.
4 Share House: a kind of flat sharing, which recently gained popularity in Japan. It often involves the renovation of the single-family house, which is no longer lived in.

IMAGE CREDITS

A Photograph by Ryu Fukuda.
B Photograph by Yasuaki Morinaka.

Alan-Miguel and Rubén Valdez

# Technocentric Neoliberalism and Okness

The Shaping of the City

Cities are not stable entities. The physical component, represented by buildings and infrastructure, may appear solid, but urban flows and networks that take place within these are in a state of constant movement, driven by the social and economic contexts surrounding them. These flows and networks are the concrete embodiment of a population's economic and political policies.

A neoliberalist-oriented market adapted to specific contexts has been a key feature of the western world's ideal economic policies, with a pervasive effect on all dimensions of society, including (for good and for bad) the reconfiguration of urban areas. A mix between the will of economic interests and the implied correctness of democratic politicians and city officials has clearly ruled the development of the cities in the last 40 years.[1] It is no novelty that space itself is a market commodity which has been poorly regulated by most state institutions[2], and that the city itself offers great profitability. Money, power and economic interests have set the rules for how we build the city almost since its existence and have greatly defined the physiognomy of contemporary urban zones.

However, it is interesting to note that, in the last 20 years, economic speculation with the city's space has been in juxtaposition with the discourse of sustainability, efficiency and competitiveness that has culminated in the emerging vision of the smart city. We cannot neglect the advantages of smart cities and architecture mentioned in the discourse if they are sustainable, competitive and efficient. Nevertheless, it is worth reflecting on the contradictions within this juxtaposition of values.

Recently Koolhaas stated that: "As a substitute for the French Revolution's liberté, égalité, fraternité, a new universal trinity has been adopted: comfort, security, sustainability."[3] We can hardly argue against the authoritarianism of correctness – the lactose- and gluten-free city

A    A $250 device from august you attach to your existing deadbolts that allows you to control your door lock through your smartphone via Bluetooth.

B    Songdo City, South Korea. One of the world's first specially designed "smart cities".

shouldn't disturb us because it is being shaped for our own good, for us to have a better quality of life and more opportunities.

On the other hand, as much as state institutions have been drawn into ever more explicit forms of creative destruction of urban built environments in order to promote even more intensively marketed land-use regimes[4], speculation is no longer only about space but is about automated life and about smart cities shaping smart citizens who are digitally savvy, efficient and entrepreneurial.

Last June, Google's Sidewalk Labs was announced as "An urban innovation company that will develop technology at the intersection of the physical and digital worlds, with a focus on improving city life for residents, businesses and governments."[5] The head of the project, Dan Doctoroff, mentioned in the company's official announcement that: "We are at the beginning of a historic transformation in cities. At a time when the concerns about urban equity, costs, health and the environment are intensifying, unprecedented technological change is going to enable cities to be more efficient, responsive, flexible and resilient. We hope that Sidewalk will play a major role in developing technology products, platforms and advanced infrastructure that can be implemented at scale in cities around the world."[6]

Technocentric neoliberal utopianism which unquestioningly assumes that technology development and business growth will automatically improve the quality of life within the city and its space is not only a feature of Google. An immense number of entities are hands-on on the smart city and its market, basing this on promises of a better life. By being so, they are completely changing the way we move, inhabit and read the city, creating an incredibly vast and unprecedented infrastructure of services directly related to it, not only redefining existing cities, but already defining those to come.

Ironically, what may have been Le Corbusier's idea that a house is a machine for living has been extended to the whole city, empowered by Lewis Mumford's [7] conception of large hierarchical organizations as mega-machines – machines using humans as their components. Here, the city becomes a machine for living, a digital one, and life itself consequently becomes subject to technological automation with digital placemaking substituting an actual sense of place, and digital capital replacing social capital. The digital and physical spaces merge in the contemporary city, completely changing the creation of a place and therefore the people defining it.

The smart city's digital place is almost as present in our consciousness as the physical one. Our relationship towards the city depends increasingly on the screen as an interface to inhabit, perceive and share it. The architect has never been alone in the shaping of the city, but never before has he or she been more accompanied in defining the relationships towards the city space. An army of software engineers, entrepreneurs and investors are slowly kicking the architect out of imagining the future city, or are using him as a necessary marketing accessory. The discipline may not disappear or be substituted by graphic designers [8] in the near future, but the role of the architect as the catalyser of the space available to citizens in their pursuit of a meaningful relationship with the city is at stake. For how long will the discipline remain relevant in such a scenario?

## AUTHORS

Dr. Alan-Miguel Valdez (Guadalajara, Mexico, 1978) is a Research Associate in the Department of Engineering and Innovation at the Open University. His current work further develops this early-market niche perspective within the smart transport work package of MK:Smart, a £16m smart city programme.

Rubén Valdez (Zacatecas, Mexico, 1986) studied architecture at the Accademia di architettura di Mendrisio and contemporary art at ECAL (École cantonale d'art de Lausanne). After doing an internship at Miller & Maranta Architekten in Basel and Estudio Toga in Mexico, he worked independently in Guadalajara, México on several single housing projects. He has been a participant in different architecture and art exhibitions such as "Monumental Masonry" at Sir John Soane's museum (London), "Vertige des correspondances", curated by Julien Fronsacq at ELAC (Lausanne), and "Life is a Bed of Roses", curated by Stephanie Moisdon at Fondation Ricard (Paris).

## NOTES

1. Peck J., Theodore N. & Brenner N. (2009), Neoliberal Urbanism Models, Moments, Mutations SAIS Review.
2. Ibid.
3. Koolhas R., April 2015 Artforum International Magazine.
4. Peck J., Theodore N. & Brenner N. (2009), Neoliberal Urbanism Models, Moments, Mutations SAIS Review.
5. sidewalkinc.com
6. Ibid.
7. Mumford, L. (1971). Technics and Human Development: The Myth of the Machine, Vol. I. Harvest Books.
8. In the frame of the 56th Venice art Bienale, Shawn Maximo for DIS magazine on Styles and Customs in the 2020s.

## IMAGE CREDITS

A   Image taken from august.com.
B   Image taken from songdo.com.

Cristina García Baeza

# Architecture Construction Process

## A Molecule

"Architecture has many aspects (…) we analyse architecture as a complex fact so that all the elements may find their balance in every project."[1]
Cruz y Ortiz arquitectos

### Architectural construction process as a molecule and the anamorphosis [2] of its atoms

As society evolves, the realm of knowledge increases in complexity and new disciplines have to be taken into account for the development of construction processes. Social complexity and the evolution of the cities require and establish a constant readjustment. Architecture is a multidisciplinary process involving artistic, technical, economic and social concerns. There is no doubt that, historically, architecture has always connected different realities: the material used to humanize the natural space, the individual and social needs that move architecture, the site conditions, the economic impact of construction, or public policies. This complexity has been growing over time but we are now more aware of the importance of how all these disciplines may modify the conception of architecture in the different stages of construction.

This is why architects are becoming part of continuously growing architectural teams, where professionals from different disciplines work more closely together than ever: engineers, quantity surveyors, landscape architects, topographers, sales assistants to name but a few. As in molecules, the construction process in architecture increases in complexity with the addition of new components inside the process molecule.

In my experience, within the perspective of architecture as a set of disciplines, I have seen that concerns may arise resulting from the potential risk that architecture could be trivialized, losing its leading role in the construction process. In this sense, the influence of emerging local and global factors and conditions in the entire building process is definitely changing the realm of architecture. These changes might be considered as a threat and as an opportunity since the result of their evolution will determine the new role of architecture.

The type of construction process relies on the number of agents and disciplines involved (atoms), and can have an impact on the construction of the project (molecule). Different circumstances (social-political-economic context, people involved, type of design, budgets, materials, etc.) will always have an impact on the concept of architecture. Due to this complex hybridization, architecture can no longer be defined as a clearly bordered activity, but as a blurred concept determined in every single situation by the atoms that compose and structure the final activity. The architectural trunk is branching out, and even though the upcoming new branches still belong to the same entity, some gaps are beginning to develop amongst them, creating differences and singularities. Evolving architecture is plural. Therefore, from my point of view, architecture is a consequence of the evolution of its components. It is not a fixed or pre-established concept. As a matter of fact, it seems to me that architecture shares this mutable quality with other phenomena as an immanent principle of our society.

This leads to anamorphosis, a phenomenon that may somehow clarify what happens inside the molecule of the construction process. We note that, depending on its set position inside the "architecture molecule" and the extension of its scope, architecture can be seen in many ways. In fact, the position of the key economic factor within the "molecule" will itself influence the whole process, inducing the emergence of new

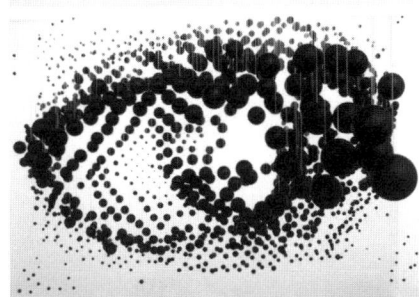

A   "The perceptual Shift" by Michael Murphy.

B   Muslim Fortress and Roman Theater by OAM arquitectos and Jesús Granada.

architectural characteristics or the disappearance of historical features. From the position of each atom, where the whole process is perceived in a determined way, the architect should coordinate all parts of the process in order to achieve the most optimized and balanced architecture. Special attention should be given to clients or promoters/developers and particularly to the user needs, since the former act as a catalyst and the latter are the deepest reason for the architecturural process.

## Construction's economic crisis as a positive aspect for architectural development

The economic crisis in Spain has deeply affected the construction industry as the most important business in our country. However, this global crisis, almost as an oxymoron, has encouraged the development of good practice models in Spain. Maybe because fewer construction processes are under development, architecture teams are investing much more time in each one of them, and reaching more imaginative and streamlined design solutions. Our first work developed as OAM arquitectos [Fig. B], is a good example for the molecular construction process described above.

## Experience 1:
## Landscape restoration and new access to the Muslim Fortress and Roman Theatre, Málaga, Spain by OAM arquitectos

This construction process was very special both because of its location – a palimpsest place in the city of Málaga, where unequalled monuments of the Roman City (1st century) and Muslim City (11th century) coexist in the heart of the historic centre alongside the Picasso Museum-Buenavista Palace (16th century) and Aduana Palace (18th century) – and from an architectural, urbanistic and heritage point of view. Many agents were involved in it. Currently, it is not completely open to the public (broken link in the molecule) [Fig. F], since the visits must be organized by agreement with local authorities. One of the main concepts in this project is the addition of minimally invasive new material for the construction process through the use of assembly systems that will allow the future reversal of actions in the light of new needs or restoration theories. We chose COR-TEN steel plates as a very strong material, close to old stone, to limit sunken pathways. This choice of material worried and divided the local archaeologists of the Andalucía Heritage-Architecture Office in Málaga, who scrutinized the design. Some of their technicians considered it an inappropriate material because of how it had been unwisely used in other heritage architectural interventions in this city. Due to these fears and concerns, the process slowed down considerably. Andalucía Heritage Office, for the first time in Málaga, delivered neither a positive nor negative report, but a "non-adverse" report.

During these months of uncertainty and the various meetings between our team, the Urban Municipal Office technicians and Andalucía Public Administration technicians, our office took advantage of the delay in construction to develop and "purify" the original proposal's construction details, and to fully adjust the design and budget. Seven months after our first meeting with the Andalucía Heritage-Architecture Office, the construction process began. The first contractor was dismissed because of its budget proposal (first broken link inside the molecule) and was replaced by a second company. Apart from the initial difficulties, the process developed well. The team meshed well, with meetings taking place in situ three times per week and we tried to enhance the final result despite the low budget for the design.

Analysing this landscape-heritage architecture project molecule, we find that the biggest atoms are the public administrations: promoter and heritage supervisor office, and that the powerful links are public administrations-architect and builder-architect. These two binomials were the core of this work. Good relations between them were essential to achieve very satisfactory work. As said at the beginning: Architecture is a complex fact so that in every project all the elements may find their balance. Therefore, architects should find their balance when coordinating all the atom-agents. In this context, it seems fundamental to me to consider architects as global agents who are not only able to visualize or understand the architectural molecule-processes, but also to design these in order to achieve optimal frameworks for developing architecture. These primary molecule-designs [Fig. E, F] will ensure, or at least help in the search for excellence in architecture. Harmony is the key.

AUTHOR

Cristina García Baeza (Sevilla, Spain, 1985) studied architecture at Seville University School of Architecture and the Technische Universität Graz Faculty of Architecture in Austria. In 2010 she joined OAM arquitectos as Head Architect together with architect Iñaki Pérez de la Fuente. She has been Guest Professor at Seville, Huelva, Málaga and USJ Zaragoza Universities. She was a commission member of the III International workshop 'New materials in architecture' at Málaga University. In 2014, OAM was selected to design a pavilion by Seoul Design Foundation at Dongdaemun Design Plaza by Zaha Hadid in South Korea. The OAM design for DDP was exhibited at Seoul Architecture Festival 2014. Prior to this, her work was selected for the 11th Biennale Archittetura di Venezia 2009 and the 5º Biennal de Paisatge Barcelona 2009.

NOTES

1 'La arquitectura tiene múltiples aspectos (...) nosotros la analizamos como un hecho complejo para que en cada proyecto todos esos elementos encuentren su equilibrio', Antonio Cruz. Cruz y Ortiz arquitectos. Diario de Sevilla. 12/07/2015.
2 Anamorphosis (OED definition): distorted projection or perspective requiring the viewer to use special devices or occupy a specific vantage point to reconstitute the image.

IMAGE CREDITS

A Michael Murphy. The perceptual Shift. I.M.A.G.E. Gallery. Brooklyn, New York. 2015.
B Photograph by Jesús Granada.

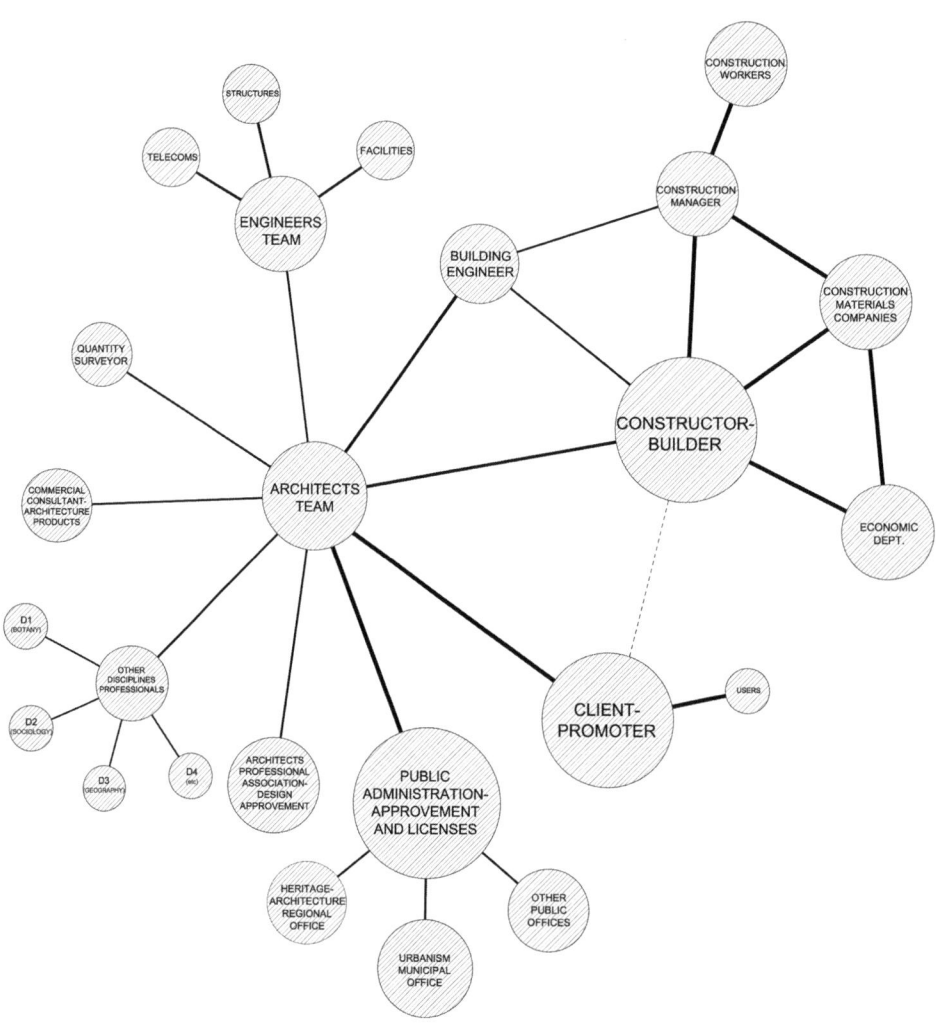

E    Molecule (architecture construction process) and atoms (construction agents). From the architect's point of view in Spain.

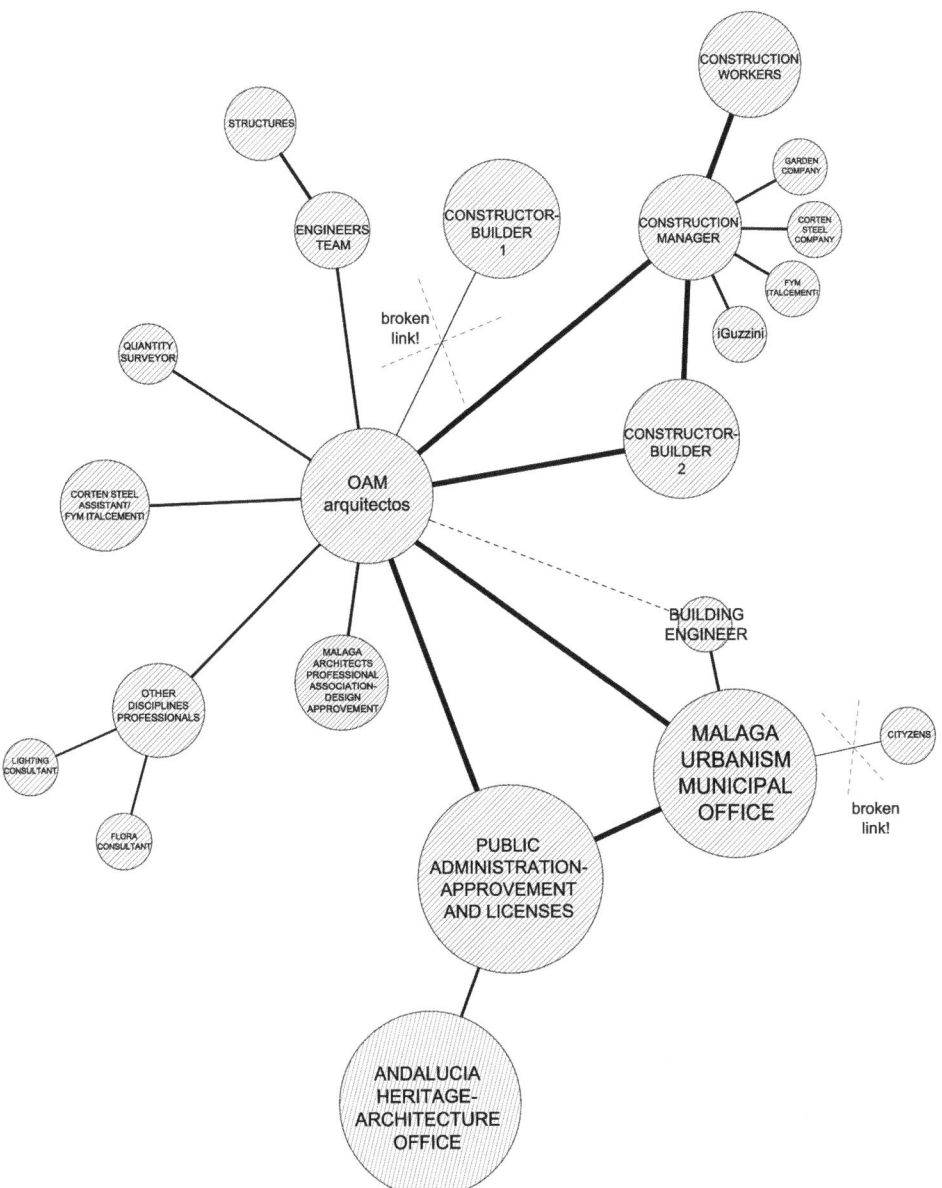

F   Construction process molecule in Landscape restoration and new access to the Muslim Fortress and Roman Theatre, Málaga (Spain) by OAM arquitectos.

Vicente Nequinha

# Fernand Pouillon

The Modern Master Builder

When we listen to classical music, even if it is inattentively, we can understand that there are a large number of musicians playing together with the common goal of creating a harmony. Each one of them has the responsibility to dominate the instrument and the music sheet. However, it is necessary that someone co-ordinates the whole orchestra; there cannot be a violin playing a wrong note or an oboe that is not on tempo. At the tip of the Maestro's fingers, the leader of all the musicians, a *Battuta* is held. With it, he conducts the how and when of the orchestra's performance.

Just as in music, it is also possible in building to find a person who is in charge of a group of specialists and workers: the architect. Amongst the characteristics of the architect we can recognize the possibility, or the impossibility, of assuming the role of a master builder: the one who not only designs but also sees his designs through to their completion, taking the construction site under his responsibility.

The persona of a master builder was easily recognizable during the Middle Ages, where this character embodied the functions of the contractor, the mason, the engineer and the architect. Recognizing the master builder as a figure of prime importance, Fernand Pouillon wrote the novel *Les pierres sauvages*, in which he described the story of a character who faces all the difficulties of the living and working conditions in the construction at the Cistercian Abbey at Le Thoronet, and in whom he recognizes himself, "I was applying my own character as it might have been within the context of such a magnificent architectural period."[1]

Pouillon was not interested in finding a theoretical discourse that could define his work, avoiding the search for a stylistic tendency and thereby going against the spirit that fed the architects of his generation in the 1930s. "Pouillon was a modern architect, but he was not a modernist"[2], staying away from architects' meetings, such as the Congrès Internationaux d'Architecture Moderne (CIAM), in order to remain focused on practical issues of architecture, and avoiding taking an ideological stance towards reality. It was this attitude that allowed him to develop some necessary assets, such as decision making and efficiency, which would later allow him to act as he did. He acknowledged the act of building as a response to homelessness, as a need about which he felt passionate.

His reputation as an architect was reinforced when he developed a lot of apartments within a tight schedule in Aix-en-Provence, being responsible for all phases of the project, from urban design to architecture and construction. "Two hundred housing units at two hundred metres from the city centre, built in two hundred days, for two hundred million francs. (…) I planned the construction in cut stone, a Pouillon system of flooring, a Pouillon method of load-bearing brick walls, a Pouillon vaulted structure. This represented a housing development of simple invention, achieved at lowest possible cost and within a schedule that nobody believed."[3] This achievement convinced the newly elected mayor of Algiers, Jacques Chevallier, of his efficiency, leading him to invite Pouillon to be the Architecte en chef of the Algerian capital, where he was commissioned to design three large-scale housing developments.

Some years before his arrival in Algiers, Fernand Pouillon was responsible for the creation of the Société d'Etudes Techniques (SET) in France. This technical consulting office was in charge of the supervision of construction sites, time planning, and coordination between different constructors and entities, showing how the design, the development concerns and the construction can work together, testing the boundaries of the architect as an artist and inventor, the

A    View of the construction site from a high point of the Frais Vallon Valley.

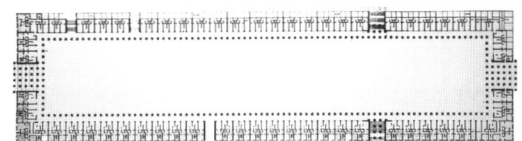

B    Plan of 200 Colonnes.

C    200 Colonnes under construction.

client as a developer and the general planner as a manager. With this model of a work process, Pouillon assured that the architect was able to coordinate all the design and construction stages.

The project for the cité Climat de France, in Algiers, together with the cités Diar-es-Saada and Diar-el-Mahçoul, was one of the most important commissions for Fernand Pouillon. During the 1950s, the French government started several social housing initiatives in response to the decadent social climate present in the North African colonial territories, Pouillon being in charge of one of the largest housing projects constructed in North Africa at that time. Situated at a high point of the Frais Vallon Valley in the Algerian capital, it was developed as a "gridded"[4] urban proposal, challenging the strong inclination of the site. Combining a variety of small and large buildings, it explored different dwelling typologies in order to understand and give a proper answer to the particularities of the Muslim cultural demands.

One of the most peculiar elements of this project is a rectangular housing block that defies the limits between the monumental and domestic scales. This search for a scale variation is easily perceived in the contrast between the closed character of the outer facade and the colonnade in the inner courtyard composed of 200 columns – giving the building the name "200 Colonnes". A strategy used by Pouillon to emphasize the cohesion among all the buildings involved in the project was an attentive choice and use of materials, opting for a system of modular stone blocs, conceived by him, to cover the walls of the buildings and, at the same time, to give the modest construction a "monumental spirit".[5]

The particularity of his approach towards this commission was the fact that he did not face it just as a designer, "More and more I started to orient myself towards rapid and economic construction. I elaborated a method, a technique. I reworked the organization of the construction process in order to make it more rational. I had to solve three problems: prices, deadlines, comfort (…). I was the first one to think simultaneously as an organizer, a financier, an engineer, an inventor and an artist."[6] This attitude towards architecture becomes a work of coordination, just like the Maestro and his orchestra. A capability to control all the stages of a project, from the design to its construction. For Pouillon, the most important role of an architect, as a master builder, is the capability to implement ideas and to find opportunities in the constraints that all projects present.

But how realistic is this master builder nowadays? It is difficult to compare the master builder of the Middle Ages and such a figure nowadays for various reasons; the cultural and social demands are not the same, and neither are the construction techniques and tools. However, there is a critical understanding that we can recognize in this medieval character – besides his *savoir-faire* put at the service of a collective work, he had the desire to take complete control over the task at hand as a way to perceive what was being proposed. In Fernand Pouillon, we must recognize this attitude, not as result of nostalgia or admiration for an unachievable period, but as an intellectual capacity, as an architect, to critically understand how to operate in the reality that we are about to change.

AUTHOR

Vicente Nequinha (Bragança, Portugal, 1991) is a student of architecture at the Department of Architecture of the University of Coimbra. He was an editor of Revista NU from 2009 to 2013 and vice-director in the academic year 2012-13. He moved to Switzerland to do an exchange in a students' programme at the École Polytechnique Fédérale de Lausanne, where he developed his interest in Fernand Pouillon with Professor Jacques Lucan's theoretical essays. Afterwards, he completed an internship at Atelier Cube Architectes, in Lausanne. He is currently developing his Master thesis on Fernand Pouillon's work in Algiers during the 1950s.

NOTES

1  Pouillon, Fernand, Mémoires d'un architecte. Paris: Éditions du Seuil, 1968, p. 439, 4 pp.
2  Caruso, Adam and Thomas, Helen, The Stones of Fernand Pouillon. Zurich: gta Verlag, 2013, p. 6, 3 pp.
3  Pouillon, Fernand, Mémoires d'un architecte. Paris: Éditions du Seuil, 1968, p. 141, 3 and 4 pp.
4  Avermaete, Tom, "Climat de France. Fernand Pouillon's re-invention of modern urbanism in colonial Algiers (1955 – 1957)". In OASE Journal of Architecture #74. p. 120, 7 pp.
5  Pouillon, Fernand, "La monumentalité". In Marrey, Bernard (ed.), Mon ambition. Paris: Éditions du Linteau, 2011, p. 123, 1 pp.
6  Pouillon, Fernand, Mémoires d'un architecte. Paris: Éditions du Seuil, 1968, p. 78 and 102, 4 and 2 pp.

IMAGE CREDITS

A–C  Images taken from www.fernandpouillon.com.

Walter Achermann

# The Team Captain

Notes from a Life of Building

The following notes are the result of a request from CARTHA's editorial group to Walter Achermann to share his privileged view on the evolution of the construction industry and the role of the construction manager in it. He chose three projects: the first construction site where he acted as construction manager; a second one where the construction environment started to be affected by the introduction of new technologies; and a third one that presents a huge contrast of scale to the previous two and is relatively recent.

Construction site no. I

- 1978, Engelberg (Lucerne)
- Construction duration: 15 months
- Cost: 2.5 million CHF
- 2 housing buildings, vacation apartments, 2 × 12 APP
- 10 companies involved, ca. 60 workers in total

Working processes and tools:

The *Bauleiter* (construction manager) took over the whole construction process, starting from where the architect had left, the concept phase. The *Bauleiter* looked after the detail plans, the description of the materialisation and construction techniques to be used, and dealt with the local officials, the few specialists and the client.

At this time there were no computers or photocopiers to provide support at work. All correspondence was written on typewriters with a carbon copy. A transfer matrix (*Umdruck*), had to be made to produce copies of submission papers. Plans were drawn by hand on transparent paper with ink by a Rapidograph (instrument of drawing).

Precision and detailing in the *Ausschreibung* (submission) phase were quite reduced when compared to today's practice. This had two direct consequences: it was much faster and simpler to do, but it required a more "hands-on" approach to the management of the construction site. This was only possible because when one wrote, for example, "brick walls and concrete ceilings", the construction worker and the contractor knew exactly what this meant and what the architect expected. Construction techniques were somehow less variable and the construction workers had a better understanding of the relation between different materials and building techniques. One can say that the workers were more qualified than now.

This quality and know-how from the workers allowed the construction site manager to be more relaxed, to trust the contractors and workers when it came to competence during the building process.

The only specialist needed for this project was the structural engineer. All the other aspects (electricity, sanitation, heating, so on…) were handled by the contractors, from the planning until the construction phase. There was a lack of specialisation; the skill sets needed to bring the planning and construction processes to their successful completion were held by general contractors and planners that handled the relatively simple act of building. The *Bauleiter* was also responsible for the coordination and correctly handled execution of these special technical skills.

## Construction site no. II

- 1989–1992, Hergiswil (Lucerne)
- Project duration: 2.5 years
- Cost: 9 million CHF
- 8 Single family houses, lakeside villas
- 25 companies involved, around 150 workers in total

Working processes and tools:

The known developments in building technologies during the 1980s and 1990s as a consequence of the oil crisis and increasing ecological and economic concerns, led to the multiplication of consultants and specialists. New categories and sub-categories within the previous disciplines were born: thermic specialists and energy consultants now had an input when it came to heating and insulation techniques; a geologist had to be called in to deal with the risk of landslide into the lake etc.

Also in the planning phase, the *Bauleiter* had the representation of his inputs and detail plans drawn by draughtsman. This had consequences: the further interpretation of the desired materials and techniques by another person.

Beginning of the use of computer as a tool for the submission phase: material and construction techniques were now described using a computer program and a standard method (BKP and NPK from CRB). With this "help", the submission documents could be more detailed. This was a new process to a lot of contractors and they did not understand the standardized descriptions, which meant more work (explanations) for the *Bauleiter*.

A system of coordination drawing known as *Tochterpause* was used to implement the knowledge and needs of each specialist into the project. The *Bauleiter* would draw the construction plans based on the architect's plans on a piece of paper.

This piece of paper would then be sent to the sanitation planner, who would draw directly on it. He would then send these plans to the heating planner, and so on, until all the consultants had drawn their contribution on the original construction plan. This would take around two months.

It allowed for the prevention of planning mistakes as the planners knew where they could draw at first hand; it was clear on the plan they had in front of them. A meeting would then be held at the end of this process where all the specialists would meet and discuss minor details that had to be solved on the plans. A final coordination plan would then be drawn and the construction could start with a certain certainty that the layering of the consultants' inputs would work correctly.

Local authorities only had rudimentary control over the project. The submission plans had to be approved and there was a zoning plan for the area but the presence of local authorities on the construction site was close to none. The single inspection was at the end of the construction process, before the owners moved in.

### Construction site no. III

- 2006–2009, Basel (Basel City)
- Project duration: Planning 2.5, Construction 2.5 years
- Cost: 98 million CHF
- 1 building in the Novartis Campus St. Johann (Office and Laboratories)
- 10 consultants and specialists involved
- 32 companies involved, around 1150 workers took part in the construction phase
- The main architect was David Chipperfield; Burckhardt + Partner acted as local architect and construction manager.
- The architect was in charge of the plans, including detail plans.
- The local architect was in charge of the submission and budget calculation, and served as a specialist/consultant for local laws and construction processes, accompanying the project from the planning phase onwards.

Working processes and tools:

This project took advantage of all the technologies that are available nowadays. Computers were used for both drawings and the production of texts/documents.

An ever-growing wish for optimization and cost reduction on the construction site had been gradually changing the methods and techniques. More and more, the construction elements and materials are pre-fabricated and processed in order to reduce the assembly and mounting time on the construction site.

Very high demands regarding safety and security meant a lot of additional work for the *Bauleiter*, who had to check and adjust what was not in accordance with the regulations of the law and of the client.

The number of companies involved combined with the tight time schedule meant the additional task of managing weekly coordination meetings with the local architect – led by the *Bauleiter* – with the consultants, specialists and companies currently working on the site. At the end of the project, over 130 minutes of meetings from these construction meetings had been written down.

Adhering to increased regulation by the authorities, the *Bauleiter* needed much more time for the approvals of every single action, especially with regard technical equipment.

There is one aspect that did not change during this time and throughout these projects: The *Bauleiter* had overall responsibility for costs, time schedule and correctly executed construction.

AUTHOR

Walter Achermann was born in 1953 in Lucerne. After four years of high school, he started and finished an apprenticeship as a draftsman. He went on to complete a diploma in theology and then studied adult education for three more years. Since then, Achermann has worked both on a self-employed basis and as an employee in the construction area, building projects that range from single family houses to multi-million public and private facilities.

CARTHA

# Joël Tettamanti

A Visual Contribution

Mathieu Bujnowskyj on Joël Tettamanti

## The Photographic Ambiguity and the Artification of Architectural Communications

Born in Cameroon and a graduate of Ecal in Lausanne, Joël Tettamanti is a Swiss artist and photographer. He is mainly known for his meticulously composed large-format photographs of alpine landscapes, and for "local studies" of various remote locations, from the African savanna to Arctic harbours. If there are generally very few protagonists in the composition of Tettamanti's pictures, the human presence and influence on the environment is a recurrent theme that can be understood in the line-up of the New Topographics[1] exhibition. His images testify to moments in the human alteration of environments – construction, utilisation, the decrepitude of artefacts or landscapes.

It is interesting to note that Joël maintained two twin websites for a long time: *tettamanti.ch* and *tettamanti.li*. A white one for his personal projects, and a black one for various commercial works commissioned by architects, international brands and magazines. The present selection of Tettamanti's photographs has been taken from these two collections, mainly from his personal works. In the context of MANNSCHAFT, his ambiguous status between independent artist and commissioned photographer allows us to think about the position of artistic photography in the valorisation cycles and communication strategies of contemporary architects.

In an era of speed and digital fluxes, Tettamanti still captures his observations of natural and built environments through large format (4×5) film cameras mounted on tripods. These heavy traditional tools that he carries with him around the world allow him to slow down the photographic process. Even in commissioned projects, each picture becomes unique and strongly authored by Tettamanti because of low flexibility and very small series. His workflow has intrinsic qualities and aesthetics that support his particular vision of the subjects captured, and differentiate him from many other architectural photographers who work digitally with extended series and options. This phenomenon reinforces his authorial (artistic) status.

From the early days of 20th century, Modernism emerged along with the birth of a new kind of Promethean architect.[2] This is well illustrated, for example, by personalities such as Le Corbusier, Mies van der Rohe or, more recently, Rem Koolhaas. Architects presented as charismatic visionaries with ambitious responsibilities for society. These architects understood well the continuous logics between the efforts invested in the development/construction of a building and its presence in the world afterwards.

Architectural communications developed exponentially with this necessity to valorise ideas and built production as much as possible in order to consolidate the architect's status. An increasing number of architects started to invite artists and photographers to document the evolution of their projects under construction, and to portray their representation once finished. The images were then used in various publications such as monographs and magazines, supporting the visibility and the credibility of the architects.

These produced images can be understood both as the representation of an architectural product as well as an autonomous image supporting an artistic statement where architecture acts only as inspirational subject. The presence of this iconographical duality creates an "artification" of the architectural communications. It showcases, honestly or not, a supplementary cultural value through artistic collaboration. The reputation and the universe of the commissioned artist or photographer are transferred to the documented building through his production, to the benefit of architects.

### AUTHOR

Mathieu Bujnowskyj (1990) is a French architect graduated from Swiss Federal Institute of Technology (EPFL, 2016) He worked for Philippe Rahm Architectes and Herzog & de Meuron. In parallel of his architectural practice, he co-founded the French critical review QNDMC where he worked as editor-in-chief (2011 – 2015) and the research platform about postdigital architecture makecollaborate.net (2015 – on going). Mathieu was guest lecturer at ENSA-LYON and is now architect in residency at the CCA Kitakyushu for 2016–2017.

### NOTES

1  Jenkins, William. New Topographics: Photographs of a Man-Altered Landscape. Catalogue. Rochester, NY: International Museum of Photography at the George Eastman House, 1975.
2  Ratti, Carlos, Claudel, Matthew. Open-Source Architecture, Thames & Hudson, London, 2015.

### IMAGE CREDITS

Photographs by Joël Tettamanti.

II MANNSCHAFT

# III
# SANTÍSIMA TRINIDAD

| | | | |
|---|---|---|---|
| 196 | **CARTHA**<br>Editorial | 232 | **Enrique Peleaz**<br>There's something about Clients |
| 200 | **Rubén Valdez, Interview**<br>Marco Serra | 236 | **Laura Bonell and Daniel López-Dòriga**<br>A Portrait of Stone |
| 206 | **Tanguy Auffret-Postel**<br>Gears of Utopia | 242 | **Tiffany Melançon**<br>Artist's Loft House Renovation |
| 210 | **Rabih Shibli**<br>Ghata – A Cover against Herculean Odds | 248 | **Pedro Bragança**<br>The Quasi-Temple of Architecture |
| 216 | **Albert Palazón**<br>Back in the Caves | 256 | **Visual Contribution**<br>Onnis Luque |
| 220 | **Bernardo Menezes Falcão**<br>Pre-Architect | 263 | **Onnis Luque**<br>USF \ DF Appropriation Techniques |
| 229 | **Fritz Barell**<br>The Tree from the Triangle | | |

III SANTÍSIMA TRINIDAD

## The inevitability of the triangle

When dissecting the building process, we found that we could pin down three main interventionists; client, architect and user.

The client is the source of the process. He/She is the will and the birth of the whole discussion. Without the client, there would be no project, no building.

The architect is the means to an end. He/She is the negotiator between the client's wishes, the user's needs and his or her own views.

The user is the end, the individual who gives meaning to the built environment, who projects him or herself onto it, appropriates and lives in it, with it.[1]

These three entities are always present even if they are absent. This is possible due to the collective and societal nature of man, which allows individuals to assimilate empirical knowledge about the built environment and to take an active role in its construction. The built environment and its language are the result of the constant, either conscious or unconscious, dialogue between this trinity.

If we were to understand the role of the client as a specific entity that starts the project, follows it through to its conclusion and ends up profiting from its use, we could argue that, for example, in the "Torre de David" project[2], the figure of the original client was replaced by an informally organized group of people that started taking over an unoccupied structure. For them, the project started as soon as they moved in and had to transform the raw structure into livable quarters.

We could use the same example to discuss the absence of the role of the architect. Even though there was no architect involved in the planning and execution processes of the "finished" structure, the concept of what architecture is, was extremely present. The materials used, the disposition of the rooms, the placing of the household amenities – these are all decisions that are deeply influenced by the perception these people have of their built environment, which, in turn, is influenced by architects.

In this same situation, the final user was not the originally intended one. As the original project came to a halt, a new potential user started to appear, a user that was detached from the one idealized by the client and the architect, but was still a very valid one. The people that took over the Torre gave purpose to this otherwise dead skeleton; they won it over and brought it to life by projecting their needs and wants onto it.

This realization of the inevitability of the triangle is both comforting and disturbing for architects, for even though it is known that architects will always be indirectly present, it is also known that they do not have to be present per se. This reinforces the strength and responsibility of architecture as a social event but questions the role of the architect as an individual.

In our present situation, these figures have become disconnected to the point that, for instance, an investor from Suriname that is unknowingly backing a real estate developer in Zurich via his stock market portfolio, might end up being the end user of the luxury housing complex this developer builds in Italy. The triangle can be multiplied but, in the end, it is just a matter of proximity; it can always be brought down to the three original vertices.

With this issue, SANTÍSIMA TRINIDAD, we aim to take a look at the current conception of the client-architect-user relation, the influence it has on our reality and how it is influenced by it in return.[3] As one might see when reading this issue, the presence of the three entities is mostly volatile; sometimes the three vertices have exploded into multiple dots, sometimes one of the vertices is engulfed by the other two [4], other times all of the vertices becomes a sole point.[5] But again, it is a matter of proximity, the triangle is always there.

NOTES

1 as brilliantly explored by the work of Onnis Luque "USF \ DF", featured in this issue
2 see "Back in the Caves" by Albert Palazón
3 see "Gears of Utopia" by Tanguy Auffret-Postel
4 see "Ghata – A Cover against Herculean Odds" by Rabih Shibli
5 see "A Portrait of Stone" by Bonell and Dòriga

III  SANTÍSIMA TRINIDAD

Rubén Valdez

# Marco Serra

Interview

Few architects probably understand the complexity of the relationships between the client, the user and the architect as well as Marco Serra. As a chief architect for Novartis, with a robust trajectory behind him, Serra has engaged at eye level with most of the vertices involved in architecture, acquiring an unrivalled understanding of the completeness of the architectural process and its different players. Italian-Swiss, born in Zurich in 1970, he studied architecture at the ETHZ, graduating in 1996 under professor Hans Kollhoff. After working in the office of Adrian Meyer from 1996 to 1999 and for Diener & Diener Architects from 1999 to 2002, Serra started working at Novartis in 2003 and is currently responsible for Campus master planning in Basel. From 2002 to 2005, he was the architect in charge of the design for the main gate and the car park project of the Campus in Basel. Since 2006, he has been the design architect responsible for the conversion project of the Abadia Retuerta into a hotel with spa in Valladolid, Spain. He has also been chief architect at Global Novartis since 2014.

**Referring to our current call for papers, what is your opinion on the architect, the client and the user, the way they relate to each other and the different situations between them?**
Rather than a trinity, it's a new form of architect.

**One single entity that produces its own architecture for its own use?**
More than one single entity, what I have in mind is how I believe the ideal architect should work. Today's culture has the tendency to see architecture as equal to design. Unfortunately the tendency is going more and more in this direction, and I consider this a problematic development. The basis of architects has been reduced to a very thin area and has been detached from the construction sites and from the implementation. The practice shows that architects are involved, depending on their profile, above all on a very high level and at the very beginning. This presumes that architecture can be reduced to the elegant movement of the architect's hand. The architect as a complete, universal actor is disappearing more and more.

> Today's culture has the tendency to see architecture as equal to design. Unfortunately the tendency is going more and more in this direction (…).

**Whether we see the architect as an entity that manages all the different parts of his discipline or as a person that builds a language through architectonic gestures, how would you define your position within your personal work in relation to the trinity of user, client and architect?**

First of all, I would like to define my ideal character of the architect. I think the architect should be neither a manager nor a coordinator, nor would I reduce him to a coordinator of disciplines. The important part in an architect's work is to be able to absorb the different disciplines and make them become one in what is the result of his activity. The architect should be able to converse with all disciplines at the same eye level without falling into the trap of becoming a superficial generalist. If you have a look at the way medieval monks used to build their facilities, you will be astonished by the exemplary way they did their work. What fascinates about medieval architecture is its coherence.

**Probably the coherence comes from the fact that the architect was the user and the client at the same time?**

Having had the opportunity to work for a decade on the restoration of an ancient monastery, I saw that the coherence did not, at first, come from an architectonic will, but from the circumstances under which the projects were set up. The monks would define the strategy and the location of the monastery. They would define the architecture, including details, construction and materials. They were also the constructors themselves and, last but not least, they were also the users. Their buildings do nothing else than reflect these circumstances. That is where the coherence comes from. Having said this, I do not argue for regression. I argue for completeness in the architect's work. *Les pierres sauvages*, written by Fernand Pouillon, describes the life of a monk building a monastery in southern France, which I think it is a fantastic illustration of the topic.

**Going back to the *Santísima Trinidad* subject: in your position as a global chief architect, what would be your role in this comprehensiveness of the architecture?**

First of all, I'm far from being a modern monk, overarching all disciplines. But one of the particularities of my work is that the first discussions in projects do not happen about architecture, but about project circumstances. Also, having the possibility to see into different areas and stages of the project gives me the opportunity to see things that you generally don't see as an external architect. Take the start up or the hand-over phases of a project. These are important phases, but despite this, architects are often not present during these discussions. The start-up is the phase in which you lay out the project basis and therefore have the most influence over it. The hand-over is the moment when you can learn from all the mistakes. These are very valuable insights.

**Talking about design and experimentation, have the usage and building restrictions of the Campus been in contradiction with the architects' will to experiment?**
There is no general answer to this and it varies from project to project. It also depends on how much engagement the company has put into the project. Beyond that, it is not only about the architect, but about the whole team: the general planner, the user and the client. Depending on the cooperation and the energy the stakeholders have put into the project, the result is better or worse. The better the team, the higher the probability of finding good answers to what you call restrictions.

**So that in order to achieve a satisfactory building you need to work again as a single entity: the client, the user and the architect together?**
Considering that cooperation is crucial to the result, the question is how you set up teams. Good projects begin by picking the right members and this is why the choice of the architect and his team is so important. You can mitigate mistakes and improve quality by setting up a good structure, but much more effective is the right choice of people. The other aspect with which you can influence the quality is how you set up roles and responsibilities.

> Beyond that, it is not only about the architect, but about the whole team: the general planner, the user and the client. Depending on the cooperation and the energy the stakeholders have put into the project, the result is better or worse.

**So more precisely, how do you choose an architect?**
Probably the most important aspect in the choice of the architect is trust. Reference projects are also good but experience is more important. The only way to understand these qualities is to interview and talk to people. Particularly in an environment of very sophisticated communication, face-to-face talks become more and more important. Think about the extraordinary ability of studios to visualize projects. It is really hard to distinguish what has been built and what not. This brings us to the next point which is important in the choice of teams, and this is the visiting of projects. Only by looking at realized buildings can you distinguish the quality of the studios. This is why I think that competitions do not a priori lead to the best result. Irrespective of whether you do a competition or a direct commission, I prefer discussion as a first step. We have had the experience that competitions are not simple because the immediate interaction between planner and client is lacking. Also, in competitions you need to have a very clear briefing; this is why some companies begin with intermediate discussions in competitions.

**Since the early 20th century, various companies like Olivetti, Nestle and Ford have undertaken wide-ranging research into the working space, its consequences on productivity and its social implications. However, they have often chosen one architect in long-term collaboration. Has working with such a large group of different architects on the same campus added an extra level of difficulty in developing projects?**
I think that the choice of architects is linked to the overall philosophy of the company. I have a very high respect for long-term thinking, but the longer the timeline, the more difficult is it to continue working with one structure over the whole project. The highest value of working with different architects is that you can learn from them. The challenge is how you transfer these insights from project to project. We have tried to do that by keeping continuity within the team and have therefore integrated experienced employees in different projects. You can integrate learnings into guidelines, but the best way to transfer learnings is through people.

> So in this sense you would say that the client experiences constant learning from different practices and that this enriches his or her existence as a client?

Yes, I would say so.

Thinking about the building in an international and local context, apart from the users inside the building, there is another kind of user that perceives the building from the outside. How would this constellation of architects and clients insert itself not only in a Basel context but in an international context?

What are you relating it to, what kind of perception?

> Of course there is an image of the values that the company wants to present. By hiring several different architects you send a completely different message than you would by just hiring one.

I think one of the important messages that you send out is the attention to quality. This has both an internal and external dimension. For the external aspect, I think it is related to the company's expectations, which is to attract talents. By setting high expectations for yourself, you also set high expectations towards the outside. Working with the best teams sets the expectations that we want to be attractive for the best employees, and this is related to the ambition of becoming the most attractive company for the best people. Good people create good companies. The same is true for the internal aspect. By caring for the people, you send a strong signal, that people are important to the company. The first target of the project is not architecture, but the employees. The idea of attracting and working with the best employees has been instrumental to the idea of working with the best planners. We believe that the best work environment will create and retain the best people.

IMAGE CREDITS

Courtesy of BoB, Photograph by Maria Gambino.

Tanguy Auffret-Postel

# Gears of Utopia

On the "plateaux" of the Ecole de Nantes
by Lacaton & Vassal

Thinking about the relationships between clients, users and architects really comes down to examining the *relations de pouvoir*[1] that exist between these three entities. Of course, in some cases, the wills of the three might align for better or worse. But those scenarios do not provide interesting case studies for this paper, as we are unable to distinguish the strategies of the different players and therefore question them.

The Ecole de Nantes by Lacaton & Vassal provides us with a more intriguing example. A client (the French Ministry of Culture, which runs the schools of architecture) chooses an architectural practice (Lacaton & Vassal) which offers a project destined to enable its users (teachers and students) to inhabit it more intensely or, rather, differently. To do so, the architects created, among many other architectural features, large spaces called *plateaux*, which could be described as large slabs of concrete that stand between the actual programme (classrooms, library, etc.) and the polycarbonate façades. These *plateaux* were destined from the beginning to host what could not happen in the defined areas of the programme. Visiting the building today, five years after its opening, raises a few questions. What can we learn from Nantes to make it the prototype for an ongoing suite of buildings and not an isolated burst of optimism?

**Life is the show, architecture is its stage.
An architect's fantasy.**

Architects have for a long time understood their ability to forge systems that can influence the way life happens inside them. This consciousness of their power culminated in a hardcore modernism that proclaimed that it could invent a new man. The Dom-Ino system[2] might be the paroxysmal and yet strangely the most minimalist example of such systems. By updating the idea of the

A  Interior view of the Nantes school of architecture.

B  Example of coevolution.

primitive hut[3], it concentrated its means on providing a skeleton for life. The fascination it has inspired since probably draws its intensity from the openness of interpretation it allows. Indeed, while the world discovered the conceptual danger of an all-powerful environment, architects also envisioned strategies to put their power to the service of a progressivist view. They believed in their ability to create genuinely new spatial systems as well as in new emancipated ways of life.

Fascination and trust in technology nourished a series of emblematic projects of which Cedric Price's fun palace might be the most influential.[4] Lacaton & Vassal have many times cited their admiration for its poetry and radicalism. Their project for Nantes, although often described as austere and low-tech, openly places itself in the footsteps of this high-tech and joyful chef d'oeuvre.[5] But where Price's fantasy sadly stayed on paper, Lacaton & Vassal actually brought their machine to the real world, with all its complexity.

When visiting the school today and discussing with its users, one can only witness the acuity of the initial ambition. Invention and appropriation appear to be everywhere: from the pink trailers that host a café to the badminton classes, the exhibition, concerts and the final reviews.

Students and professors have integrated this mute space into their everyday life and praise its many qualities: proportions, light, views. Nevertheless, the *plateaux* are now threatened to become a caricature of themselves. The school administration is controlling more and more closely what can and cannot happen in these structures, limiting their use to more classic appropriation scenarios. Furthermore, the space is now being rented out to host external events for clients in search of a creative *décor*. This driftage reminds us of the risk that many innovative social and spatial structures face once the image of their freedom becomes more important than their actual freedom.

## Imagining the contemporary agora. The strategies of Lacaton & Vassal to create "espaces capables".

The idea of public space as the centre of democracy is deeply rooted in our cultural history. So many projects try to refer to or invoke it that we have reached a point where it has become a completely washed-out concept, rendered hollow by its ubiquity. Intensity of life has become mandatory for all projects. Perspectives of crowded piazzas with happy children are now everywhere; from malls to museums they only contribute to emphasising the loss of influence of architecture. Should great empty spaces be the only alternative? Should architects abandon their ideal of meaningful configurations of space? Lacaton & Vassal's work is a powerful antidote to those who think that flexibility and intensity are neoliberal values only. Making Cedric Price's statement their own, they reaffirm the idea that space can empower people rather than constrain them while providing new solutions regarding its implementation. Indeed, the silent and powerful structure in Nantes derives its force not only from the high techs.

Taking clues from architects who decided to counter the modernist dictate by reconnecting to permanent figures and reaffirming the inner logic of architecture, Lacaton & Vassal use their controlled architectural vocabulary to produce spatial quality. This attitude is not meant to detach architecture from its political context but rather to allow life to happen on its own, as if architecture offered an antidote to its own power. It also ensures that all means focus on creating the best possible space. This approach has recently been described by Jacques Lucan as a *style de l'absence* in reference to Roland Barthes and the *degrée zero de l'écriture*.[6] Indeed, Lacaton & Vassal's work is sometimes presented as non-architectural, or rather as an architecture that focuses mostly on peripheral strategies (cost, climate, etc.) and on simple research for maximum space efficiency. Yet, when visiting their buildings, and particularly Nantes, one can only agree with critics[7] who describe the building as a powerful architecture in the complete understanding of the word. The school and particularly the *plateaux* offer strong statements regarding tectonics, space and materiality. In Nantes, Lacaton & Vassal achieved an architecture that welcomes new uses but does not dictate them. This also implied that the potential for social inventions is left to the users. Spaces could have stayed empty and lifeless without interfering with the core functions of the school. This is a risk the architects are willing to take in order to leave things open. In Nantes, they gave (almost) no clue as to what should happen. There are no big signs to tell you how much fun you are supposed to have, no fancy furniture to position a resting area, no flashy colours to instigate a playful atmosphere. Those initiatives and choices were left to the users. This confidence in the community's ability to invent is what sets apart those plateaux from a "googletopia".[8] But for reality to live up to the radical expectations of the project, users must be able to grasp opportunities and explore concrete ways to appropriate space.

## Architectural Coevolution. Inventing social frameworks to enable new spaces. And vice versa.

Coevolution refers to a concept of natural science first described by Charles Darwin, which postulates that plants and insects have evolved in a continuous *va et vient*. According to this theory, evolution by one of the entities encourages the other to develop structures (pistils, trunks, etc.) that work in close relationship with the first one. The idea that sustains this theory is that iterative adaptation is more efficient than a siloed development as a way to reach a complex system of interaction. One could postulate that architecture and social structures are the same. Taking the examples of Swiss cooperatives like *Kraftwerk*, one can see that the amazing typology developed by architects has been made possible because groups of inhabitants invented a framework over time to update what community life means today. If architects had acted alone by inventing everything from the ground up, failure would have probably been right around the corner. Looking at the world and its current state, one can only hope that architects will continue to reflect upon the relationships between their creations and the life they welcome. This evolution will be even more fruitful if concrete examples, good or bad, nourish their reflection. The intense life inside the Nantes School shows us that the desire for new ways of inhabiting our daily surroundings is still vivid and full of poetic and political potential. But it also shows us the perils that inevitably threaten these bubbles of liberty. For other contemporary fun palaces to see light of the day, users should maintain a certain level of control over their destiny. To help them do so, architects must finely tune their building to provide opportunities and desire. A lesson from Nantes is that a strong yet open form is a first step in this direction.

AUTHOR

Tanguy Auffret-Postel, born in 1985, studied architecture in Rennes and Versailles. He now lives in Lausanne, where he collaborates with local architecture offices and develops personal research projects. He has been an assistant at the Versailles School of Landscape and is currently an assistant to atelier architecten de vylder vinck taillieu at EPFL. He is also part of the curatorial team of gallery TILT in Renens.

NOTES

1  About architecture and power, see Michel Foucault, Surveiller Et Punir (Gallimard 1975).
2  Le Corbusier designed the Dom-Ino project in 1914 to offer a solution for rapid reconstruction of destroyed regions. He envisioned two concrete slabs resting on pillars and linked by a staircase. In his vision, people would freely complete the skeleton with architectural solution of their choosing. The goal was double, to offer maximum flexibility but also to maintain a coherence beyond individual choices.
3  San Rocco #8, What's wrong with the primitive hut, multiple authors, Milan, 2013.
4  J. Stanley Mathews, From Agit-Prop To Free Space: the architecture of Cedric Price (Black Dog Pub Ltd 2007).
5  Fernando Márquez Cecilia and Richard C Levene, Lacaton And Vassal, 1993/2015 (El Croquis 2015).
6  Jacques Lucan, Précisions Sur Un État Présent De L'architecture (Presses Polytechniques et Universitaires Romandes 2015), p. 247.
7  Iñaki Ábalos in Anne Lacaton and Jean Vassal, Lacaton & Vassal (Gustavo Gili 2011). p. 4.
8  Google has been among the first companies to communicate about its offices, praising the added value of a fun and flexible workplace. Yet many people have questioned this strategy, arguing that this joyful atmosphere was first and foremost a tool to intensify workload.

IMAGE CREDITS

A  Photograph by Marine Mallédan.
B  Wikipedia, Amegilla Cingulata On Acanthus Ilicifolius' en.wikipedia.org/wiki/Bee accessed 4 December 2015 under CC license 4.0.

Rabih Shibli

# Ghata

A Cover against Herculean Odds

As an architect born two years after the outbreak of the Lebanese civil war (1975–1990), I have witnessed lots of destruction (my family's same house three times) and flawed reconstruction processes, repetitive waves of displacement, and the rise and fall of grandiose ideologies. My perception of space and place has become tied to uncertainties. This is also true of my clients, who are at the same time the end users. The specificity of each project that I have designed in the past decade is based on the nature of the struggle facing my clients, where politics, anxieties, longings, and capacities intersect to develop the built environment. My latest project Ghata has been conceptualized to address the plight of Syrian refugees during their protracted and temporary stay in Lebanon, and to draw on the significant role of proactive architecture in response to unfolding crises.

### The Struggle

The seismic pressures that followed the uprisings have caused deep rifts among local constituents of the "Arab Spring" countries and in many cases, contravened the covert and overt aspirations of the "New Middle East". Syria is a stark example of the inherent complexities of a region that cannot simply absorb hasty transformational agendas without paying a high bloody price.

Since the outbreak of protests in March 2011, almost half of the Syrian population has undergone internal displacement (7.6 million) or has sought shelter, mainly in Turkey, Lebanon, and Jordan (4.5 million). With the direct engagement of regional and international players in the Syrian war(s), the refugees' stay in neighbouring countries is expected to be prolonged while abilities to host them are diminishing. Accordingly, the past year witnessed a new trend of displacement as thousands of refugees marched across Europe

A

B

in search of asylum. Meanwhile, millions are enduring severe conditions while living in collective shelters and formal camps or informal tented settlements that are supported by humanitarian agencies operating with conventional methods in unconventional times.

To date, Lebanon is hosting the largest concentration of refugees per capita worldwide. Around 1.2 million registered Syrian refugees and an unknown number of unregistered are dispersed along 1700 locations in the country's geographically small (10 452 square metres) and politically fragile landscape. Fatigue in the structural governance body has resulted in a vacancy in the presidency since May 2014, the postponing of parliamentary elections twice since May 2013, and the absence of a well-structured national response plan for the Syrian refugee crisis.

Following the first year of the crisis and the engagement of regional and international forces in the Syrian quagmire, the protracted nature of the civil war loomed as a palpable fact. Although many humanitarian programmes modified their operations in order to respond to the critical repercussions of the long-term stay of the refugees, implementations did not yield impactful results.

## The Cover – Ghata

As a director of the Center for Civic Engagement and Community Service (CCECS) at the American University of Beirut (AUB), I launched the Syria Relief Project (SRP) in December 2012 to address the refugees' worsening conditions. During the first phase of the project, CCECS collected and distributed clothes donations, and supported students' initiatives and activities. The project unfolded to engage most faculties across the university, tackling a wide number of sectors that include water sanitation and hygiene, education, food safety and nutrition, trauma and mental health, and shelter.

C

D

In my expertise as an architect leading the SRP, I designed the Ghata, meaning "cover" in English, to serve as a multifunctional structure for refugees. The guiding principles of the Ghata are based on the (a) simplicity and portability, (b) adaptability and scalability, (c) climatic responsiveness, (d) economic efficiency and endurance of a design that is aimed to ensure decent shelter conditions for Syrian refugees facing a protracted stay on mired Lebanese ground.

AUB student volunteers assembled the first unit in August 2013 in an Informal Tented Settlement (ITS) in South Lebanon. This basic 20 m² structure was modified and adjusted by the user refugee family to correspond to their daily needs. Unit 2 was assembled on the campus of the American University of Beirut (AUB) for further testing and modifications. Units 3 and 4 were assembled in ITS's, as classrooms and literacy programs were delivered by local partners to refugee students. Children constitute the highest percentage of Syrian refugees in Lebanon (53.2%) and only 14% (90 000) of them are accommodated within the already overcrowded public schooling system.

## Assembling Portable Schools

In May 2014, CCECS partnered with the local NGO Kayany under the project titled "Ghata: Bringing Education to Refugees in Informal Tented Settlements". To date, 6 Ghata schools have been assembled in Beqaa, the district hosting the largest number of Syrian refugees in Lebanon. Each school is built to cater for an average of 700 refugee students (age groups 4 to 14) on a double-shift basis. A unit of 40 m² proved to be the most efficient to function as a classroom that accommodates an average of 40 students. The ground floor area needed for a Ghata school campus is around 1 200 m². Each school includes:

E

F

9 classrooms, 1 office space, 4 dry sanitation latrines, a kitchen, and a storage area. Structures are laid out in a U form incorporating an outdoors activities area.

The Malala foundation funded a Ghata Vocational Training Center that was assembled in Beqaa and consists of 6 workshops (60 m² each). Each workshop is equipped with tools and machinery with an objective to train female refugees (age groups 14 to 18) in skills that will help them find suitable jobs in the host country, and that will prepare them for active engagement in the reconstruction of Syria in the aftermath of the war. Malala Yousafzai inaugurated the Center on June 12, 2015 and celebrated her 18th birthday with the refugee students.

Situated within tented settlements, Ghata schools also serve as distribution hubs used by relief agencies during school breaks. The schoolyards are suitable for unloading shelter equipment and supplies, clothes donations, hygiene kits, food rations, wood logs and the like. Awareness campaigns are frequently held in Ghata classrooms addressing practices that include hygiene, child protection, gender-based violence, and resilience. The open, outdoors central area (school yard) of every Ghata campus hosts events that are celebrated by refugees to celebrate their traditional cultural values. Schools shift function to community shelters in times of severe weather conditions. Following a snowstorm that hit Lebanon last winter (causing four children to freeze to death in Beqaa), refugees residing in settlements adjoining the portable schools sought warmth in the Ghata classrooms. The physical and mental wellbeing of refugees emerged as essential needs to be addressed within the holistic approach of the project. Accordingly, the intention is to situate a 60 m² Ghata clinic with a focus on primary and mental health care within every school campus.

G

H

Currently there are more than 3000 refugee children that have been able to enjoy a sense of normality in the Ghata schools amidst the surrounding madness. However, according to UNICEF, more than 700 000 Syrian refugee children are "unable to attend school because the overburdened national education infrastructure cannot cope with the extra student load" in Lebanon, Turkey and Jordan.

## Healing for the future

Ten years ago I founded and directed Beit Bil Jnoub (House In The South), a non-profit organization that was heavily involved in the reconstruction process following the 2006 Lebanon War. Working closely with hundreds of families who had lost their memories and in many cases their beloved ones under the rubble of their destroyed houses, enabled me to realize the significance of design and architecture in the recovery process of war-torn societies. Designing for refugees who are enduring a protracted stay on mired ground has been a more challenging task to accomplish. In addition to the needs and requirements of the end users, the design had to respond to inherent local concerns and to political complexities.

Accordingly, architecture in contested landscapes is the composition of a design that absorbs deep-seated anxieties, and a spatial configuration that is the direct product of resilience. It is imperative to institutionalize this process into the design and architecture theory in an era where we are witnessing the emergence of a nation of 60 million refugees, according to data gathered by UNHCR in 2014. The psychological profile of the increasing number of different user groups is charged with tensions and will require healing environments that are constructed by this responsive, progressive architecture. The practice

I

needs to embrace unconventional users, who own nothing but shattered memories and undetermined futures.

AUTHOR

Rabih Shibli is the director of the Center for Civic Engagement and Community Service at the American University of Beirut and the founder and director of Beit Bil Jnoub (House In The South), a non-profit institution. His latest research and projects focus on the Syrian refugee crisis and its impact on Lebanon.

IMAGE CREDITS

Photographs by Rabih Shibli.

Albert Palazón

# Back in the Caves

Hummingbirds are master crafters. They are true nest builders. Their skills in the field of architecture are simply astonishing. These hummingbirds build a tiny, knot-like structure attached to a tree branch with spider silk. The nest structure is crafted from bark, leaf strands and silk fibres, which make it strong and stretchable. The nest is covered on the outside with lichen for camouflage and lined on the inside with hair or feathers for insulation. A craftsman heritage that has helped their species survive while providing a solution to a very specific need.

The nest-building tradition among hummingbirds originated thousands of years ago. In actual fact, these tiny flying creatures were already building such highly-developed architectures while we humans were still living in caves. Recalling the beginnings of the human race, it is interesting to note that the first nomad communities in prehistoric times did not design or build their living environments. Their survival depended on their ability to "find architecture": interpreting a place and adapting to it. Inside the sheltered space of a cave, a flat surface could be seen as a sleeping spot or a gathering place; a crack in the rock could become a fireplace or maybe room for storage. Architecture was in the eye of the beholder. As opposed to the bird's nest, which represents the achievement of an "ideal" design with a very specific purpose, the cave is an ambiguous place that enables the user to solve his needs in a flexible manner.

Caves made us develop a basic framework and sense in the whole process of adaptability, which became the basis of what we call "architecture" today. This analogy: nest (planned environment) versus cave (adaptive environment), as a depiction of two different paradigms, was the starting point of Sou Fujimoto's conference at the *Seminario de Montevideo 13* in Uruguay in October 2012. Fujimoto's thoughts on the adaptable aspects of indeterminate places give clues about the true nature of contemporary architecture. Could architecture be much more detached from the traditional notion of client-architect-commission that we have? Do architects have a significant role in that scenario?

In the year 2012, the photographer Iwan Baan and Urban-Think Tank studio were together awarded the Golden Lion at the Venice biennale for the graphic depiction of a vertical self-made favela growing in the fabric of an abandoned skyscraper in central Caracas. Their series of pictures gave vivid evidence of how users create architectures by interacting with their surrounding contexts.

The *Torre de David* project proved that architecture not only needs to be the act of designing a place but, most importantly, needs to have the ability to read it in order to dwell in it. London-based artist Nadav Kander highlights the same reality of human adaptability by means of the photo series he took during his three-year Yangtze River photo project: Sunday Picnic at Chongqing is a revealing picture of how a humble family can transform the residual space under a massive concrete motorway into an impressive daytime living room by the river.

From my humble perspective, not that many architects have shown awareness of people's fluctuating needs and adaptation skills. Even fewer have used that knowledge as a design tool. In the year 2003, Alejandro Aravena and Elemental studio together carried out a housing experiment at Quinta Monroy, Chile. The core concept of their project was to design a housing complex which would allow users to expand their own homes and inhabit their places in a personal way. One could argue that Quinta Monroy in Chile reproduces the same social phenomenon as the *Torre de David* but in an environment planned by the author. Aravena's proposal produced an

A   Towhee bunting and egg. Drawn from nature by A. Wilson, engraved by A. Lawson.

B   Torre David – gran horizonte.

C   Chongqing IV. Sunday Picnic: vimeo.com/29879295.

incredibly rich and successful outcome. The project was flexible enough to allow an assorted variety of situations within it. Its main strength consisted of accepting the fact that adaptation is part of survival. It is fascinating to observe how buildings and spaces drastically evolve over time and move away from their original function. That natural process is strongly related to both the notion of "cave architecture" and the notion of adaptation as a mean to survival.

Giles Gilbert Scott was a brilliant English architect of the early 20th century. His work comprises significant buildings such as Liverpool Cathedral, the Battersea Power Station and the old Bankside power station in London. He mastered the art of brickwork and was the author of some of the most valuable industrial architectures of the last century. Little could Gilbert Scott have ever imagined that, long after his death, the Bankside power station would eventually become the new international cathedral of contemporary art;

now widely known as the Tate Modern. Whether aware of it or not, Gilbert Scott designed a superstructure which was flexible enough to house any possible scenario. Herzog & de Meuron, the Swiss team which led the renovation of the Tate Modern, saw the opportunities in the original fabric. A stigmatized non-functional brick power station became one of the most significant cultural and urban landmarks in Europe. The Tate Modern is an excellent example of what adaptation is: an essential process necessary in every ecosystem, environment or architecture that aims to stay alive.

Modern life is evolving faster than ever. We architects must understand that contemporary architecture has to be adaptable to constant change. There is an increasing necessity to design buildings that can have multiple lives, buildings which can cope with almost any situation and which guarantee future adaptation. At the end of the day, a very specific need required by a

D     Quinta Monroy Chile by Alejandro Aravena and Elemental Studio 2011.

specific client is only a fleeting situation in time. For this reason, I believe that the role of the client is slowly fading away in favour of both users and designers. An architecture that doesn't want to expire cannot be defined by a single client's need. Many other future clients, users and even architects will have to find new opportunities in a building that aspires to be long lasting. We will perish and die, but our buildings will be left behind in the fabric of our cities, and they will have many other future lives, some of which will be surprisingly unexpected. Bear in mind the *Torre de David*, the Bankside power station and Quinta Monroy in Chile.

Let's leave things open and in flux. Maybe we should just project architectures which are more like "caves", where nothing is ever meticulously designed, but where there is always a chance to find shelter and a "home".

AUTHOR

Albert Palazón (Barcelona, 1987) is an architect, 3D artist and music producer from Barcelona, now based in Madrid. He has worked as a project architect at Mansilla+Tuñon studio since 2012 (nowadays called Emilio Tuñon architects: emiliotunon.com). Albert Palazon was trained as an architect at the Architecture School of Barcelona (ETSAB), the Edinburgh College of Art in Scotland and the Faculty of Architecture in Montevideo, Uruguay (FARQ, UdelaR). During his studies, he became involved in various architecture practices, such as Enric Ruiz Geli's interdisciplinary team at cloud 9 in Barcelona. In 2012 he was awarded with the Arquia Foundation National Scholarship, which led him to Madrid. He received mentions under his own name at Europan 13 Finland and the Asemas national master thesis contest. He is currently working on his next music album, which will soon see the light of day.

IMAGE CREDITS

A     American Ornithology; or The Natural History of the Birds of the United States by Alexander Wilson.
B     Photograph by Iwan Baan.
C     Photograph by Nadav Kander.
D     Photograph by Cristobal Palma.

# Pre-Architect

There was a time when the urban planner or architect was a public figure. He or she was the expert mandarin of a technocratic society, the public intellectual, the celebrated artist, or the popular leader of a participatory movement. The erosion of these public positions has produced a slumbering malaise within the discipline. But more importantly, it points to a general incapacity to engage coherently in the public sphere, in the legitimisation of public actions.[1]

Some months ago, on the occasion of a study trip to Berlin, I visited the BigYard, a recently built half-block residential complex in the historical neighbourhood of Prenzlauer Berg. Our host was Sascha Zander, a resident of BigYard and an architect co-founder of Zanderroth Architekten, the office responsible for this co-housing project.

Zander and Roth initiated their practice at the end of the 1990s and decided to choose the projects they would like to build. Since then, they have developed an effective building model which enables them to generate their own architecture design commissions. While leveraging on the popular co-housing schemes of *Baugruppen*, the architects subtracted the developer from the building equation, not only to provide more affordable houses, but also to reclaim responsibility for defining the urban and social impacts of their projects within the city.[2] Self-initiative led them to consider additional tasks concerning the classical practice of architecture while also starting to deal with the factors that precede it, i.e. that make architecture possible in the first place.[3] Philipp Oswalt coined this modus operandi as "Pre-Architecture".

## I A tour around the BigYard

At Zelterstrasse, the sober playfulness of the 100-metre-long, panelled façade distinguishes the new building from the surrounding five-storey homogeneous blocks of the neighborhood Prenzlauer Berg, in a respectful manner. From the street, what intuitively appears to be an apartment building, with apartments stacked on each other, reveals itself to be a row of four-storey townhouses disguised by a unifying façade. This volume is only breached by a covered pedestrian passage, which provides access to the backyard. An oblong courtyard garden mediates between the longitudinal street volume with 23 townhouses, and a parallel one at the back with 22 housing units. Here, three-storey penthouses with direct access to the communal roof terrace are stacked on top of three-storey garden houses a step away from the courtyard garden. In total, 135 people dwell in the BigYard; four of the 45 units are shared and intended to host guests.

Given the early hour and as agreed between residents, we are not allowed to cross the courtyard on the way to visit the communal roof terrace. In this regard, Sascha elaborates on the village character of the project and refers to the founding principle of providing an atmosphere similar to a village, where a high density of occupation intersects with the desire for an individual house under the conditions of permanently negotiated close proximity.

This project addressed the wishes of middle-class families earning average incomes – "separate dwellings, large garden, green roof, open outlook, front door onto the street, parking behind the house"[4] – who didn't have the chance to gain access to the housing market and become homeowners within the inner city. According to the architect, the goal was to offer a lifestyle that combined the urban and suburban condition in a central location: "the project expands our ideas about contemporary urban housing. Housing is no longer confined to simply providing accommodation for people. It has more to do with the spatial organization of leisure time spent at home. Housing should contribute to recreation."[5]

Sascha describes the building model process that allowed them to set up this residential complex from its first spark, tracing the most significant tasks carried out as well as their phasing over a period of four years, between 2006 and 2010. With approximately 9000 m² of total floor area, this project represents a total investment of 15 million euros.

According to the architect, it all started with the choice of the plot to be developed and the search for its owner, with whom they signed a one-year "option to buy" contract, thereby assuming the initial risk themselves. This time span was helpful in light of one of the main challenges of their model: the need for a long lead time in order to develop the project and to complete the organization of the *Baugruppe* to fund it. This illustrates well one of the main challenges of their model: the need for a long organizational lead-time. With a clear concept in mind regarding the usages and their target audience, they developed the concept design and the submission project during the first months, in order to get official approval. Still without any clients, the architects took on the economic risk. Once the project had been officially approved, the architects launched an advertising campaign to sell the housing units on the *SmartHoming* website.[6] This is the "sister" company of Zanderroth Architekten, which is dedicated to marketing, project management and client care. A brochure with all the necessary information for purchasing an apartment – location, list of the different flat typologies available,

A    Courtyard of the "BigYard".

floorplans, area quantities, visualizations, prices – was made available to the public. The aim was to find clients – and future users – to participate in the BigYard *Baugruppe*. As more people joined, the *Baugruppe* gradually grew under the legal framework of a civil law association. Members signed a partnership agreement – GbR (*Gesellschaft bürgerlichen Rechts*) – that outlined who was to obtain which apartment and which share of the total cost it represented. From this point onwards, the clients' collective shared all the financial risks, and the liability of each member was proportional to the respective share of ownership. Likewise, all the decisions represented a consensus between all the members of the group. As soon as the required capital for construction had been gathered from the members' funds, the *Baugruppe* acquired the plot and Zanderroth Architekten proceeded with the construction project.

From this moment onwards, the architects organized monthly group meetings with the members of the *Baugruppe* both to report on the progress of the project, and to collect the participants' points of view. One-to-one meetings between the architect and each one of the clients also took place during the final stage of the construction project in order to fine-tune aspects related to the organization of domestic spaces and to define interior coatings, floorings and furniture in each apartment. Construction took approximately two years, evolving efficiently under the architects' control. By assuming construction management, the architects managed to cut time and costs in the process. Once built, keys were delivered to the house owners. The architects also became residents.

With the development and maturation of this *Baugruppe* building model, Zanderroth Architekten have managed to develop and consistently implement multiple co-housing projects within Berlin's inner districts over the last ten years.

B   BigYard – View from the communal roof terrace.

## II Baugruppen and the Self-made City [7]

Zander and Roth started their practice by drawing up a catalogue of empty plots in Berlin, and found more than 1000. After selecting a few, they researched their ownership and devoted themselves to persuade landowners of their ideas for these sites. This pro-active and entrepreneurial attitude earned them their first commission.

Indeed, Berlin is labelled a "self-made city". Self-initiated projects have become a mainstream phenomenon within the last 15 years, providing paradigmatic cases of architecture and urban development, particularly in the area of housing. This singularity is rooted in Berlin's squatter movement "tradition" of the 1980s, when artists and activists broke in, took control of and made inhabitable vacant buildings in the Kreuzberg neighbourhood following the cancellation of the government's ambitious plans for a new highway that would have torn the neighbourhood apart.

In 1987, IBA Altbau tapped into the do-it-yourself energy of the squatter movement by fixing up these old buildings and then handing them over to their residents as rightful owners.

After the fall of the Wall in 1989, social housing (government-subsidized, rent-controlled, pre-fabricated concrete housing) made up most of the housing throughout Berlin. In turn, the old centre of East Berlin was a no-man's land, with over 25 000 unoccupied apartments. In the early 1990s, a strong associative and self-made culture developed among people occupying these run-down buildings. There were countless self-initiated projects in the form of clandestine bars, clubs, galleries, shops, cultural institutions, meeting and working places. On the other hand, the focus of development in the city after political reunification in 1990 turned eastwards, and profit-oriented investments focusing on the renovation of these buildings had a disruptive impact on these associations. Despite this, the governmental programme *Bauliche Selbsthilfe* (Self-Help Building) enabled over 300 squatted buildings and self-organized housing projects to be legalized between 1984 and 2003 through private self-initiative. Indeed, Berlin's transformation years were the foundation for do-it-yourself project makers.

In 2002, Germany's economic recession led the State to cut funding for housing programs and investors to stop building housing. Berlin's urban fabric was left with numerous empty building sites. These small "holes" presented the very special potential of Berlin and were the catalysts for a new type of development in the inner city.[8]

At that stage, affordable living spaces in the city had become limited and the economic pressure on residents and users had risen dramatically. Nevertheless, families wanted to stay in the city and people showed interest in owning their own apartment; both to ensure a stable cost of living and to dwell in more personalized living spaces. Working on the basis of this generalized desire, Zanderroth Architekten started to develop architecture projects themselves, carrying out designs to fill the existing "holes" in the urban fabric.

The formation of *Baugruppen* is the framework condition that enables them to substantiate these enterprises. These *Baugruppen* are the outcome of a specific legal and cultural context and constitute a condition *sine qua non* for the necessary generation of usages, clients and funding, for the generation of usages, clients and funding necessary for the realisation of the architecture project.

Zanderroth initiated their first *Baugruppen* in 2005, forming a small group of clients with whom they proposed to share the responsibility of design. While demonstrating alternative solutions, it is the possibility that architects present for people to take charge of determining their own living environment that reveals a valuable resource in urban development created in the area of tension between freedom and need.[9]

## III Production of desire

The success of Zanderroth Architekten's approach is related both to the affordability and the flexibility of their residential units. Middle-class people earning average incomes are enabled to become homeowners within the inner city. In addition, the opportunity to obtain individually tailored living space adds inestimable value to the investment of a lifetime.

After understanding that after understanding that developers in general earn a 20% average profit on each project – the difference between production costs and sales price – Zander and Roth decided to determine their own framework. With this building model, there is no developer to assume the risk and make a profit. Instead, the coordinated design and construction processes enable the architects to finance additional spatial qualities by reducing production costs. Cost-effective projects are obtained as there are fewer people involved, and time-saving decisions are taken along a centralized and optimized construction process. When compared to the prices provided by the real-estate market, the final cost per square metre is far below the market average.

Furthermore, their clever strategy also makes use of the discovery of plots which are less valuable from the real-estate investors' point of view. The conscious choice of a "difficult" site is one of their trump cards: within a cheaper plot they manage to create assets that add value both to the site and the new buildings, and ultimately to their surroundings. Zanderroth consider themselves to be responsible, together with their clients, for creating a meaningful design not only for the housing units and the building, but also for the urban space, emphasizing the importance of the interface between the public and private. Through an urban-oriented architectural design that goes beyond the investor's urgency to create built financial assets, Zanderroth put into practice the capability to transform a disadvantage into an advantage. Their first project for the RUSC *Baugruppe* illustrates this aspect well.[10] At the north-oriented corner site between Schönholzerstrasse and Ruppiner Strasse, the architects created a public square within private property. This square is completely open to the neighbourhood, and the *Baugruppe* has undertaken to take care of it for the next one hundred years. The constraint typical of a Berlin block corner, where light doesn't adequately reach most of its rooms, was regarded as an opportunity to enhance the urban character of this intervention, and led to an "atypical" solution. It resulted in the separation of the programme into two buildings, with apartments facing three sides – towards the street, the new square and the backyard. The architects and clients' collective took on responsibilities that reached beyond their own property and buildings, creating new possibilities in the neighbourhood and encouraging interaction with the surrounding urban environment.

Another pillar of this building model is the "design deal" arranged between the architects and their *Baugruppen* members. The architects state a priori that the clients are to keep what would be the profit margin of the developer; in exchange, they demand total freedom for each project's design, except for the domestic interior spaces, as mentioned before in the case of BigYard.

Concerning the design of the housing units, Zanderroth's concentrate on optimizing spatial organization in terms of maximum economy and flexibility of space, as well as on interpreting the spatial requirements of a specific target audience. In the BigYard project for example, a project conceived to house young families on average incomes, architects define the spacious kitchen as the living core of the house, with a 4.20 m height that allows it to have visual contact with two floors, and a balcony towards the backyard. On the other hand, the housing units are generally provided with smaller surface areas than those delivered by the real-estate market, simultaneously allowing for a certain number of adjustments regarding the compartmentalization of the unit – the number of bedrooms for example. Through the design of "atypical" but nevertheless smart typologies, architects manage to produce projects with high-density occupation, thus generating more affordable housing units.

On an urban scale, the projects carried out by *Baugruppen* are gradually growing in size both due to the recent scarcity of small infill plots and to the unification of different collectives with compatible wishes regarding the conceptualization of public space. The challenges posed by these new urban interventions bring an added complexity to *Baugruppen* processes. Nevertheless, these challenges also reveal new potentials for architects to explore while shaping pieces of the city.[11]

A large scale project involves, first of all, the necessity of admitting other programmatic usages into the project in order to offer adequate urban living conditions. Finding the mechanisms to integrate infrastructural facilities like supermarkets, schools or day care centres, is one of the challenges currently being dealt with by the architects. According to the architects, the hypothesis is to call on companies or institutions to become part of *Baugruppen* from the beginning in order to facilitate integrated solutions. This integration may allow, for example, cases of "cross-subsidizing", where profit-oriented supermarket chains are brought on board on condition that they contribute to the lowering of housing unit prices.[12]

Commenting on their recent project in the borough of Friedrichshain, within a plot covering 8 000 m², the architects also identify their aim to widen the socio-economic range of people that can afford to join *Baugruppen*. Leveraging on a more substantial critical mass, they managed to offer a wider range of prices for the apartments by diversifying unit sizes and relating these to their vertical position in the building – size plus height equals price. This redistribution strategy allowed them to offer penthouses with a price per square meter that is almost double the price they offer for other apartments within the same building project. On the other hand, they have also foreseen the option for merging and separating two adjacent apartments, arguing for evolution of the needs of the tenants over the course of their lives, and the possibility for enabling rentals. They conclude: "Nevertheless, it would be naïve to believe that, like some kind of Robin Hood for the housing market, we could ever compensate for the major political failures that exist in Berlin due to the complete lack of a socially sustainable housing policy."[13]

## IV The public role of the architect

While initiators of their own projects for co-housing buildings, Zanderroth Architekten assume and conciliate multifarious pre-architectural tasks – land procurement, expertise in law, financial modelling, market analysis, marketing, *Baugruppen* mediation and client care – alongside the architectural design typical of the "classical" practice of architecture, as we know it.

Nonetheless, and despite the fact that they do not put forward an unprecedented building model, both their discourse and designs seem to propose a "fresh approach" within the architecture debate, arguing in favour of the possibility for architects to play a public role.

In fact, there are multiple examples of architectural practices that integrate services and optimize building processes in order to deliver cheaper turnkey projects. This is usually the case with market-oriented strategies with underlying profit margins, where users are not part of the building "equation".

On the other hand, housing cooperatives are also a pertinent practice, offering a parallel to *Baugruppen*. Often created to provide affordable housing, their relevance is much related to the absence of the mentality of private property ownership in the first place, thus avoiding any motivation for real-estate speculation. According to Zander and Roth, reality nonetheless shows that a newly founded cooperative is not as financially powerful as a *Baugruppe*, as it must raise the entire budget for the building project from scratch.[14] Moreover, the current European economic context is revealing itself to be arid ground, since the states have gradually abandoned these social mechanisms, facilitating the growth of private housing companies and stimulating the real-estate market, which is thought of as a catalyst for "urgent" economic growth.

In this regard, it is worth mentioning a particular case: the Fideicomiso, a legal framework that resurged in Argentina after the national banking crisis in 2001 and enabled local architects to initiate their own building models.[15] This framework gives architects and clients the possibility to sign a kind of fiduciary contract based on trust, which allows the architect to take on the risk of a development and use the residents' collective assets to buy the land, fund the project and deliver the scheme. As with *Baugruppen*, this scheme encourages clients to participate in the design process, and the final price of the apartments is thought to be 20 to 30 % cheaper than on the open market. Yet, and despite having contributed during the last ten years to the revitalization and densification of low-valued neighbourhoods across Buenos Aires, *Fideicomiso* projects have few arguments to produce any significant impact within a broader societal context, given their small scale.

In turn, the Zanderroth Architekten building model reveals new faculties that instil added value into the design project. Catalyzing on the strength of *Baugruppen* – culturally assimilated and legally matured within Berlin's context –, their practice distinguishes itself for channelling this ability of dealing with the possible uses, clients and funding, towards the production of a critical intervention in the city. In order to produce an effective impact by reaching beyond plot boundaries, this model either challenges or engages with the societal status quo, ultimately doing this through design. That is what Pre-Architects do: they put forward a social agenda.

Regarding "classical" architectural practice, the Pre-Architecture displays a reaction to the "self-amputation" to which postmodernism had condemned the professional field of architecture, since the 1960s and 1970s. Criticism of technocracy, rationalism, and utopianism led architecture back to its own discipline, thereby screening out questions that went beyond it, allegedly undermining architecture. The increasing reduction of architectural discourse to questions of form blocked out the question as to how architecture could be created in the first place. But architectonic design can gain relevance only if it answers the question of how it can be created.

The proposal of this new professional role is to go beyond the narrower field of architecture, i.e. to go beyond the architect as the exclusive artistic genius serving a private client, and to turn instead to pre-architectural themes, to act as an inclusive, engaged architect who plays a public role. While leading to the re-politicization of the architectural debate – who builds with which resources and to what end?[16] – the advent of the Pre-Architect testifies to the democratization of architecture.

In this regard and against the background of the persistent image of the master architect, it may be pertinent to draw attention to the multifarious relations between the architect and the public in the postwar context, as systematized by Avermaete.[17] Whether it was a question of the syndicalist who questioned the social status quo – the populist who challenged professional conventions, the activist who fought for spatial justice by transgressing the action boundaries of the profession, or the facilitator who engaged inhabitants to realize an ambitious project – all of these intervened in society by dealing with pre-architectural tasks, thereby contributing to the empowerment of the people.

In fact, the political load of architecture manifests itself today once again, this time reacting to the backlash of neo-liberal times and its disruptive effect on the urban condition. The Pre-Architect is therefore once again called upon to develop the skills that allow him to engage coherently in the public sphere and in the legitimisation of public actions. The Pre-Architect is a public figure.

AUTHOR

Bernardo Menezes Falcão is a Portuguese architect. He holds a postgraduate Diploma on Sustainable Cities and has completed a Master of Advanced Studies in Urban Design at ETH Zurich as a scholar of the Geisendorf Foundation. His project 'Inside-Out' for the informal settlements of Cairo – developed in collaboration with Grigorios Dimitriadis and Shinji Terada – was exhibited in the 2015 Bi-City Biennale of Urbanism and Architecture in Shenzhen and Hong Kong, and in the Egypt Urban Forum, organized by UN Habitat in Cairo. As a practitioner since 2007, he has collaborated with urban planning and architecture offices in Lisbon, Zurich and Rotterdam.

NOTES

1. Dehaene, Michiel. "On the Difficulty to Make a Public Proposition, or the Chance Encounter of the Panopticon and the Boyle Air Pump on a Drawing Board." Ed. Salomon Frausto. NAi Publishers/Berlage Institute. Hunch – Publicity. 14. 2010: 28 – 37. Print.
2. Wohnen in Gemeinschaft – Living in a Community. STAATBAU GmbH – Netzwerkagentur Genertionen Wohnen & Senatsverwaltung Für Stadtentwicklung, 1 May 2015. Web. 25 Nov. 2015. stadtentwicklung.berlin.de/wohnen/wohnungsbau/download/wohnen_in_gemeinschaft.pdf
3. Oswalt, Philipp. "Pre- and post- architecture." Department of Architecture. ETH Zurich. Urban Mutations on the Edge. 2015. Lecture.
4. Zander, Sascha, and Christian Roth. "Architecture Without Developers." Reinventing Construction. Ed. Ilka Ruby and Andreas Ruby. Comp. Julia Von Mende. Berlin: Ruby, 2010. 419 – 432. Print.
5. Projekte – SmartHoming. SmartHoming. Web. 25 Nov. 2015. smarthoming.de/de/projekte/
6. Title of the book: Ring, Kristien / AA Projects. Selfmade City: Berlin – Stadtgestaltung Und Wohnprojekte in Eigeninitiative =Self-initiated Urban Living and Architectural Interventions. Berlin: Jovis, 2013. Print.
7. Ring, Kristien / AA Projects. "Selfmade Not Readymade." Selfmade City: Berlin Stadtgestaltung Und Wohnprojekte in Eigeninitiative= Self-initiated Urban Living and Architectural Interventions. Berlin: Jovis, 2013. 14 – 25. Print.
8. Ring, Kristien / AA Projects. "Project Rusc." Selfmade City: Berlin - Stadtgestaltung Und Wohnprojekte in Eigeninitiative = Self-initiated Urban Living and Architectural Interventions. Berlin: Jovis, 2013. 76 – 77. Print.
9. "Inductive Urban Development." Concept. Zanderroth Architekten. Web. 25 Nov. 2015. zanderroth.de/en/profil/konzept
10. "Fideicomiso – Self-providing Housing Trusts in Argentina Initiated by Entrepreneurial Architects..." Motivating Collective Custom Build. 24 Apr. 2013. Web. 2 Dec. 2015. mccbhomeimprovements.wordpress.com/2013/04/24/fideicomiso-self-providinghousing-trusts-in-argentina-initiated-by-entrepreneurial-architects/.
11. Avermaete, Tom. "The Architect and the Public: Empowering People in Postwar Architecture Culture." Ed. Salomon Frausto. NAi Publishers / Berlage Institute. Hunch - Publicity 2010: 48 – 63. Print.

IMAGE CREDITS

A  Photograph by Simon Menges.
B  Photograph by Bernardo Menezes Falcão.

Fritz Barell

# The Tree from the Triangle

"Fritz Barell" is the fictitious name of someone who gave us access to the information that builds up this diagram but doesn't want to have his/her name published. This diagram relates to the overall project structure typically developed for the construction of a typical production plant for a major company. The graphic work of Max Frischknecht on the project structure makes use of identical modular units arranged according to the hierarchy imposed by the client's approach to the process of planning, managing and building. The architect is one of many figures in corporate architecture; the triangle is, a long-gone fantasy replaced by a tree-like shape of highly hierarchical relations between an exponential number of interventionists in the project, a structure where the client never really comes into contact with the architect. Why has this relationship come to this point? Is this way of proceeding productive? How is the built reality influenced by the replacing of the triangle by a tree?[1]

NOTES

1  See the articles of Enrique Pelaez, Pedro Bragança and the interview with Marco Serra for further insights on this specific topic.

IMAGE CREDITS

Graphics by Max Frischknecht.

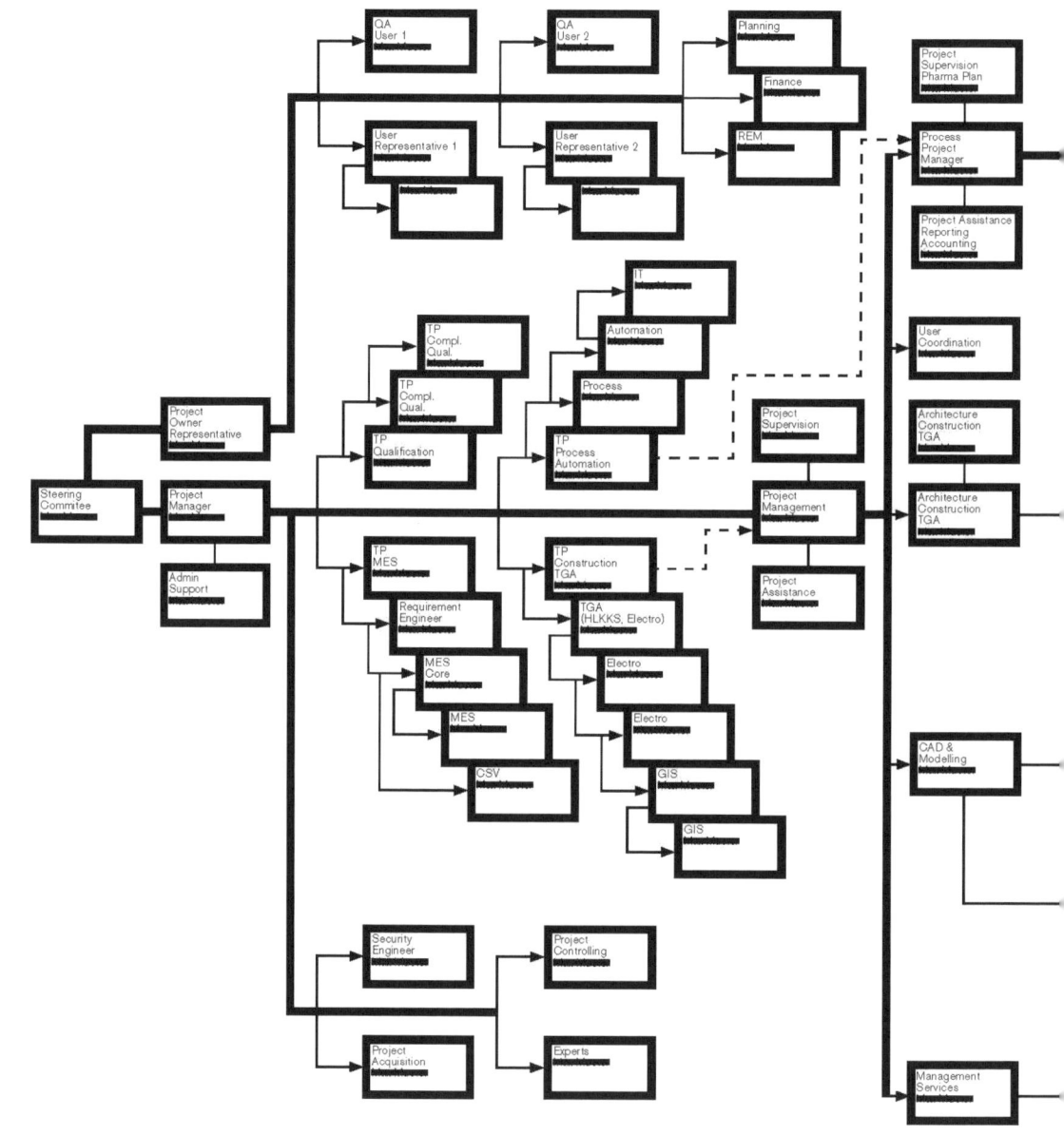

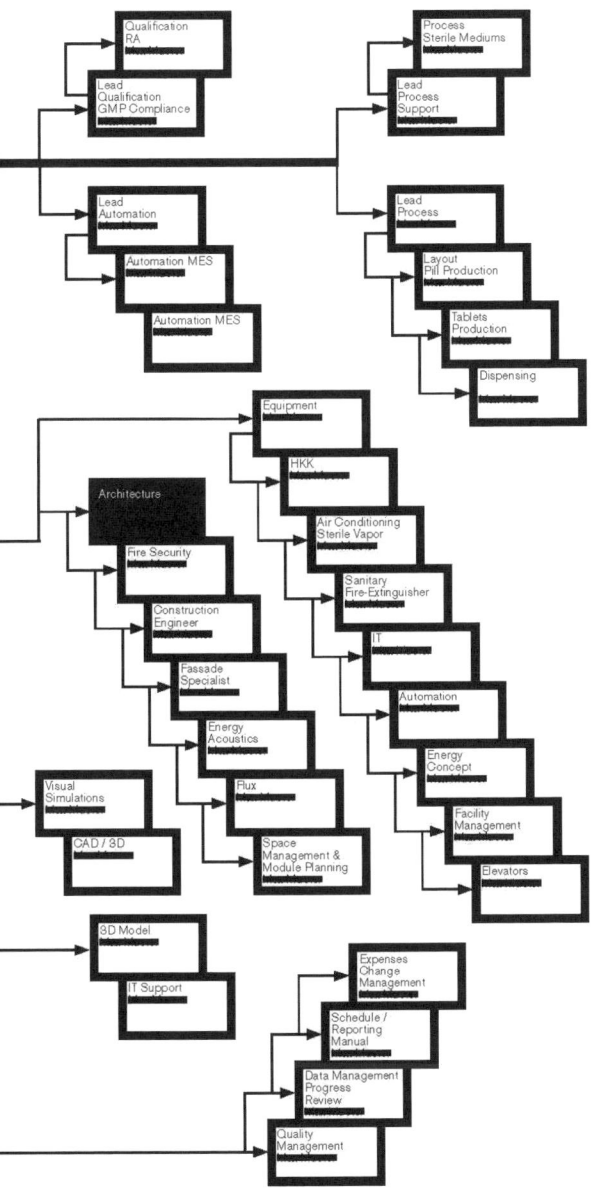

Enrique Peleaz

# There's something about Clients

## A client in the broad sense: "the inception"

Saenz de Oiza, a famous iconoclastic Spanish architect, whose work became prominent in the 1950s and 1960s, used to say that projects are as good as clients can be.

Nowadays, when delivering architectural projects it is hard to define what a client is, and more importantly, to identify the client in complex project structures where the figure of the client can take on multiple forms. Is the client the one who pays the fee? Who will enjoy the project once accomplished? Whether a client has some commercial connotation or not, a client is the point of departure of a project, the place where everything begins, the source of a need that looks forward to the creation of something that has never been done before.

## The client's expectations in the construction industry

The uniqueness of the construction industry – as opposed to the manufacturing industry which has the aim of providing serially-produced goods under conditions of controlled risk – is rarely appreciated by clients who only seek profit and who see architects as unnecessary to projects and as adding excessive costs. Nevertheless there are some other clients who invest time in explaining their needs so that these can be translated into a vision that facilitates discussions and will ultimately result in the kind of rich dialogue which all architects would wish for when doing their work. Both types of client, despite not being the only ones, can be part of legitimate process, as long as the expectations are set from the very beginning.

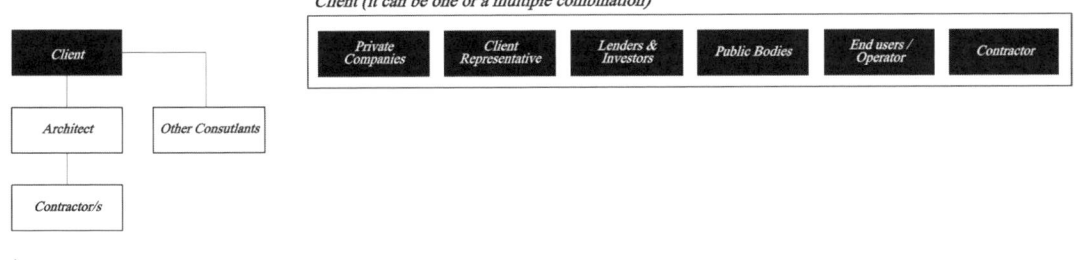

A

## Client types, complex structures

There is a range of client types which may be categorised by key characteristics. Some of the categories of client that are likely to be encountered in practice include: public bodies, including local authorities, who are experienced and have a large and wide portfolio; large commercial developers; and large and small companies who build to improve and extend their businesses and are thus owner-occupiers. These different client types will have different needs that must be explored in order to build up a fruitful relationship from which the project can benefit. It can be said that clients in general are increasingly adopting a project culture in all aspects of their business. Added to the usual stakeholders surrounding a project, this situation results in high demands and constraints when an architect is being appointed. This is something that should not necessarily be badly received, since working with limits is a challenge rather than a threat in a design process. However, these complex client structures are likely to end up in a misalignment of the project goals and in a lack of decision-making.

During the life of a project and within the spectrum mentioned above, clients are mostly linked to stakeholders. These stakeholders range from operators/end users who can actively participate by expressing their needs regarding the project, to contractors who could even become clients in design and build contracts, to lenders and investors who expect to obtain a return on the project investment, to public bodies whose interest is to bring something of value to the community/society.

The role of client representative also exists. As the name implies, a client representative represents the interests of a client. This set-up is frequently used by those clients who do not have the in-house knowledge to cope with the project, preferring instead to delegate the management of

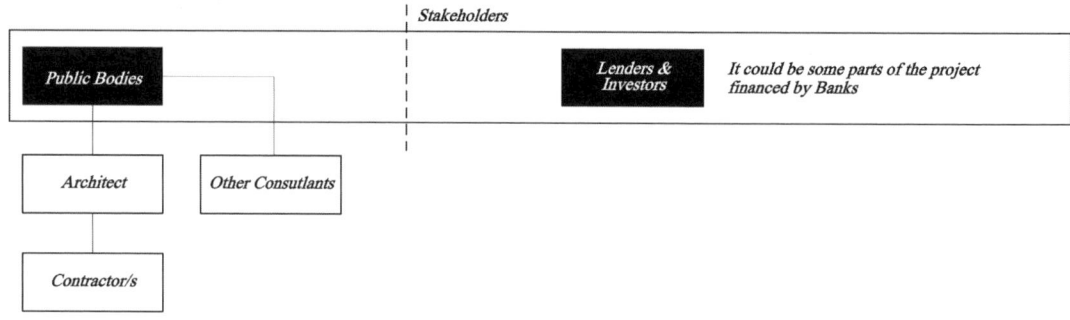

B    Public Hospital Project.

the project to another professional entity. These different roles occur in multiple combinations but irrespective of the term used, it is always a question of a client.

An example would be a hospital project. In a public hospital [Fig. B], whose capital expenditure is funded by the public administration, the client is concentrated into one or perhaps two entities. In the case of a public hospital developed in a PPP (Public Private Partnership) mode [Fig. C], on the other hand, a specific entity called a SPV (Special Purpose Vehicle) takes on the financial, technical and operational risks of the project, and the client consists of several parties.

with clients, as opposed to the times when Saenz de Oiza realised his work, and are consequently becoming machineries that react and respond to their clients' needs. To do so, they have to be equipped with multidisciplinary teams with a great variety of skills and backgrounds, not only to provide enough confidence to clients but also to manage the expectations of both client and architect, and to understand the scope of the project in the sea of interests which can frequently be found in a project. In the end, a successful project can be seen as that which best captures the needs of your client, a result which, regrettably, might not be remarkable architecture.

### How to maximise the architect relationship with a client, "bridging the gap"?

With this in mind, it is inevitable that architectural practices are continuously empathising

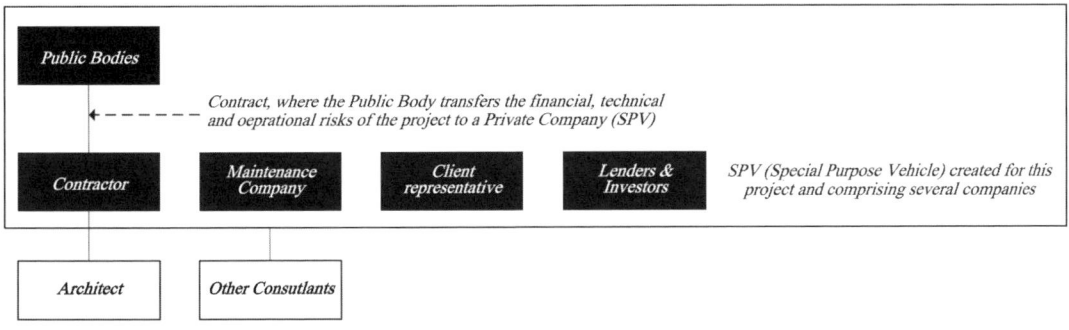

C   Public Hospital Project (PPP).

AUTHOR

Enrique Pelaez (born in Spain) is a chartered project manager surveyor and a member of the RICS (Royal Institution of Chartered Surveyors). He studied architecture at the University Camilo Jose Cela and also graduated as a technical architect from the Polytechnic University of Madrid. He holds a Master in Project and Construction Management from the ETSAM (Madrid), and an MBA in Real Estate. At present, Enrique works for Herzog & de Meuron in Basel as a project manager and he has previously worked as a consultant for EC Harris, working for clients on numerous international large-scale projects.

IMAGE CREDITS

Graphics by Enrique Pelaez.

Laura Bonell and Daniel López-Dòriga

# A Portrait of Stone

A person stands in the middle of an old structure and marvels at what was once a home:

> At the audacity of its natural enclave,
> At the scenography of its exteriors,
> At the wise use of its materials,
> At the bold combination of its elements,
> At the proportions of its spaces.

It was built 80, 200, 2 000 years ago. Its owner was its creator was its user. It was a house made for oneself. Or was it oneself turned into a house? "This house, my portrait of stone. A house that looks like me, or said in another way, a house like me. But which me?"

Upon reading Curzio Malaparte's words, a very specific kind of client emerges: one who does not need an architect to project the way in which he will live. In other words, if there is an architect, he is not important. While it is not uncommon for clients to impose their wishes on the spaces they are going to inhabit, often to their architects' disbelief, rarely does the result manage to generate consensus and go on to become a lasting piece of architecture, a masterpiece, admired by future generations. The idea that a person's character can be set in stone, that ideals can be translated into living spaces, speaks of the genuine personality of these creators/clients.

I

The oldest example that comes to mind is the emperor Hadrian, who projected Villa Adriana for himself in the 2nd century AD. In *Memoirs of Hadrian*, Marguerite Yourcenar imagines him writing: "Each building stone was the strange concretion of a will, a memory, and sometimes a challenge. Each structure was the chart of a dream."

Having been a conqueror, a traveller and a nomad, he envisioned his own house as his final

A – D  Villa Adriana, Tivoli.

encampment; tents and pavilions made of jasper, porphyry and obsidian.

## II

Sir John Soane greatly admired the remains of the villa when he visited it as part of his Grand Tour of Italy. The opulent marble was long gone, and all that was left was the brick structures of what once had been. The toplit ruined vaults, however, left a lasting impression on him.

In spite of his being a renowned architect of his time, Soane is almost better known as an art collector[1], and the home he built for himself is certainly not a typical architect's house.

Inside, walls are hidden from sight, covered by objects upon objects. Mirrors are placed strategically, multiplying the feeling of a never-ending cabinet of treasures and curiosities. However, architecture is not hidden but enhanced, as the carved-like maze of room upon room becomes a treatise on how to get natural light inside a building and how to light a work of art.

No architect without an art collection would have built a house like this; no art collector without the knowledge of an architect could have built a house like this.

> "To study Soane is to be faced with the problem of the expression of personality in architecture, for it is surely possible to find in his work reflections of the edginess and vanity, the persecution complex and the unyielding Old Testament morality, the inner conflicts, uncertainties and introspection, which we know were fundamental to his character."[2]

In his search for the "poetry of architecture"[3], his house is in essence more aesthetic than it is comfortable. It is a museum more than it is a home.

B

## III

Not one, not two, but three (and maybe even four) architects[4] were commissioned to build El Carmen Blanco (1916 – 1928), the house and atelier that José María Rodríguez-Acosta envisioned in the mountains of Granada, just outside the Alhambra palaces. All the architects contributed in some way, but the result is essentially Rodríguez-Acosta's.

> "Every spot in the space of this unusual place registers an intention that is emotional or aesthetic. (...) Imprinted are the keys of his artistic thoughts, of his talent, of his curiosity and of his desires."[5]

Rodríguez-Acosta projected this place as if he were painting. It is a delicate balance of masses and voids, construction and nature, modernity and classicism. As in Sir John Soane's Museum, each of its fragments is defined individually, but sums up to the result of its complex totality.

## IV

On the opposite side of the spectrum stands Casa Malaparte (1937 – 1939). Its appearance upon arriving from land or sea is that of a monolith on a cliff. There is no sum of parts, but an absolute whole: a purely shaped piece of architecture that looks like a wrecked ship, a bunker and a temple.

Its hard materiality reminds us of the rock on which it stands, its roof resembles the sea's horizon; but its rotund symmetry is a reminder of its artificiality. It is not the creation of nature but the creation of a man: of his character and of his life experiences, which become embedded in its formal expression. As with his writing, the house is surreal and poetic and inflexible. It is not a home; it is a stage for a life, albeit a very particular one.

c

A person looks at pictures of a new structure and marvels at what is, right now, a home:

> At the audacity of its natural enclave,
> At the scenography of its exteriors,
> At the wise use of its materials,
> At the bold combination of its elements,
> At the proportions of its spaces.

It is an ongoing construction that started on 1968. Its owner is its creator is its user. It is a house made for oneself. Or is it oneself turned into a house?

V

Set in Esplugues de Llobregat, on the outskirts of Barcelona, sculptor Xavier Corberó's house has been generating interest and curiosity for a while. He bought the land almost 50 years ago, and slowly but steadily, he has been building a home that is not a house, but an intricate labyrinth of modernly interpreted classical shapes bathed in sunlight.

It has the volumetric complexity of Ricardo Bofill's "cities in space" projects from the seventies and the playfulness of English follies. In spite of this, it is profoundly personal. It has no other purpose but to be the home of his sculptures and a source of daily inspiration for him and the artists he has in residence.It is also the closest we can get to learning the process of one of these houses in real time. These words are all his own[6], but they seem to define the minds of others:

> "I wanted to create, as far as was feasible, a continuum; a place in which the real space is not as important as the mental space."

Corberó or Hadrian?

D

"I always consider things in themselves. Rooms are considered to remain exactly as they are, and maybe to lodge a sculpture, or some piece of furniture. The room possesses utility in itself, not a defining function."
Corberó or Soane?

"What I try to do does not stem from reason. It comes from life itself. I use reason to build things up, so they don't fall to pieces. But the motives behind all the rest are aesthetic, ethical and, if you will, divine."
Corberó or Rodríguez-Acosta?

"The outcome of what I do has to be poetry, which I believe is the measure of all things."
Corberó or Malaparte?

An emperor, an art collector, a painter, a writer and a sculptor. Only one of them was an architect, or were they all?

### AUTHORS

Laura Bonell and Daniel López-Dòriga (Barcelona, 1987) both studied architecture in ETSAB. They each spent one year away during their studies, in Accademia di Architettura di Mendrisio and Technische Universität München respectively. They started their office together, Bonell+Dòriga, in 2014, where they work on projects at various scales: from small private commissions to public competitions. Among other places, their work has been published in the famed Casabella magazine, as part of its 85th anniversary issue focused on young architects.

NOTES

1. In Google Maps his house is described as "Sir John Soane's Museum. Former home of eccentric art collector".
2. "Soane and his contemporaries", David Watkin. Part of the book "John Soane" (Academy Editions / St Martin's Press, 1983).
3. In his conferences and classes, Soane often talked about the „poetry of architecture" as the impressions created by the picturesque effects of his projecting.
4. Ricardo Santa Cruz, Teodoro de Anasagasti, José Felipe Giménez Lacal were the official architects commissioned. Modesto Cendoya, then the Conservation Architect of the palaces of Alhambra, has been said to have been consulted at some point, especially in regards to the architecture of the gardens.
5. "Cada punto del espacio de este insólito lugar lleva inscrita una intención de orden emocional o estética. (...) Allí quedarán impresas las claves de su pensamiento estético, de su talento, de sus inquietudes y de sus anhelos." Miguel Rodríguez-Acosta, nephew of the painter (Translation by the authors).
6. Extracts taken from the video "In Residence: Xavier Corberó", by Albert Moya for Nowness.

IMAGE CREDITS

Photographs by Laura Bonell.

Tiffany Melançon

# Artist's Loft House Renovation

Latent in every architectural project is a tension between the designer's ambitions and the user's needs. Architectural photography reveals this tension when it shows a building unoccupied, with furniture rearranged, or the personal effects of inhabitants erased. This essay discusses the subtle wrangling between authorship and ownership in architecture, often played out through a camera's lens, by presenting 'before' and 'after' images of my own home renovation project near Basel, Switzerland.

The house was built in 1963 as an artist's loft and apartment for the Swiss painter Hans Weidmann. He lived on the ground floor and worked upstairs in the studio made to his specifications: only northern natural light and a 3.5 metre high ceiling. Fifty years later, my husband and I acquired the property and transformed it into a three-bedroom home for our young family, acting both as the architects and the users of the project. Seeing the renovation as a continued dialogue with the house's former life, we imagined the original architect, Renee Tofel, and the original user Weidmann as additional 'clients' with specific wishes to be negotiated.

Tofel designed the house as a classic modern picture, self-consciously set apart from the nineteenth century cottages of its surrounding suburban context. He made a simple industrial 'box' with perfect spatial reduction (four walls, ribbon windows and a flat, accessible roof) and punctured the concrete stair tower with sporadic, tapered window openings, thus referencing Le Corbusier's Ronchamp, built only eight years before.

To preserve its clear modernist appearance and open loft quality, we chose minimal intervention, adapting our own user needs to the house rather than the house to the typical user needs. This meant programming the more public space of living, kitchen and dining on the upper loft floor, and the private, divided spaces of bedrooms and bathrooms on the ground floor, where we

utilized oversized sliding doors to modulate different degrees of opened and closed. Because the loft had only one band of north-facing windows, we introduced new discreet window openings placed like framed pictures hung on the studio walls.

The photos in this essay ask together: How do the stories architects tell about the design-object-house differ from the stories we tell about home? What context and life is edited out of the images we construct, and how does architecture construct the life it claims merely to house? These pictures of a modern artist's loft turned into an architect's home reflect on the ways ambitions and needs are often nested, one inside the other.

AUTHOR

Tiffany Melançon (born 1972, United States) is an architect based in Basel, Switzerland and a principal at Melancon & Co. Before starting independent practice in 2013, she worked with Flubacher-Nyfeler + Partner and Herzog & de Meuron in Basel and Bond Street Architects in New York City.

IMAGE CREDITS

Photographs by Tiffany Melançon.

Pedro Bragança

# The Quasi-Temple of Architecture

The advent of modern capitalism has changed everything and architecture is no exception. These last few decades, in particular, resemble an acute transition, when everything moves at speed and is more and more difficult to track. The relocation of the world's centres, accomplished by the new geography of production and capital, reflect a new balance that has also got its own dark side of poverty and disparities.[1]

Architects probably still hope in a very optimistic sense that creative work can always become a front in order to reverse the constraints arising in society. However, "creativity has always been absorbed by capital" and "the creative professional was never *outside* accumulation, but an essential part of it."[2] To an economic and political supremacy corresponds a disciplinary mainstream which works as an enabler of the establishment. Or, better said, it is the establishment itself.

While it is dominant, the establishment is in no way absolute, and that is why we have the moral obligation to challenge it. I am trying to do so here by formulating a possible way out that takes into account the obstacles raised by fragmentation of the discipline of architecture.

This essay is a contribution written in a specific circumstance and in a concrete geography, and is influenced by both. It is impossible to deny (and I do not intend to) the subjective and, in a sense, autobiographical dimension that a text of this kind acquires.

## Compartmentalization of the design process

Like almost all disciplines, architecture tends to a progressive specialization, and herein lies a great paradox: if learning more about a certain specific subject can enable significant gains in knowledge, it can also make architects lose control of the entirety the design process, making them hostages of a very particular task or matter. Furthermore, the process of specialization within the discipline of architecture ultimately means its compartmentalization. Over the last decades, some major studios have changed the established procedures of the design process, yielding to the pressure of the entrepreneurial spirit. They have started to break the common alignments, dividing them into isolated tasks and distributing them to their draughtsmen or draughtswomen, mere executors, whose repetitive routine has established an excessive gap between practice and criticism. Resulting in a substantial increase in productivity, this can also be very advantageous to investors and to the market engine because, if the project should always be a political act, the more isolated and absent architects are from an entire vision, the more the market ideology can reign. And if it reigns, it will impose its own moral, aesthetic and constructive codes under a supposed objectivity.

Even if this is putting it in somewhat simplistic terms, I can find here a helpful and clarifying binomial between the market goals – profit and accumulation – and architecture. And if, as Joseph Rykwert said, "Architecture is primarily concerned with the public good (...), private profit can only enter into its calculation negatively as an extra-curricular matter."[3] Thus, the market will reply with infallible cohesion to the compartmentalization of the design process and to the subsequent fragmentation of the discipline.

Compartmentalization is also the result of the segmentation which the merchant status imposes: while architects are highly specialized technical designers, customers become promoters or investors and dwellers become consumers. One could suppose that the design process would become more discussed and diverse with the proliferation of *stakeholders* and *skills* (keywords of the market lexicon), but it doesn't seem to be that simple. Among all these *agents* there is a field of struggle and dispute over power and dominance.

When the market rules the world, the architects themselves sometimes begin to occupy a peripheral space in the design process. This is the scenario of the second loss, when they are not victims of the specialization that I mentioned above, but victims of their own desire. Even if those architects formally and legally maintain their centrality, they become pure bureaucrats of accumulation, whose mission is to apply generic trends to a specific geography. *Fare di più con Meno*[4] (Do more with less), a very successful book by Stefano Boeri, is a good example of how an idea of architecture can surrender to the dominant spirit of austerity, and then create a kind of new reductionist aesthetic.[5] Instead of being, as it initially seems, a brand new discourse, it remains the official rhetoric of the establishment.

Considering this paradox, I wonder whether it is possible for architects to formulate, in their own disciplinary space, a balance that implies at the same time, openness and cohesion, individuality and plurality, autonomy and commitment. Suddenly, the return to the Self becomes an imperative route.

## The Radical Self

The Self can be an irreplaceable field of work and criticism: a minimum, indivisible and impenetrable compartment of individual thought. The borderline of ambiguity and confusion which architecture sometimes reaches requires successive actions of retrospection and revision, where the architect, in an exercise of great concentration, seeks a kind of reorganization of his own discourse.

A    Johannes Vermeer, Christ in the House of Martha and Mary, 1655.

It seems to me that there are great similarities between the importance of the Self to the discipline of architecture and the religious concepts of *contemplation and action*. The dichotomy of contemplation and action has been developed by several schools of thought, based on the biblical episode in Luke 10:38 – 42 *(at the home of Martha and Mary)*, where two sisters receive Jesus into their own home. Martha, the active one, is occupied serving, while Mary, the contemplative one, devotes herself to the Word of the Lord. Numerous interpretations have emerged from this episode and the enigmatic assertion "Mary has chosen what is better", with which Luke concludes. They have found their expression in, i.e. treatises, religious texts and works of art.

Beyond the religious calling of the scripture, I think it is essential to retrieve this simultaneously contemplative and active sense as a mutually complemented binomial. Active life is the current practice – by this I mean the design work we do on a daily basis (details, construction projects, budgets, etc.). It remains an intellectual task, but it is totally distinct from contemplation. Contemplation is about reflection, synthesis and concentration; it is a great individual effort, limited in time, where the architect becomes involved with his *radical self*. And I use "radical" here not in its common sense. The *radical self* is an intellectual redoubt of revision and invention, located in the roots of each person.

It is just in these crucial moments that the architect, the client and the user are absolutely the same. Not because they are, in fact, the same person (indeed they don't need to be) but because a kind of objective coincidence, or a contemplative state of fullness, may give back to architecture its essential condition of pleasure and delight, like a "spectacle of deepest harmony".[6] What I am speaking about is an incursion and a deep ethical commitment that the author sets himself in the form of an ethics that merges with practice: in other words, a nexus between contemplation and action. It seems to me that only the art of or, rather, only the artistic practice of design is able to promote the necessary conciliation of these two worlds.

In the pursuit not only of the reorganization of a discourse and of a thought but also of the primary and essential condition of that discourse and that thought, architects made some works that can be thought of as trial pieces. The term "quasi-temples of architecture" may be used to describe these syntheses, which gather a sought essence within a project while at the same time becoming great experiments.

## Quasi-temple

The *quasi-temple* is an inventory and a device of meditation in which the architect places both a statement of principles and a symbolic universe. It is about anonymity and discretion, ethics and *métier*, like a laboratory – a space of experience and ongoing discussion – where he formulates and tries out his substantial discourse.

I say *quasi* because the ideas of essence and sufficiency arise here as unreachable horizons and not as owned realities. In fact, the total temple is an impossibility in the same way as absolute essence and sufficiency are. So the possible temples arise from these exercises.

I can collect numerous examples of *quasi-temples* throughout history that correspond exactly to this intention. Some of them are remarkable treatisesor hypotheses and speculative exercises that defined turning points in the history of architecture: Laugier's primitive hut, Corbusier's Domino house or Rossi's Teatro del Mondo, just to remember three very obvious examples. But contrary to what one might think, they do not have to be merely theoretical manifestos or intangible works, nor world-famous icons. I am thinking, for example, of a small, enigmatic chapel dedicated to Our Lady of Conception, built around 1540 in Tomar (Portugal). Its authorship and the circumstances of its construction are clouded by uncertainty, which turned it into a kind of artefact of curiosities about which several authors have invented multiple hypotheses. Let's follow, in my opinion, the most exciting of these, which is also considered by contemporary scholars to be the most consistent.

In 1972, the American art historian George Kubler suggested[7] that the author was João de Castilho, a royal architect who was involved in the main works of the Portuguese monarchy in the first half of the 16th century. Among these works is the expansion of the Convent of Christ, a colossal religious complex whose construction went through many stages over an extremely long period.

Considering that the chapel is located just a few metres away from the convent, it appears that the two works were developed in parallel by the same author. If we accept the thesis recently put forward by Celso Ramos[8], the Conception was to be a mausoleum that never received the remains of the king who commissioned it, John III. And the Convent of Christ was a royal site. So if Kubler's theory is correct, we would be presented with two simultaneous works with the same client, the same author but two opposite statements.

While the project of the Convent of Christ was subject to all the formal and stylistic constraints that any royal work had to be, being supervised by intermediaries of the king, the tiny chapel appeared as an exercise in freedom and novelty. For Kubler, the Conception "recalls so many other kinds of building that it may have been intended as an architectural experiment or

B    The Chapel of Our Lady of Conception.

C    In this image we can see the isolated chapel and in the background the Convent of Christ, drawing by Albrecht Haupt, 1888.

trial piece, never repeated, yet allowed to remain as a curiosity, like certain experimental ships and trains which need to be built only once".[9]

We can imagine Castilho confronting himself with the restrictions and failures of the super-ornamented style and of the resources that he had spent part of his life using. As Kubler pointed out[10], *Manueline* rule was unsustainable and impossible to continue and Castilho could have realized this earlier than others. In this sense, this early experience, advanced for his own time, was precipitated by the urgency of launching an alternative to the mainstream. The sequence of the historical events that followed proved him right. If we believe what Kubler is currently advocating, Conception was Castilho's own *quasi-temple*, where he worked until his death – a final essay, which turned itself into an ideological and ethical testament.

I am quite sure that many troubles that people, and particularly architects, are facing in the present day under the atrophy and the absence of alternatives, can find great parallels in the past. Just like Castilho, we probably now need to stop, rethink and start over again.

It is very hard nowadays to find examples of quasi-temples, but this is not because they no longer exist or exist less frequently. It is because, being a deposit of reflection and intelligence, a *quasi-temple* does not dispense but rather compels the maturity that only time can give. And even if they are detached from a specific time or period, a certain critical distance is required to find them and think about them. Not being particular about style or appearance (but also being so about both), a *quasi-temple* can, as a new mannerism, be revealed in several expressions and authors. It is a complex construction whose interest lies in the intellectual structure that is behind each building.

In speaking of a new mannerism, what immediately occurs to me is the work of the Chilean

D    San Francisco Lodge, Cecilia Puga.

architect Cecilia Puga, which I have followed with great curiosity (which is not easy considering the anonymity that she maintains).[11] She says her project is "sparing in formal elements, concrete in the technique employed", and that it tries "to avoid militant affiliation to a given historical or formal moment". Behind these words lies a very strong proposition that is reflected in her work.

In San Francisco Lodge (2005), a low-budget second residence located 300 km south of Santiago, Puga builds and makes her paradox explicit, taking it almost to the limit. Between an extreme, almost intimate, personalism and sufficient contextualism, the project becomes a complex challenge with which she herself engages.

I am sure that the true coherence of Puga's project method is only fully understood in a global vision of her work. And although this conclusion may seem somewhat general and trivial, it makes perfect sense here. However, this project, in particular, contains an advanced exploration work on themes and elements that were still clues in Casa de Campo in Marchigue (2000) and Casa Bahia Azul (2002). The building sits on a concrete plinth that clearly makes it stand out from the ground, as a great declaration of autonomy and emancipation, but it is at the same time committed to the geography by having, for example, a resemblance to the slope of the hill behind in its roof pitch.

This is a work full of ironies – the one to which I have referred can be considered just one of many – where her statement, quoted above, is literally transposed. There is no real formal, material, historical, stylistic or technological commitment. Only a strong bond to the programme and to the very idea of wide inclusion.

By translating her proposition into a specific project, Puga is, I would risk saying, working hard in her own *quasi-temple*.

The many political, economic and social crises of the present day appear to be a huge destructive and unpredictable hurricane. Apparently this can be a blocking force to architects, but I must remember that it is also precisely in the eye of the hurricane that a strange feeling of stillness can suddenly become its reversal.

The *quasi-temple* is the celebration of the architecture. It is not determined by the power of a state, a king, or a market, nor does it incorporate the ethical and moral values of each one of them. And although we must accept "the impossibility of an absolute value judgment", as stated by P. V. Aureli, we can and must speak of our own disciplinary corpus with its intrinsic values, which underlies the so-called autonomy of architecture.

With this possible definition of a quasi-temple, I want to state that it seems urgent to me to rescue for architectural praxis the ability to question and challenge the status quo rather than being a guardian of it. The self-induced refusal of the impositions of a dominant mode and the pursuit of alternatives are currently acts of resistance and courage that are still scarce and increasingly urgent for architecture. The best, if not the only, way to resist is to preserve the completeness and the integrity of the discipline. And the *radical self* is the proper field in which to do this, trusting that a real plural subject lies in the deepest individuality.

AUTHOR

Pedro Bragança (Oporto, Portugal). Master in Architecture at the Faculty of Architecture of the University of Porto (MIARQ-FAUP, 2014). PhD student. Post-graduation in 2015. Integrated Researcher at Centre for Studies in Architecture and Urbanism (CEAU) of the Faculty of Architecture of the University of Porto (FAUP), in the research group Architecture: Theory, Project, History (ATPH). His research program is developed on issues of contemporary territory. Editor of the Unidade Magazine. Member of the Young Architects Committee of the Union Internationale des Architectes (UIA), appointed by the national bureau.

NOTES

1. Rather than confirm, this fact counters the expectations of the ecumenical progressand common growth dynamics that underlie and legitimize capitalism itself. The hope of laissez-faire has always been placed on the supposed benefits of the trickle-down effect, a concept that defines the redistributive potential of capital accumulation. But instead of being dissipated, in society as in the world, the differences have been deepened and, as Thomas Piketty recently argued, they have reached levels only similar to those of the nineteenth century.
2. Goodbun, Klein, Rumpfhuber & Till, The Design of Scarcity, Strelka Press, 2013, p. 6.
3. Joseph Rykwert, "Architecture and the Public Good", Research and Practice in Architecture, Alvar Aalto Academy, Helsinki, 2001.
4. Stefano Boeri, Fare di più con meno. Idee per riprogettare l'Italia, il Saggiatore, Milano, 2012.
5. To learn more about this: Aureli, P. V., Less is Enough, Strelka Press, 2012.
6. Walter Benjamin, "The Destructive Character", in Walter Benjamin, Selected Writing. Vol. 2 (2), 1931-1934 (Cambridge, MA: The Belknap Press of Harvard University Press, 1999), 541 – 542.
7. Walter Benjamin, "The Destructive Character", in Walter Benjamin, Selected Writing. Vol. 2 (2), 1931 – 1934 (Cambridge, MA: The Belknap Press of Harvard University Press, 1999), 541 – 542.
8. Celso Ramos, A Capela de Nossa Senhora da Conceição em Tomar, Faculdade de Arquitectura da Universidade do Porto, 2013.
9. George Kubler, Portuguese Plain Architecture: Between Spices and Diamonds, 1521 – 1706, Wesleyan University Press, 1972, p. 33.

10  Idem, Ib.
11  It became easier after the GG monograph (2G; 53) and through Cristobal Palma impressive photographs.

### IMAGE CREDITS

A  Google Art Project.
B  Photograph by Celso Ramos, 2013.
C  Haupt, K. Albrecht, Auswahl von Illustrationen zur Geschichte der Renaissance in Portugal, Hannover, 1888.
D  Photograph by Cristobal Palma.

CARTHA

# Onnis Luque

A Visual Contribution

Onnis Luque

## USF \ DF Appropriation Techniques

This photo essay throws light on the everyday tactics of appropriation elaborated by inhabitants living in – and living with – one of Mexico City's most outstanding modernist heritage sites: the 1957 Unidad Habitacional Santa Fé by Architect Mario Pani. Photographer Onnis Luque playfully presents the creative tensions between architecture and improvisation, space and time, project and everyday life. He provides us with deep insights into the multiple functions, forms and facets of the lively transformation process this social housing estate is undertaking day by day.

IMAGE CREDITS

Photographs by Onnis Luque.

# EPILOGUE

266  **Samuele Squassabia**
Beyond the Hall of Mirrors

269  **George Kafka**
CARTHA Is Worth Sharing

Samuele Squassabia

# Beyond the Hall of Mirrors

I believe that some sort of idealism is the fundamental base of the architect's work. This kind of commitment lies beyond the architect's attitude and contributes in giving shape to his personal ambitions. In a conversation with John Peter about the future of architecture, Mies van der Rohe states:

> There is obviously visible now, a reaction to my approach in architecture. There is no question, but I think it is just a reaction. I don't believe it is a new approach. It is a reaction against something that is there. The reaction is a kind of fashion.[1]

Without dealing with the creation of a future scenario (what Mies would call new approach), architecture is merely reacting to the complex conditions it faces. It only reacts without being able to express a critical point of view. I believe that one of the biggest issues obstructing a possible evolution in this direction today is the supremacy of the image in the way we comprehend architecture. The image imposes the architect's authority above the design and fixes the project's expectations. Despite it being a powerful tool to communicate the architectural virtues with, the power of the image has increased to the point where it seems to be nearly the only medium to communicate about architecture. Sometimes even becoming the goal of the design process itself.

However, I would like to recall now a slightly different notion of image, one that concerns the way we think about architecture through visual references. Static images, or their ghosts we carefully keep, act as advisors in the process of understanding architecture. They are a personal set of fixed configurations that help translating the physical realm of buildings into the abstract realm of ideas (in the process of both conceiving a new building as well as interpreting an existing one). They take a role in discerning many aspects of a project, including not only the expression but also, for example, some programmatic, spatial and technical issues.

Despite whatsoever conceptual apparatus, a visual reference informs the way we think about architecture. It might be that as long as we think about architecture through those static images, we cannot think about architecture differently. With an old instrument, it is difficult to face the future. This might be the hall of mirror described by Martin Reinhold when searching a way to get rid of our old ghosts:

> There may indeed be no escape from this hall of mirrors. But in this realm of materialized spirits, which is a realm of real conflicts and real solidarities, also lurks the potential for a new kind of project [...]. By this I mean a form of thought that neither attempts narcissistically to render its own past present nor mourns their passing. Instead in looking back it reorients its gaze towards future yet to come. It does this by probing its own claustrophobic interiors, its many histories, not as some kind of defeat but in search of a strategic, topological reversal, where the further inside you go the further outside you get.[2]

Images isolate the objective realm of architecture in a claustrophobic interior that can be controlled. Architects get trapped in this idolatry and forgo a further search that can expand the conceptual process. The release from this supremacy might be a way out of this hall of mirrors, the above-mentioned reversal towards an evolution, in which we consider again all its constitutional elements from another perspective.

I firstly became aware of the possibility of a different approach to design through an exchange with Japanese architects in the recent past and through direct confrontations while working together with other architects. I realized how design could evolve without the need to relate to a pre-conceived expression, or representation of space. Considering the project as a tool to reach an intention rather than a goal in itself, it is possible to study a multitude of its undertaken relations to achieve a purpose. Architecture in fact establishes relationships on many levels, and they do not only concern the contingency of a building but also a broader abstract environment. Thinking of the process in this way, takes us through an unforeseen path that somehow releases the project from the architect's imposition. Therefore this is the essential difference between an image and a relationship: the former is still and static, the latter is a dynamic entity.

CARTHA's first cycle is called "Relations in Architecture". But besides the obvious presence of "relations" as a topic, I see in the magazine's curatorial concept the same approach I propose towards the architecture. By opening its platform to a multitude of entities whose only common ground is the presence on the platform itself, cartha creates an environment where unsuspected relations between apparently distant points can be perceived and nurtured. The result is here for us all to explore, project ourselves onto it and extract whatever we might find.

By focusing on relationships, we can try to open architecture from its own isolated realm and connect it to a reality that today appears fragmented. It might help to overcome the Tafurian[3] isolation of language and to define a continuity that we can share. The mutual interaction with the reality can change the way we see it and new possible meanings for architecture can be discovered. It might become a challenge for the new generation to be embraced, it might.

AUTHOR

Samuele Squassabia (Mantova, IT 1984) studied Architecture at the Politecnico di Milano and the Accademia di Architettura di Mendrisio (Diploma with Honors in 2011). He worked as a teaching assistant at the Accademia di Architettura di Mendrisio, the ETH Zurich and the Politecnico di Milano. In 2015 he co-edited the book Kazunari Sakamoto. Lecture, published by Quart Verlag. Since 2014 he has worked as an independent architect in Zurich.

NOTES

1. J. Peter, Converstaion with Mies, in The Oral History of Modern Architecture: Interviews with the Greatest Architects of the Twentieth Century, Harry N. Abrams, New York 1994, p. 173.
2. R. Martin, Utopia's Ghost: architecture and postmodernism, again, University of Minnesota Press, Minneapolis, 2010, pp. 178 – 179.
3. M. Tafuri, The Sphere and the Labyrinth: Avant-Gardes and Architecture from Piranesi to the 1970's, MIT Press, Cambridge, Massachusetts 1987, pp. 267 – 290, originally published under the title La sfera e il Labirinto: Avanguardie e Architettura da Piranesi agli anni '70, Giulio Einaudi Editore, Torino 1980.

George Kafka

# CARTHA
# Is Worth Sharing

I recently attended a talk at Berlin's Technical University by a globally respected architect. Speaking eloquently on the topic of building, they addressed an audience of students on the relationship between the human body's five senses and architecture. Asserting that we live in an era which over-emphasises the optical, the conclusion of this particular section of the talk was a frank, if a little surprising, declaration that "Architecture represents the antithesis of everything digital".

Considering the audience demographic (mostly Berlin's architecture students, under-30, Gen Y, millennials). I doubt I was the only person in the room to feel a little startled, even defensive, when told by a member of a different (older) generation that the entire system of communication around which our understanding of the world revolves stands in direct opposition to the field in which we work, the built environment.

Of course, the architect's statement is not completely without merit. It has become a truism to state that the dominance of visuals in digital spaces can be problematic for architecture. One need look no further than the annals of ArchDaily or the troll-infested discussion boards of the "Brutalist Appreciation Society" Facebook group to notice the reduction of architectural communication to one of 2D aesthetics (at best).

But perhaps this is as far as our architect has looked. For it is equally clear for those who may delve deeper into what the digital era has to offer in the world of architecture, that our speaker's vision is short-sighted.

Yet is this surprising? In 2016 we find ourselves in an era in which nearly all aspects of society are defined by severe divides: politically, economically, technologically and culturally there is a polarisation that can be largely ascribed to the cataclysmic shift in global relations brought about by digital technologies and the internet.

Architecture is no exception to this. Not only has the rise of digital mapping, construction and visualisation software expanded the possibilities of what can be built but, perhaps more importantly, the way in which the field of discourse around architecture – be that in the spread of images, opinion or otherwise – is expanding as a result of digital media has created two poles.

On one hand, there is the freely accessible yet hyperactive and clickbait-led InstaFeeds of Dezeen, Architizer and others: Architecture expressed and understood via saturated photos, hyperreal renders or flash animations. These scrolling walls limit the viewer's interaction with built structures to that of consumption; the sculpting of space becomes content, data, 1s and 0s.

On the other hand, there is the intellectually and logistically inaccessible highbrow, high quality text-led analysis from the old guard: the ARs, AJs and ADs of this world. Equally dislocated from the realm of the built, these bastions of architectural intelligentsia maintain a superiority hiding behind internet paywalls and subscription fees. Those who break through find an echo chamber of obscure theory and insider industry gossip.

A void emerges between these two branches as they dismiss each other as vapid and exclusive respectively. This is a tragedy – of all the topics of crucial importance today, discussions around the environments we inhabit should not be defined by impenetrable walls, opposing fronts.

Crucially there are signs that these voids are being addressed. While the internet has contributed to generational divides, it has also been vital in breaking down the once rigid borders that defined creative disciplines. The once fixed identities of Artist, Musician, Engineer, Programmer, Publisher or Designer are increasingly fluid.

Where job descriptions once isolated individuals into their office cells, today the artist and the architect can be one and the same thing (see Assemble) and the traditional gatekeepers are being challenged, even made obsolete.

CARTHA is one such challenger.

This young magazine has already become an essential voice in architecture by bridging that divide which threatens both the accessibility and quality of the discourse. In occupying this middle ground CARTHA takes the virtues of both extremes of contemporary architecture publishing – free access and quality writing – and presents them on a platform that combines class, expertise and, most importantly, curiosity.

Look no further than the Editorial of Issue I (CONFRÈRES) and the inquisitive approach of CARTHA's young team is made clear in the amount of questions posed. 'How do architects relate to each other nowadays?…What are the types of relation among colleagues?…Where is the focus in the binomial "I" versus "we"? Are the current relations amongst architects more affected by the idea of collaboration and of a social agenda? Is the focus coming back to the "we", to a broader social-politic dimension of architecture?'

Questioning is what we, millennials, do. Striding uncertainly into a foggy world, it seem there can be no room for dogma in our context of structural, environmental and political instability. What good did solid borders do for us anyway? Instead we ask questions and try to dismantle those walls, borders, divisions and establish *relations*.

For what else would CARTHA's first year be devoted to? In its commitment to 'Relations within the architectural spectrum' the team demonstrate an awareness of where they stand within this spectrum, facilitating open debate for established critics and newcomers alike as well as intrigue and stimulation for the reader. The accessibility of CARTHA cannot be understated. To quote Andrew Mackintosh from Issue I: "Through the accessibility of communicating by drawing, ideas are able to to continuously resonate in our discourse of Architecture and enable borderless debates without the need to be physically present." Not just drawing, but also the digital reality of an online architecture magazine will allow architectural discourse to progress beyond factionalism and contribute to the societies it seeks to construct.

Publishing in the post internetpostinternet world is uncertain – perhaps too uncertain for those who preceded it to comprehend – but in accepting uncertainty and embracing the borderless debates of the present, CARTHA points to the future of architectural publishing. For now, as we ricochet between oversharing and worthy exclusivity, CARTHA is worth sharing.

AUTHOR

George Kafka is a writer and editor based between London and Berlin. He has written on architecture and cities for uncube, Metropolis, The Spaces, Huck and Port.

# Acknowledgment

CARTHA wants to thank all the contributors featured as well as all the photographers who have provided their work for this publication.

**Prologue**
Rebekka Kiesewetter

**Issue Ø**
Diogo Seixas Lopes
Francisco Nogueira
Roland Remaa
Rubén Valdez
Vera Sacchetti
Juan Palencia
Ganko
Guido Guidi
Mark Minkjan
Antoine Prokos
AbdulFatah Adam

**Issue I**
Grafton Architects
Andrew Mackintosh
Benjamin Krüger
Luis Pedro Pinto
Rasmus Norlander
A.S. Bramble
Whoodstudio
Maria Barreiros
Atelier Angular
Migrant Garden
Victoria Collar Ocampo

**Issue II**
Samuel Schultze
Joanne Pouzenc
Joël Tettamanti
Mathieu Bujnowskyj
Fabrizio Ballabio
Mio Tsuneyama
Alan-Miguel Valdez
Cristina García Baeza
Vicente Nequinha
Walter Achermann

**Issue III**
Marco Serra
Rabih Shibli
Tanguy Auffret-Postel
Albert Palazón
Bernardo Falcão
Onnis Luque
Fritz Barell
Max Frischknecht
Enrique Peleaz
Laura Bonell
Daniel Lopez-Dòriga
Tiffany Melançon
Pedro Bragança

**Epilogue**
Samuele Squassabia
George Kafka

A warm thank you to our sponsors who made this book possible and to the graphic design studio for their expertise and vital work on it.

**Sponsors**
Burckhardt + Partner Architekten
Laufen
Rapp

**Institutional Sponsor**
Fundaçao Serra Henriques

**Graphic Design**
Studio HübnerBraun

# Imprint

**Editorial Board**
Aurélien Caetano
Elena Chiavi
Pablo Garrido Arnaiz
Matilde Girão
Francisco Moura Veiga
Francisco Ramos Ordóñez
Rubén Valdez

**Graphic Design**
Studio HübnerBraun

**Layout, Typesetting**
Esther Lohri

**Copy Editing**
Carolyn Kenny

**Proofreading**
Raneen Nosh
Fiona Shipwright
Edward Haynes

**Cover Photo**
Joël Tettamanti

**Printing and Binding**
CPI Books, Ebner & Spiegel GmbH, Ulm

© 2016 CARTHA and Park Books, Zurich

www.carthamagazine.com

Park Books
Niederdorfstrasse 54
8001 Zurich
Switzerland

www.park-books.com

ISBN 978-3-03860-037-4

All rights reserved; no part of this publication may be reproduced, stored in a retrieval system or transmitted in any form or by any means, electronic, mechanical, photocopying, recording or otherwise, without the prior written consent of the publisher.